The 2023 U. S. Merger Guidelines

A Review

Editor
Sean P. Sullivan

Foreword by Ilene K. Gotts

106 West 32nd Street, Suite 144 New York, NY, 10001, USA
www.concurrences.com
book@concurrences.com

First Printing, April 2024
978-1-939007-33-9 (Hardcover)
Library of Congress Control Number: 2024934041

Cover Design: Yves Buliard, www.yvesbuliard.fr
Book Design and Layout implementation: Nord Compo

Concurrences Books

Tributes

James F. Rill, *P. Lugard, J. Taladay (eds.), Forthcoming 2024*

Eleanor M. Fox – Antitrust Ambassador to the World, *2021*

Herbert Hovenkamp – The Dean of American Antitrust Law, *2021*

Frédéric Jenny – Standing Up for Convergence and Relevance in Antitrust, (Vol. I & II), *2019 & 2021*

Albert Foer – A Consumer Voice in the Antitrust Arena, *2020*

Richard Whish – Taking Competition Law Outside the Box, *2020*

Douglas H. Ginsburg – An Antitrust Professor on the Bench (Vol. I & II), *2018 & 2020*

Wang Xiaoye – The Pioneer of Competition Law in China, *A. Emch, W. Ng (eds.), 2019*

Ian S. Forrester – A Scot without Borders (Vol. I & II), *A. Komninos (eds.), 2015*

William E. Kovacic – An Antitrust Tribute (Vol. I & II), *2013 & 2014*

Practical Books

The DMA and more – Future application and margin of manoeuvre for national jurisdictions, *G. Muscolo & A. Massolo (eds.), Forthcoming 2024*

AI & Competition Policy, *A. Abbott, T. Schrepel (eds.), Forthcoming 2024*

State Aid & National Enforcement, *J. Derenne, D. Jouve, C. Lemaire, F. Martucci (eds.), Forthcoming 2024*

Competition Inspections in 25 Jurisdictions 2nd Edition – A Practitioner's Guide, *N. Jalabert-Doury (ed.), 2024*

EU Antitrust Enforcement – Law, Economics, History, *Policy & Practice, Wouter P. J. Wils, 2024*

The EU Foreign Subsidies Regulation, *Andreas Reindl, Isabelle Van Damme, 2024*

Compendium of Antitrust Damages Action – International Chamber of Commerce (ICC) – 2nd edition, *J.W.H. Denton AO, F. Brunet, S. Williams, C. Inthavisay (eds.), 2023*

Pharmaceutical Antitrust: An Analysis of US and EU Law, *M. Thill-Tayara, G. Gordon (eds.), 2023*

Innovation Paradox in Merger Control, *G. Gurkaynak, 2023*

Antitrust and the Digital Economy, *Y. Katsoulacos (ed.), 2023 (in collaboration with CRESSE)*

Judicial Review of Competition Cases, *D. Ginsburg, T. Eicke (eds.), 2023*

Competition Law Treatment of Joint Ventures, *B. Bleicher, N. Campbell, A. Hamilton, N. Hukkinen, A. Khan, A. Mordaunt (eds.), 2022 (in collaboration with the IBA)*

Information Exchange & Related Risks, *Z. Marosi, M. Soares (eds.), 2022 (in collaboration with the IBA)*

Rulemaking Authority of the US Federal Trade Commission, *D. Crane (ed.), 2022*

The International Competition Network at Twenty, *D. Anderson & P. Lugard (eds.), 2022*

Competition Case Law Digest – 5th Edition, *F. Jenny, N. Charbit (eds.), 2022*

Competition Inspections in 21 Jurisdictions – A Practitioner's Guide, *N. Jalabert-Doury (ed.), 2022*

Perspectives on Antitrust Compliance, *A. Riley, A. Stephan, A. Tubbs (eds.), 2022 (in collaboration with the ICC)*

Turkish Competition Law, *G. Gürkaynak, 2021*

Competition Law – Climate Change & Environmental Sustainability, *S. Holmes, D. Middelschulte, M. Snoep (eds.), 2021*

Merger Control in Latin America – A Jurisdictional Guide, *P. Burnier da Silveira, P. Sittenfeld (eds.), 2020*

Competition Inspections under EU Law – A Practitioner's Guide, *N. Jalabert-Doury, 2020*

Gun Jumping in Merger Control – A Jurisdictional Guide, *C. Hatton, Y. Comtois, A. Hamilton (eds.), 2019 (in collaboration with the IBA)*

Choice – A New Standard for Competition Analysis? *P. Nihoul (ed.), 2016*

PhD Theses

The Economics of Digital Markets – Essays in Theoretical and Empirical Industrial Organization, *E. Arnoud-Joufray, Forthcoming 2024*

Abuse of Platform Power, *F. Bostoen, 2023*

Reform of Chinese State-Owned Enterprises, *X. Bai, 2023*

Competition & Regulation in Network Industries – Essays in Industrial Organization, *J-M. Zogheib, 2021*

The Role of Media Pluralism in the Enforcement of EU Competition Law, *K. Bania, 2019*

Buyer Power, *I. Herrera Anchustegui, 2017*

General Interest

Why Competition? Voices from the Antitrust Community and Beyond, *D. Crane, D. Gerard, R. Tritell (eds.), Forthcoming 2024*

Global Dictionary of Competition Law, *D. Healey, W. Kovacic, P. Trevisan, R. Whish (eds.), Forthcoming 2024*

Great Antitrust Enforcers, *W. E. Kovacic, 2023*

Competition – How to Speak Like an Expert, *E. Combe , 2023*

Women and Antitrust – Voices from the Field (Vol I & II), *E. Kurgonaite & K. Nordlander, 2020*

e-Book versions available for **Concurrences+** subscribers

Contributors

Logan Billman
Gibson Dunn & Crutcher LLP

Peter C. Carstensen
University of Wisconsin Law School

Joseph Farrell
University of California, Berkeley

Merritt B. Fox
Columbia Law School

Eleanor M. Fox
New York University School of Law

Kristen Limarzi
Gibson Dunn & Crutcher LLP

Diana L. Moss
Progressive Policy Institute

Maureen K. Ohlhausen
Wilson Sonsini Goodrich & Rosati

Taylor M. Owings
Wilson Sonsini Goodrich & Rosati

Menesh S. Patel
UC Davis School of Law

Jeremy Sandford
Compass Lexecon

Loren Smith
Compass Lexecon

Sean P. Sullivan
University of Iowa College of Law

Gregory Werden
Mercatus Center at George Mason University

Nathan Wilson
Compass Lexecon

Overview

Foreword

Ilene Knable Gotts
Wachtell, Lipton, Rosen & Katz

> "These finalized Guidelines provide transparency into how the Justice Department is protecting the American people from the ways in which unlawful, anticompetitive practices manifest themselves in our modern economy. ... The Justice Department will continue to vigorously enforce the laws that safeguard competition and protect all Americans."[1]

1. The issuance of the much-trumpeted new Merger Guidelines ("2023 Guidelines") on December 18, 2023 are true to the above statement of Attorney General (AG) Merrick Garland: they (and the more extreme draft guidelines)[2] provide an accurate portrayal of how the U.S. antitrust enforcement agencies under the Biden Administration have been applying the antitrust laws. They also mark a dramatic shift from the Guidelines issued previously over the last four decades. As demonstrated by the discussion in the articles in this compendium, opinions differ regarding whether being "faithful to the law" (as Assistant Attorney General (AAG) Jonathan Kanter indicated)[3] in the cited legal precedent reflects modern legal and economic advances over these last four decades or a step back to an earlier era of populist merger enforcement.[4] Also, as Professor Emeritus

---

1 U.S. Dep't. of Justice Press Release, (AG) Merrick Garland (Dec. 18, 2023), https://www.justice.gov/opa/pr/justice-department-and-federal-trade-commission-release-2023-merger-guidelines#:~:text=%E2%80%9CThe%20Guidelines%20we%20release%20today,competition%20is%20our%20North%20Star.

2 Diana Moss posits that "[w]hile the final guidelines will govern the antitrust agencies moving forward, it is important to reflect on key changes to the draft version to understand where antitrust ideology in the United States is today. These changes were far from cosmetic. Rather they reflect pressure to move the merger guidelines away from the far left of the ideological spectrum. The final version of the 2023 guidelines clearly represents a compromise document that attempts to balance and resolve strong feedback."

3 U.S. Dep't. of Justice Press Release, (AAG) Jonathan Kanter, "The Guidelines we release today are faithful to the law. ...." *See also* Lina Khan, "The 2023 Merger Guidelines ... ensure fidelity to statutory text and precedent." (Dec. 18, 2023), https://www.justice.gov/opa/pr/justice-department-and-federal-trade-commission-release-2023-merger-guidelines#:~:text=%E2%80%9CThe%20Guidelines%20we%20release%20today,competition%20is%20our%20North%20Star.

4 As Moss's article indicated, 60% of the cases cited were decided before the 1980s and "elevating the importance of certain cases highlight the dangers of 'selective' citations in promoting strong enforcement." At the same time, Ms. Moss points out that "there is post-1980 caselaw that supports stronger enforcement on a wide variety of important merger issues. A reluctance to give credit to more recent administrations for stronger merger enforcement telegraphed a more polarized ideology."

Eleanor Fox writes, "it remains to be seen whether the Guidelines are likely to gain the sympathy of the judiciary."

2. This compendium consists of ten articles, written by leading practitioners, economists, academics, and public policy advocates. Several of the articles discuss the historical evolution of merger law and policy, and the underlying bases for the precedent. Some of these articles provide in-depth retrospectives on the various topics raised (or omitted) in the Guidelines. These articles are not only interesting, but are important for assessing the Guidelines and their objectives. They highlight what Diana Moss notes is missing from the Guidelines: "The 2023 Guidelines missed an important opportunity to marshal evidence from past mergers to provide transparency and context. .... This omission of important economic and business analysis seems oddly out of sync with the guidelines' priority of introducing citation to legal precedent. On the whole, however, it is consistent with the theme of relegating non-legal analysis and precedent to a secondary role in the 2023 Guidelines." As philosopher George Santayana stated: "Those who cannot remember the past are condemned to repeat it." These chapters and their illuminating discussion fill some of this missing element of the Merger Guidelines by providing a more fulsome context of the past.

3. A major change in the merger review paradigm from the 2010 Guidelines involves the methodology specified for market delineation. Economist Gregory Werden (who was involved in preparing the 1982 Guidelines and the subsequent guidelines prior to the new Guidelines) condemns the 2023 Guidelines for "abandon[ing] some critical principles that governed market delineation since 1982.[5] The [Agencies] ... evidently contemplate gerrymandering markets as in the 1960s, when the relevant market in merger cases was whatever collection of products and places made the best case against the merger." Dr. Werden describes the return to the "dark ages" that does not use the "hypothetical monopolist test" (HMT) to delineate the relevant market – or even requires the specification of the boundaries of the relevant market. Dr. Werden finds flaws with each of the four market delineation tools described in the 2023 Guidelines: (1) direct evidence of substantial competition between the merger parties can demonstrate that a relevant market exists, even if the precise metes and bounds of the market are only broadly characterized;[6] (2) direct evidence of the exercise of market power can demonstrate a relevant market

5 *See* Joseph Farrell who provided a different view, suggested that with respect to key parts of the Guidelines (*e.g.*, the scope of merger control, the approach to market definition, market shares, and concentration measures, and the discussion of the risk of coordinated conduct), the points were made in previous market guidelines but the new 2023 Guidelines "say them more often and louder, and that matters.")

6 In contrast, Sandford et al. indicate that while this can be read as subordinating the market definition exercise to a competitive effects analysis, it may be appropriate to demote market definition in importance. In fact, they suggest that the Agencies "do (appropriately) give primacy to competitive effects analyses over market definition (particularly during their internal evaluations). Thus, this change may accurately and helpfully reflect their practice."

in which that power exists, particularly in cases posing a "risk that a dominant position may be entrenched, maintained, or extended";[7] (3) the use of the practical indicia of *Brown Shoe* even if resulting in market definitions that the HMT cannot adequately support;[8] (4) failure to apply the principles of controlling the size and shape of the relevant market through the "Circle Principle" and the "Smallest Market Principle" of the HMT; and (5) modifying the HMT by disassociating the delineation of the relevant market from the assessment of competitive effects. Dr. Werden concludes that the result will be that "defendants are apt to assert that the alleged relevant markets were gerrymandered, and courts are apt to agree if they find that the alleged relevant markets make little sense. Defendants also are apt to invoke market delineation principles that the [2023 Guidelines] ... abandoned, and courts are apt to hold that the [Agencies] ... acted arbitrarily and capriciously in abandoning them."

4. Other authors focused on the departure of the 2023 Guidelines from the 2010 Guidelines in providing market structure presumptions at pre-2010 levels and eliminating "safe harbors."[9] As pointed out by Ms. Moss, the draft guidelines went even further in "present[ing] what appeared to be quasi-bright-line tests for determining whether a merger is illegal" that departed from effects-based analysis under the consumer welfare standard. Although some of the authors were displeased with the final Guidelines replacing the quasi-bright-line test with a rebuttable "presumption of illegality,"[10] others point to the evolution of economic thinking beyond the Structure–Conduct–Performance paradigm for discrediting the inclusion of the 30% share presumption.[11] In addition, Drs. Sandford et al. criticized the "myopic view of non-horizontal [i.e., vertical and conglomerate] mergers articulated in the [Guidelines] ... seems predicated on the belief that nuance unduly favors the merger parties," citing to the Agencies' track record in such merger challenges. Finally, both the Sandford, and the Ohlhausen/Owings articles, noted the greater reluctance in these Guidelines to recognize merger efficiencies, and even "several

7 Sandford, et al. find that the term "market power" "lacks a consistent definition" and therefore "it can be challenging to credibly establish market power by methods other than defining a market and demonstrating large shares in that market...." They believe that this approach may be useful to address the "cellophane fallacy" but that "it remains to be seen just what the agencies intended with this new language."

8 Sandford, et al. indicate that although the *Brown Shoe* indicia have not been expressly referenced, these factors *could be* relevant *to support* the HMT findings, but *not* because they offer "appropriate contours of the relevant market outside of the HMT framework."

9 Farrell indicates that there were never safe harbors, but, a better term would be there was a "presumption of no harm."

10 *See, e.g.*, Cartensen, "The presumption only operates to shift the burden of persuasion to the defendants. This limited presumption makes policy sense only if there is substantial reason to believe that major mergers are in fact likely in a significant number of cases to have positive effects associated with such combinations. ... The empirical data and economic theory point against the likelihood of [there being likely to be a number that either would not harm competition or that would provide unique positive results with respect to innovation or both] in the vast majority of ... [mergers involving significant market shares]."

11 *See* Sullivan article.

suggestions that acquisitions leading to an improvement in the merged firm's performance would violate the antitrust laws."[12]

5. AAG Kanter indicated that "[t]he Guidelines we release today … reflect how competition plays out in our modern markets," FTC Chair Lina Khan similarly stated: "The 2023 Merger Guidelines reflect the new realities of how firms do business in the modern economy." The new Guidelines introduce five market "applications" in which the framework is applied: (1) trends toward concentration; (2) serial acquisitions; (3) mergers involving multi-sided platforms; (4) mergers of buyers of inputs;[13] and (5) partial ownership acquisitions. The Billman/Limarzi and the Carstensen articles focused on buyer power mergers, and reach differing views on whether the new Guidelines expand on prior agency policy in this area. The Fox/Patel article critiqued the expansion of partial ownership discussion to include common ownership situations, noting the fundamental differences in cross-ownership and common ownership situations and their implications on the ability to influence the firms' incentives to compete. Fox and Patel rejected that the mere presence of common ownership can lessen firms' incentives to compete in the absence of any control or communication by the common owner and make suggestions on how such arrangements should be analyzed.

6. In sum, this foreword is meant to whet your appetite for consuming the contents of this book. I am delighted to have had the opportunity of reading the proofs of this book before publication and am pleased to commend it to practitioners, officials, and academics who seek to have a deeper understanding of the Merger Guidelines and their potential use in merger enforcement.

---

12 *See* Ohlhausen & Owings. The authors point to Guideline 6 (entrenchment of dominant position), Guideline 9 (multi-sided platforms), and Guideline 7 (trends toward consolidation) as examples. Sandford et al. also point to Guideline 3.3 that mandates "any benefits claimed by the merging parties are cognizable only if they do not result from the anticompetitive worsening of terms for the merged firm's trading partners." This includes if input costs are expected to decrease as a result of monopsony power. *See also* Billman & Limarzi (discussing the rejection of cross-market balancing).

13 Farrell indicates that "the 2023 Guidelines take a step toward better integrating the discussion of buyer and seller victims of enhanced power than does the not-entirely-satisfying 'analogous' idea, by using the phrase 'trading partner' (rather than 'buyer' or 'customer' or 'supplier') for the potential victim a dozen or so times throughout the document." He also points out that "much of the additional material concerns labor markets."

A Retrospective and Prospective Analysis of Monopsony Power Under the Merger Guidelines

LOGAN BILLMAN[*] AND KRISTEN LIMARZI[**]
Gibson Dunn & Crutcher LLP

* Logan Billman, Associate, Gibson Dunn & Crutcher LLP.

** Kristen Limarzi, Partner, Gibson Dunn & Crutcher LLP and Senior Fellow at the George Washington University Competition and Innovation Lab.

7. The 2023 Merger Guidelines (the "2023 Guidelines"), published by the U.S. Department of Justice (DOJ) and Federal Trade Commission (FTC) (the "Agencies"), refresh the Agencies' analytical frameworks for assessing competition concerns raised by mergers to align with developments in economics, evolving market structures, and the Neo-Brandesian modes of analysis. In several areas, the 2023 Guidelines significantly depart from and expand on prior Agency policy. Yet in others, the Guidelines are a modest refresh of well-established principles. This chapter compares the 2023 Guidelines' treatment of mergers of competing buyers to prior guidelines and enforcement actions. It concludes that the 2023 Guideline's treatments of buyer competition and monopsony power largely adheres to well-established principles for assessing monopsony power. As before, the Agencies will continue assessing mergers between buyers using "the same – or analogous – tools used to assess the effects of a merger of seller."[1]

8. The 2023 Guidelines expand on prior Agency enforcement in two areas. First, the 2023 Guidelines expound on the Agencies' framework for analyzing the effects of monopsony power in labor markets. Second, the 2023 Guidelines clarify that cross-market balancing is disallowed and confirm that injuries to sellers cannot be offset by purported benefits to consumers or other market participants.

I. Introduction to Monopsony

9. Monopsony, called the "mirror image" of monopoly, describes an economic condition wherein a purchaser has the power to affect the price of an input through its purchasing decisions.[2] In the classical economic case, a monopsonist exercises its power to lower input prices by scaling back the total quantity purchased.[3] In so doing, the monopsonist sacrifices additional sales and profits in the output market, which it makes up for by securing a lower price for the units it does purchase.

10. Monopsony sounds in antitrust law because it has the potential to harm consumers, sellers, and the competitive process without a countervailing benefit to consumer welfare. In the short run, monopsony injures sellers by forcing them to accept prices that are below the competitive level.[4] Additional injury may occur if sellers, unable to remain in the market at

---

1 Fed. Trade Comm'n and U.S. Dep't. of Justice, *Merger Guidelines*, § 2.10 (2023) ("2023 Guidelines"), https://www.justice.gov/d9/2023-12/2023%20Merger%20Guidelines.pdf.

2 Weyerhaeuser Co. v. Ross-Simmons Hardwood Lumber Co., Inc., 549 U.S. 312, 322 (2007), see John E. Lopatka & Roger D. Blair, *The US Supreme Court recognizes a limited claim for predatory bidding (Weyerhaeuser/Ross-Simmons)*, E-COMPETITIONS Feb. 2007, art. No. 47314; *see also* Todd v. Exxon Corp., 275 F.3d 191 (2d. Cir. 2001) ("The equation for measuring market power in monopsony is a 'mirror image' of the relationships that create market power in a seller.") (quoting IIA PHILLIP E. AREEDA ET AL., ANTITRUST LAW: AN ANALYSIS OF ANTITRUST PRINCIPLES AND THEIR APPLICATION ¶574, 302 n.12 (1995).

3 *See* Steven Salop's *Anticompetitive Overbuying by Power Buyers*, 72 Antitrust L.J. 669, 672 (2005) (for an economic explanation of monopsony power).

4 *See* C. Scott Hemphill & Nancy L. Rose, *Mergers That Harm Sellers*, 127 Y. L. J. 2078, 2082–92 (2018).

the sub-competitive price, are forced to exit.[5] Likewise, if, as a result of its scaled-back input purchases, the monopsonist reduces the quantity sold in an output market, consumers are injured in the form of higher prices and deadweight loss.[6] Indeed, sustained monopsony power may injure the competitive process itself, as distorted price signals – the "central nervous system of the economy" – induce underinvestment in the input market and overinvestment in the output market.[7]

11. Condemnation of monopsony power under the antitrust laws is not a new phenomenon. Since Congress enacted the Sherman Act of 1980, antitrust enforcers have understood that their mandate to preserve competition encompasses competition between buyers and have successfully prosecuted buy-side cartels, buyer-side monopolies, and conduct that artificially creates and maintains monopsony power.

12. One of the first successful prosecutions brought under the Sherman Act, *United States v. Swift & Co*, involved a meatpacking cartel that leveraged its monopsony power to gain an advantage against and exclude rival meatpackers.[8] There, a cartel consisting of vertically integrated stockyards and packers who collectively produced 60% of the meat in the United States conspired to suppress the price of livestock by rigging stockyard bids and leveraging their collective buyer power to secure unlawfully low railroad rates.[9] This monopsonistic conduct enabled the cartel to exclude rival meatpackers who were unable to match the cartel's artificially low input costs while simultaneously setting and maintaining supracompetitive fresh meat prices.[10] The district court, as affirmed by the Supreme Court, enjoined all elements of the conspiracy, including the cartel's concerted buying.

13. Likewise, the breakup of Standard Oil of New Jersey, which stands as one of the first challenges to a consummated merger, was based in part on Standard Oil's illegal acquisition and maintenance of monopsony

5 *Id.*

6 While the monopsony always reduces economic efficiency, it does not necessarily harm consumers. *See* Salop, *supra* note 3, at 674. For example, if the monopsonist sells into a perfectly competitive output market (i.e., a market where rival suppliers have elastic supply at the prevailing price), rival competitors will be able to expand their output to offset the monopsonist's reduced output, thereby preventing consumer harm. *Id.* However, in reality, monopsony often results in reduced output because markets with perfectly elastic supply is highly rare and monopsonists typically possess some degree of power in the output market. *Id.* at 674–75 (modeling the conditions in which monopsony results in sub-competitive output).

7 National Society of Professional Engineers v. United States, 435 U.S. 679, 692 (1978) (quoting United States v. Socony-Vacuum Oil Co., 310 U.S. 150, 226 n.59 (1940)), see Jarod Bona, *The US Supreme Court rejects the attempt to justify a restrictive practice on the basis of the potential threat that competition poses to public safety and professional ethics (National Society of Professional Engineers)*, E-COMPETITIONS Apr. 1978, art. No. 65451.

8 United States v. Swift & Co., 122 F. 529 (C.C.N.D. Ill. 1903), *modified*, 196 U.S. 375 (1905).

9 *Id.* at 394.

10 *Id.* Later, in affirming that the conspiracy to set artificially low railroad freight costs violated the antitrust laws, the Court observed that low input prices resulting from monopsony power were a "powerful instrument of monopoly." *Id.* at 402. ("It is obvious that no more powerful instrument of monopoly could be used than an advantage in the cost of transportation.").

power.[11] Standard Oil of New Jersey was formed in 1899 through a stock-for-stock merger between 19 petroleum companies, each a former subsidiary of Standard Oil of Ohio and collectively the Standard Oil Trust.[12] Under common ownership, the Standard Oil Trust dominated oil extraction and refining, controlling over 10% of crude oil extraction, over 50% of petroleum distribution, 75% of refining operations, and at least 80% of refined petroleum sales in the United States.[13] In its challenge to Standard Oil, the DOJ alleged that the Trust possessed monopsony power over crude oil extractors due to its dominant refining position, which it leveraged to secure lower prices for itself and impose higher costs on rivals. The DOJ alleged, and the District Court held, that this price-cost squeeze excluded rival refiners and reinforced Standard Oil's monopoly. Ultimately, the district court found, and the Supreme Court affirmed that Standard Oil of New Jersey's formation violated the Sherman Act.[14] In so doing, the Court dissolved the Trust and enjoined its members from further monopsonistic practices, such as re-consolidating or agreeing on the price of inputs.[15]

14. In subsequent years, the Supreme Court has repeatedly affirmed that harm to sellers from the exercise of monopsony power violates the antitrust laws. In *Mandeville Island Farms v. American Crystal Sugar Co.*, sugar refiners accused of fixing the price paid for sugar beets argued that their agreement was lawful because the Sherman Act only protected competition between sellers.[16] The Court rejected the position, holding that the Act protects sellers as well as purchasers, pronouncing that the Sherman Act "does not confine its protection to consumers, or to purchasers, or to competitors, or to sellers. The Act is comprehensive in its terms and coverage, protecting all who are made victims of the forbidden practices by whomever they may be perpetrated."[17] In subsequent years, the Supreme Court has held that exclusionary conduct

---

11 U.S. v. Standard Oil Co. of New Jersey, 173 F. 177 (1909), *aff'd*, 221 U.S. 1 (1911).

12 The Standard Oil Company, Inc. was founded in 1863 and, through a series of acquisitions, mergers, and trust agreements, had acquired 40 rival oil refineries and a controlling interest in more than 30 petroleum companies by 1879. *Standard Oil*, 173 F. at 180–81. In 1982, the Supreme Court of Ohio held that Standard Oil's consolidation and operation violated state law and ordered the Trust dissolved into 20 separate operating companies. *See* State v. Standard Oil Company, 49 Ohio St. 137 (OH 1892). The 20 operating companies then re-merged into a single entity under Standard Oil of New Jersey.

13 *Standard Oil*, 173 F. at 183.

14 *Id.* at 190 ("The power to vote the stock, to elect the officers of the subsidiary corporations, to control and operate them, and thereby to restrict their competition in interstate and international commerce, was illegally granted to the Standard Oil Company of New Jersey in 1899, and that company ever since has exercised [that power] unlawfully .... These are menacing and continuing violations of the Act which Congress has imposed the duty upon the courts to restrain and prevent.")

15 *Id.* at 193.

16 334 U.S. 219, 221 (1948) ("The main question is whether ... California sugar refiners who sell sugar in interstate commerce may agree among themselves to pay a uniform price for sugar beets grown in California without incurring liability to the local beet growers under the Act.").

17 *Id.* at 235–236.

targeted at rival purchasers[18] and agreements fixing compensation for collegiate athletes are unlawful.[19]

II. Treatment of Monopsony under the Merger Guidelines Prior to 2023: A Retrospective

15. The first litigated challenge to a merger under the Clayton Act based on a theory of monopsony harm was the DOJ's 1965 challenge to Pennzoil's merger with Kendall Refining Company.[20] *Pennzoil* concerned a merger between the second and third-largest purchasers of Penn Grade crude oil, a form of oil drilled and refined in the Appalachian basin. The DOJ alleged the merger was unlawful because it would have significantly increased Pennzoil's share of, and concentration in, the market for purchasing Penn Grade crude oil; eliminated competition between Pennzoil and Kendall for the purchase of Penn Grade crude oil; and removed a "substantial competitive factor" in the market. The district court enjoined the merger on these grounds.[21] Notably, the merging parties neither contested the applicability of the Clayton Act to a merger between buyers nor the district court's reliance on *Philadelphia National Bank* and other merger case law involving sell-side mergers.[22]

16. The first Merger Guidelines, published in 1968 by the DOJ, did not expressly identify the creation, enhancement, or entrenchment of monopsony power as a competitive problem or basis for challenging a merger.[23] This is because, under the 1968 Guidelines, a merger's effect on market structure and concentration were the *sine qua non* of legality under the Clayton Act.[24] Because market power was presumed

---

18 *Weyerhaeuser,* 549 U.S. 312 (2007) (holding that predatory overbuying targeted at rival purchasers is unlawful); Klor's v. Broadway-Hale Stores, 359 U.S. 207 (1959) (holding that group boycotts organized seeking to foreclose rival purchaser's access to key inputs are *per se* illegal).

19 National Collegiate Athletic Association v. Alston, 594 U.S. 141 S. Ct. 2141 (2021) (Affirming lower court's finding that the NCAA's restrictions on student-athlete academic awards and compensation violated Section 1 of the Sherman Act), see Louis K. Fisher et al., *The US Supreme Court prohibits an association from restraining student-athlete education-related benefits while recognizing the association still retains considerable flexibility to regulate such benefits (NCAA/Alston)*, e-Competitions June 2021, art. No. 101244; *see also id.* at 2167 (Kavanaugh, J., concurring) (describing the NCAA's rules as "price-fixing labor.").

20 U.S. v. Pennzoil Co., 252 F. Supp. 962 (W.D. Penn. 1965).

21 *Id.* at 985.

22 *See, id.* (citing United States v. Phila. Nat'l Bank, 374 U.S. 294 (1963).

23 U.S. Dep't. of Justice, *Merger Guidelines* (1968) ("1968 Guidelines"), https://www.justice.gov/archives/atr/1968-merger-guidelines. The FTC tacitly followed the 1968 Guidelines until 1982, at which point it jointly reassessed merger policy with the DOJ. However, the FTC ultimately declined to endorse the 1982 Guidelines, opting instead to issue a separate set of general principles for assessing horizonal mergers. *See* Fed. Trade Comm', *Statement of Fed. Trade Comm'n Concerning Horizontal Mergers* (June 14, 1982), https://merger-guidelines.com/1982-statement-concerning-horizontal-mergers#section-VI. The FTC began participating in the merger guidelines with the 1992 Guidelines.

24 *Id.* at § 1 ("Market structure is the focus of the Department's merger policy chiefly because the conduct of the individual firms in a market tends to be controlled by the structure of that market ... such as, principally, the number of substantial firms selling in the market, the relative sizes of their respective market shares, and the substantiality of barriers to the entry of new firms into the market .... Accordingly, the Department's enforcement activity under Section 7 is directed primarily toward the identification and prevention of

from increased concentration alone, inquiry into the merger's effect on competition was unnecessary, except in cases involving conglomerate mergers.[25] Consequently, while a merger between buyers was actionable under the Clayton Act, as shown by the DOJ's successful *Pennzoil* challenge, there was no reason for the 1968 Guidelines to differentiate mergers between buyers from mergers between sellers because both were analyzed under identical structuralist approaches. For that reason, the omission of monopsony from the 1968 Guidelines should not be understood as a policy choice in favor of mergers that increase buyer power but rather an artifact of the pre-Chicago structuralist approach to antitrust.

17. With the publication of the 1982 and 1984 Merger Guidelines, which marked the ascendancy of the Chicago School's economic approach to antitrust, the main goal of merger enforcement became preventing mergers that may create or enhance market power or facilitate its exercise.[26] As a consequence of their focus on market power in all its forms, the 1982 and 1984 Guidelines expressly recognized that "market power by buyers" was an independent basis for a merger to violate Section 7.[27] Every subsequent iteration of the Merger Guidelines has recognized that mergers that create, maintain, or enhance "monopsony power" and enable buyers to "depress the price paid for a product to a level that is below the competitive price" are unlawful.[28]

18. A survey of merger enforcement actions since the publication of the 1984 Guidelines indicates that the Agencies commonly investigate and challenge mergers that present a risk of monopsony harm. Between 1984 and 2023, the Agencies investigated at least 15 mergers on monopsony harm grounds and challenged 12.[29] Of the 12 challenged mergers, seven

---

those mergers which alter market structure in ways likely now or eventually to encourage or permit non-competitive conduct.")

25 *Id.*

26 U.S. Dep't. of Justice, *Merger Guidelines*, § 1 n.5 (1982), ("1982 Guidelines"). ("The unifying theme of the Guidelines is that mergers should not be permitted to create or enhance "market power" or to facilitate its exercise.")

27 *Id.* ("'Market power' also encompasses the ability of a single buyer or group of buyers to depress the price paid for a product to a level that is below the competitive price. The exercise of market power by buyers has wealth transfer and resource misallocation effects analogous to those associated with the exercise of market power by sellers."), https://www.justice.gov/sites/default/files/atr/legacy/2007/07/11/11248.pdf; U.S. Dep't. of, *Merger Guidelines*, § 1 (1984) ("1984 Guidelines") *id.*, https://www.justice.gov/archives/atr/1984-merger-guidelines.

28 Fed. Trade Comm'n and U.S. Dep't. of Justice, *Merger Guidelines*, § 0.1 (1992) ("1992 Guidelines"), https://www.justice.gov/sites/default/files/atr/legacy/2007/07/11/11250.pdf; *see also* Fed. Trade Comm'n and U.S. Dep't. of Justice, *Merger Guidelines*, § 0.1 (1997) ("1997 Guidelines"), https://www.justice.gov/sites/default/files/atr/legacy/2007/07/11/11251.pdf; Fed. Trade Comm'n and U.S. Dep't. of Justice, *Horizontal Merger Guidelines*, § 12 (2010) ("2010 Guidelines"), https://www.justice.gov/sites/default/files/atr/legacy/2010/08/19/hmg-2010.pdf.

29 The authors are aware of three investigations where an enforcer formally considered but declined to prosecute a merger based on a monopsony theory of harm: *Caremark Rx, Inc./AdvancePCS*; *Express Scripts/Medco Health Solutions*; and *Lifespan/Care New England Health System*. However, the 15 investigations figure is likely a significant underestimate because the Agencies rarely publicly announce decisions not to prosecute.

were settled by consent decree,[30] two were abandoned by the parties,[31] and three were litigated.[32] In the litigated challenges, the government prevailed on its monopsony theory of harm in *United States v. Bertelsmann SE & Co.*[33] and *United States v. Rice Growers Association of California.* In the other case, *United States v. Anthem*, the district court enjoined the merger without reaching the monopsony issue.[34]

19. From this robust enforcement record, several consistent themes emerge. First, it is well established that the Clayton Act prohibits transactions that create, enhance, or facilitate the exercise of monopsony power. Second, when assessing transactions for monopsony harm, the Agencies and courts are primarily concerned with preserving buyer competition and preventing the development of monopsony power. Third, the Agencies and courts employ a common set of legal and economic tools to assess a transaction's effect on market power and monopsony power, and these tools have not significantly changed over time.

20. In contrast, the Agencies have been inconsistent on the question of whether harm to downstream consumers is an essential element of an enforcement

---

30 *See* Decision and Order, In the matter of Grifols, S.A. and Grifols Shared Services North America, Inc., FTC File No. C-4654 (Sept. 17, 2018) (alleging merger between blood plasma collection centers would lessen competition for human blood plasma collection in three cities; settled); Complaint, United States v. Danone S.A., 2017 WL 3172888, at 6–7 (D.D.C. Apr. 3, 2017) (alleging that the acquisition of a raw organic milk processor would reduce competition in, inter alia, "the purchase of raw organic milk from farmers" in the northeast United States; settled); Complaint, United States v. Tyson Foods, Inc., No. 14-cv-1474, 2014 WL 4249929 (D.D.C. Aug. 27, 2014) (alleging that the acquisition of a competing buyer would harm competition in the market for "purchase of sows from farmers"; settled); Complaint, United States v. George's Foods, LLC, No. 5:11-cv-00043 (W.D. Va. May 10, 2011) (alleging that the acquisition of a competing chicken processor would harm competition in the market for "purchase of broiler grower services"; settled); Complaint, United States v. UnitedHealth Group, 71 Fed. Reg. 13991 (2006) (alleging the acquisition would have harm competition for the purchase of physician services in Tucson, AZ, and Boulder, CO; settled); Complaint, United States v. Cargill, Inc., No. 99-CV-01875, 2000 WL 1475752, at *1 (D.D.C. June 30, 2000) (alleging merger of competing grain traders would harm competition in "grain purchasing services"; settled); Complaint, United States v. Aetna, Inc., No. 3-99 CV 1398-H, 1999 WL 1419046, at *15 (N.D. Tex. Dec. 7, 1999) ("Aetna's acquisition of Prudential will also consolidate its purchasing power over physicians' services in Houston and Dallas"; settled).

31 U.S. Dep't. of Justice Press Release, Blue Cross Blue Shield of Michigan and Physicians Health Plan of Mid-Michigan Abandon Merger Plans (Mar. 8, 2010) (alleging that Blue Care Networks of Michigan's proposed acquisition of Physicians Health Plan of Mid-Michigan "would have given Blue Cross-Michigan the ability to control physician reimbursement rates in a manner that could harm the quality of health care delivered to consumers"; abandoned prior to issuance of a complaint); Complaint, United States v. JBS S.A., No. 08-CV-5992 (N.D. Ill. Nov. 7, 2008) (alleging that the acquisition of a competing beef packer would harm competition in the market for "purchase [of] fed cattle"; abandoned following issuance of complaint).

32 United States v. Bertelsmann SE & Co. KGaA, 646 F. Supp. 3d 1 (D.D.C. Nov. 7, 2022) (enjoining Penguin Random House's acquisition of Simon & Schuster to preserve competition for book advances paid to authors); United States v. Rice Growers Ass'n of Cal., No. S-84-1066, 1986 WL 12562, at *4 (E.D. Cal. 1986) (agreeing with DOJ's allegation that acquisition of a competing rice miller would harm competition in the market for "purchase or other acquisition for milling of paddy rice grown in California").

33 The DOJ initiated its challenge to Penguin Random House's acquisition of Simon & Schuster in November 2021, 19 months before the Agencies published the draft 2023 Guidelines, and was largely litigated under the 2010 Guidelines' principles. See Fed. Trade Comm'n, Press Release, *FTC and DOJ Seek Comment on Draft Merger Guidelines* (July 19, 2023). Therefore, it is properly viewed as a merger challenge predating the 2023 Guidelines, even if the Agencies had announced their intention to revise the guidelines two months prior. See Fed. Trade Comm'n, Press Release, *Federal Trade Commission Withdraws Vertical Merger Guidelines* (Sept. 15, 2021).

34 United States v. Anthem, Inc., No. 1:16-cv-149, 2017 WL 527923 (D.D.C. Feb. 8, 2017) *aff'd* 855 F.3d 345 (D.C.C. 2017), see Clifford H. Aronson et al., *The US District Court for the District of Columbia blocks two proposed mergers in the insurance sector brought and litigated under the Obama administration (Aetna / Humana and Anthem/Cigna)*, e-Competitions Feb. 2017, art. No. 83761.

action. While the DOJ has pursued such enforcement actions, the FTC has historically declined to challenge transactions absent evidence of downstream consumer harm.

1. Monopsony Harm is an Established Basis for Blocking Mergers under Section 7 of the Clayton Act

21. The treatment of monopsony power by courts and the Agencies makes clear that it is unlawful for mergers to harm sellers by substantially lessening competition between buyers.

22. The judicial record is unequivocal: the Clayton Act prohibits mergers that harm sellers by reducing competition and enhancing monopsony power. Since the enactment of the Clayton Act, the Agencies have sought to enjoin four transactions based on a theory of monopsony harm. In all three cases in which an Article III judge reached the merits of the monopsony claim, the government won.

23. First, in *Pennzoil*, the DOJ successfully blocked a merger between two leading refiners of Penn Grade crude oil, which would have resulted in a single firm purchasing 34% of crude produced in the Appalachian basin and producing 54% of refined Penn Grade oil.[35] Upon accepting that a market for Penn Grade crude oil was sufficiently definite for a preliminary injunction, the court enjoined the transaction, holding that it would likely eliminate substantial competition for the purchase of and substantially increase concentration in the markets for purchasing and producing Penn Grade crude.[36]

24. Second in *California Rice Growers*, the DOJ blocked a transaction that would have combined the first and third largest rice millers of California rice, resulting in a single firm controlling 64% of the market for the purchase of paddy rice in California and increasing the market's Herfindahl–Hirschman Index (HHI) from 3726 to 1598.[37] Despite holding that the government's definition of a downstream market for the sale of milled rice products was defective, the district court nevertheless enjoined the transaction based solely on the harm to California rice farmers.[38]

25. Third, in *Bertelsmann*, the DOJ blocked a merger between the largest and third largest domestic book publishers, which would have resulted in a single publisher controlling 49% of the market for anticipated top-selling books and increased the market's HHI from 2,220 to 3,111.[39] Based on the market share and concentration analysis, as well as evidence showing

35 *Pennzoil*, 252 F. Supp. at 985.

36 *Id.* at 985, 988.

37 *Rice Growers*, 1986 WL 12562 at *10.

38 *Id.* at *8–9, *12.

39 *Bertelsmann*, 646 F. Supp. 3d at 12.

the merger would have substantially lessened competition by eliminating head-to-head competition to purchase publishing rights and facilitating coordination, the district court enjoined the merger.

26. While the Supreme Court has yet to rule expressly that mergers that reduce competition between buyers are unlawful under the Clayton Act, the district court in each of these cases determined that the loss of competition between purchasers and resulting harm to sellers was either the sole basis (*California Rice Growers* and *Bertelsmann*) or an independent basis (*Pennzoil*) to enjoin the transaction. Moreover, in no proceeding did the defendant parties argue, nor did the court consider, that the Clayton Act cannot reach monopsony harms. Simply, in every instance a court has had an opportunity to rule on the treatment of monopsony power under the Clayton Act, every court affirmed that the Clayton Act prohibits mergers that harm sellers by reducing competition and enhancing monopsony power.

27. The Agencies' pre-litigation enforcement record is equally clear. In all nine cases where the Agencies determined that a transaction was likely to mean substantially less competition between buyers but an injunction was not litigated before an Article III court, the Agencies either successfully extracted a remedy that alleviated the competitive concern or induced the parties to abandon the transaction. In other words, the Agencies have a 100% success rate in challenging mergers that harm sellers.

28. Moreover, the position that the Clayton Act prohibits mergers that harm sellers also enjoys broad bipartisan support. With the exception of the first Bush Administration, the Agencies have challenged at least one merger under a monopsony theory of harm in every presidential administration since Ronald Reagan (inclusive).

2. The Primary Competitive Concern in Mergers between Buyers is the Transaction's Effect on Buyer Competition and Monopsony Power

29. When assessing transactions for monopsony harm, the Agencies and courts are primarily concerned with preserving buyer competition and preventing the development of monopsony power.

30. As a preliminary matter, monopsony power refers to a buyer's ability to influence the price of an input. Monopsony power, like market power, is as a continuum, with all firms competing in differentiated and imperfect markets possessing some scintilla of monopsony power.[40] And, as with market power, the exercise of monopsony power harms consumer

40 United States v. Syufy Enters, 903 F.2d 659, 663 n.4 (9th Cir. 1990) ("Monopsony and monopsony power are the equivalent on the buying side of monopoly and monopoly power on the selling side.") (quotations omitted); Todd v. Exxon Corp., 275 F.3d 191 (2001) ("The equation for measuring market power in monopsony is a 'mirror image' of the relationships that create market power in a seller.").

welfare by generating allocative inefficiencies and distorting producers' incentive to invest in quality and efficiency improvements.[41]

31. Monopsony power can be exercised in several different ways. For example, in the classical economic model of monopsony ("classical monopsony"), a dominant buyer exercises unilateral control over an input's market price by cutting back its quantity purchased, depressing demand below the competitive level and thereby causing the input's market price to fall.[42] By comparison, in a Nash-bargaining model of monopsony power, a dominant buyer of inputs sold in a market where prices are individually bargained for exerts control over the input prices by threatening to reduce the quantity purchased. Alternatively, monopsony power may also be used to facilitate the exclusion of the monopsonist's rivals.[43] For example, in *Klor's v. Broadway-Hale Stores*, a leading department store (Broadway-Hale) unlawfully used its "monopolistic buying power" to force appliance manufacturers and distributors to stop supplying a rival store.[44] Likewise, in *JTC Petroleum Co. v. Piasa Motor Fuels, Inc.*, a dominant asphalt applicator allegedly induced smaller asphalt manufactures through threats and bribes to stop selling asphalt to a rival applicator.[45] Indeed, the exercise of monopsony power does not even necessarily result in lower input prices, as occurs when monopsony power is used to force sellers to accept unfavorable non-price terms. Such a situation occurred in *Anderson v. Shipowners' Association*, where shipowners operating on the Pacific Seaboard agreed to only offer sailors all-or-nothing employment contracts that deprived sailors ability to select a ship, route, or other terms of employment.[46]

32. Given the heterogenous means through which monopsony power can be exercised, in assessing monopsony power, one should not conflate the

---

41 *See Bertelsmann*, 646 F. Supp. 3d 1, 24, 56 (2022) (finding that a merger resulting in "lower advances for the authors [] and less favorable contract terms" would harm consumers by "resulting in fewer books being published, less variety in the marketplace of ideas, and an inevitable loss of intellectual and creative output."); *Penn Allegheny Health* Sys., 627 F.3d at 104 (3d Cir. 2010) ("Artificially depressed" payments to suppliers result in "suboptimal output, reduced quality allocative inefficiencies, and (given the reductions in output) higher prices for consumers in the long run.").

42 *See* Salop, *supra* note 3. In this respect, classical monopsony is the mirror image of monopoly – both involve a dominant firm reducing its output in order to make its remaining sales more profitable, either by lower input costs or by raising output prices. Indeed, as with monopoly, there is no question that the artificial acquisition or maintenance of classical monopsony through exclusionary conduct, agreement, or merger is prohibited under the antitrust laws. *See, e.g., Standard Oil Co. of New Jersey,* 221 U.S. at 5 (affirming that Standard Oil's formation, which created a firm with monopsony power in several markets, violated Sections 1 and 2 of the Sherman Act); West Penn Allegheny Health System, Inc. v. UPMC, 627 F.3d 85 (3d Cir. 2010) (Allegations that the dominant hospital network and insurer in western Pennsylvania conspired to mutually reinforce each other's monopoly (hospital) and monopsony (insurer) by excluding each other's competitors sufficient to support Sherman Act Section 1 and 2 claims).

43 *See also* Been v. O.K. Industries, 495 F.3d 1217, 1222–23 (10th Cir. 2007); Sprint Nextel Corp. v. AT&T Inc., 821 F. Supp. 2d 308, 320 (D.D.C. 2011).

44 359 U.S. 207, 212–13 (1959).

45 179 F.3d 1073 (7th Cir. 1999) (Posner, J.) (reversing dismissal of the plaintiff-applicator's antitrust claims).

46 272 U.S. 359 (1926).

inapplicability of a particular model as the absence of monopsony power. For example, just because the exercise of monopsony power necessarily results in reduced downstream output in the case of classical monopsony, one cannot assume the absence of monopsony power from the evidence of constant output. Using output as a screen for monopsony power risks missing a buyer using its monopsony power to force sellers to accept sub-competitive prices or contract terms,[47] as can occurs in agricultural markets.[48] Instead, as with the assessment of market power, the inquiry should focus on the underlying market realities and the buyers ability influence that market.

33. The Merger Guideline's treatment of monopsony power is consistent with these principles. The Merger Guidelines are concerned with mergers that create, enhance, or facilitate the exercise of monopsony power by reducing competition between buyers, without distinction given to a specific model of monopsony. Indeed, the Merger Guidelines have consistently identified "market power by buyers," not classical monopsony, as the Agencies' focus[49] – indeed, the term "monopsony" only first appeared in the 1992 Guidelines.[50] In those Guidelines where the term "monopsony" is used, the Guidelines make clear that monopsony power need not rise to the level of classical monopsony to generate antitrust scrutiny. The 1992 and 1997 Guidelines make clear that "monopsony power" may be wielded by "a single buyer (a 'monopsonist'), a coordinating group of buyers, or a single buyer, not a monopsonist."[51]

34. The enforcement record is clear that monopsony power short of classical monopsony is unlawful. Indeed, only two of the 12 challenges brought against mergers on monopsony grounds (*Cargill/Continental Grain*[52] and *Grifols/Biotest*[53]) alleged the transaction was a merger to monopsony.

---

47 *See* Hemphill & Rose, *supra* note 4, at 2093–99 (applying Nash bargaining models to show that the threat of monopsony power, including the threat of reducing the quantity purchased to zero, can induce the monopsony price without a corresponding loss in short-run output); *Anthem*, 855 F.3d at 377–78 (2017) (Kavanaugh, J., dissenting) (recommending the DOJ's challenge to Anthem's acquisition of Cigna be vacated and remanded for the district court to decide whether the merger would enable Anthem-Cigna to "unlawfully push healthcare providers to accept rates that are below the competitive level).

48 *See, e.g., Mandeville Island Farms*, 334 U.S. at 223 ("Since the refiners controlled the seed supply and the only practical market for beets grown in northern California, when the new contracts were offered to the farmers, they had the choice of either signing or abandoning sugar beet farming."); Complaint, *George's Foods*, No. 5:11-CV-00043 (alleging merger would "allow George's unilaterally to decrease prices or degrade contract terms to [chicken farmers].").

49 1982 Guidelines, *supra* note 26, at § 1 n.5 ("'Market power' also encompasses the ability of a single buyer or group of buyers to depress the price paid for a product to a level below the competitive price. Market power by buyers has wealth transfer and resource misallocation effects analogous to those associated with market power by sellers."); 1984 Guidelines, *supra* note 27, at § 1 (*id*).

50 1992 Guidelines, *supra* note 28, at § 0.1.

51 *Id.* 1997 Guidelines, *supra* note 28, at § 0.1.

52 Complaint, *Cargill,* 2000 WL 1475752 at *11 ("The approximate post-merger HHIs for purchase of wheat in the Central California port range would be about 10,000, with an increase in the HHI of 7,888 points.").

53 Complaint, *Grifols*, FTC File No. C-4654, at 3 ("Respondent Grifols and Biotest US are the only two participants in the human source plasma collection market in the three [relevant markets].").

In the three litigated monopsony challenges, *Bertelsmann*[54] would have resulted in a five-to-four, *Ricer Growers*[55] a four-to-three, and *Pennzoil* a three-to-two.[56] Nevertheless, all three transactions were enjoined upon a finding that they would have substantially lessened competition.

35. Ultimately, monopsony power short of classical monopsony is unlawful under the Clayton Act because the Act is intended to "cope with monopolistic tendencies in their incipiency,"[57] and the Supreme Court has been clear that the Clayton Act's incipiency standard extends to monopsony.[58] Therefore, the government need not, and does not, prove the existence of true classical monopsony to block mergers between buyers.

3. The Agencies and Courts Have Consistently Employed a Common Set of Legal and Economic Tools to Assess a Transaction's Effect on Market Power and Monopsony Power

36. Under every Merger Guideline published since 1982, the Agencies have employed "essentially the same framework" to analyze the effect of mergers in upstream buyer markets and downstream seller markets. As the Guidelines have evolved to adopt new tools for assessing a transaction's likely competitive effects, Agencies have those techniques for both buyer and seller markets. Courts, too, adopted the Guidelines approach to analyzing buyer markets under the same or similar tools.

37. The Agencies' primary tool for assessing whether a merger is substantially likely to reduce competition between buyers and enhance monopsony power has been evidence of post-merger market concentration and market shares. Indeed, the Agencies have never challenged a merger on monopsony grounds without evidence that the merger would create a firm with a substantial share of and significantly increase competition in a relevant market.

38. As with market power in mergers between sellers, the market concentration and shares screen predominates because the screen is simple to administer and relies on readily available evidence. However, the graft of the market concentration screens developed for seller markets onto buyer markets should not be understood as lacking sound economic rationale. A market

54 *Bertelsmann*, 646 F. Supp. 3d at 46 ("The merger would distill the Big Five to a Big Four, with an overwhelmingly dominant top firm, PRH-S & S, controlling 49 percent of the market and dwarfing its nearest competitors.").

55 *Rice Growers*, 1986 WL 12562 at *11 ("RGA's acquisition of the PIRMI business will substantially increase concentration in the market by reducing from four to three the number of firms controlling over 95 percent of the market.").

56 *Pennzoil*, 252 F. Supp. at 982 (identify the three pre-merger purchasers of Penn Grade crude with any "real significance" as Pennzoil, Quaker State, and Kendall.)

57 *Brown Shoe Co. v. U.S.*, 370 U.S. 294, 318 n.32 (1962).

58 *Weyerhaeuser*, 549 U.S. at 322 (Because there is a "close theoretical connection between monopoly and monopsony … similar legal standards should apply to claims of monopolization and claims of monopolization."); *see also id.* ("[M]onopsony pricing … is analytically the same as monopoly or cartel pricing and [is] so treated by the law") (*quoting* Khan v. State Oil Co., 93 F.3d 1358, 1361 (7th Cir. 1996) (Posner, J.) vacated and remanded on other grounds, 522 U.S. 3 (1997).

concentration and market share screen effectively polices for mergers that enhance monopsony power. This is because three economic conditions must be present for monopsony power to exist, and those conditions are positively correlated with market concentration and high market shares.[59] These three conditions are: Inelastic residual demand for the input; inelastic supply; and the possession of a substantial market share.

39. Residual demand for the input (the number of inputs demanded by market participants other than the merging parties) is a key determiner of a merger's effect on monopsony power because it measures the ability of rival firms to defeat the exercise of monopsony power by increasing their purchases of the input. If residual demand is elastic (i.e., rival purchasers are willing and able to meaningfully increase production in response to a price decrease), the post-merger firm cannot credibly threaten to (or actually) reduce its input purchases, as rival purchasers will increase their consumption to offset. However, if residual demand is inelastic, a post-merger firm is less constrained by rival purchasers and has more monopsony power. Inelastic residual demand may result from alternative purchasers being too small and too few to meaningfully increase demand or tacitly facilitating the exercise of monopsony (i.e., tacit "oligopsony"), as is often the case in concentrated markets. Scrutinizing and challenging mergers that significantly increase the concentration of firms is, therefore, an effective screen for inelastic demand.

40. Similarly, an input's elasticity of supply (the sensitivity of the quantity supplied of a good in response to a change in price) is a key determiner of a merger's effect on monopsony power because it measures the ability of sellers to defeat the exercise of monopsony power by redirecting their input to other markets or switching production to a different input. Where redirecting and switching are easy (i.e., the elasticity of supply is elastic), the post-merger firm cannot substantially affect the seller's profit by reducing its input purchases. Therefore, the threatened or actual exercise of monopsony power is weak. But, where supply is inelastic, the threat of monopsony power is stronger, as sellers are effectively locked into doing business with the post-merger firm with few viable alternatives. Inelastic supply may result from sellers having high sunk costs, no equally viable alternative purchaser of their input, or the input commodity having to be sold within a narrow period or set of circumstances (e.g., the risk of spoilage makes the supply of many agricultural products highly inelastic). Because, in assessing mergers between buyers, relevant markets are defined to include all "reasonably interchangeable" buyers,[60] evidence that a merger will "result in a significant increase in the concentration of

59 *See* Phillip E. Areeda & Herbert Hovenkamp, Antitrust Law: An Analysis of Antitrust Principles and Their Application ¶575 n.14 (4th and 5th eds. 2018–2023).

60 *See Bertelsmann*, 646 F. Supp. 3d at 34 (quoting with modifications FTC v. Wilh. Wilhelmsen Holding ASA, 341 F. Supp. 3d 27, 46–47 (D.D.C. 2018)). In buyer-side mergers, relevant markets are defined based on "the cross-elasticity of supply between the product's buyers … and the substitutes for such buyers," with a properly defined relevant market defined to include all "reasonable interchangeable" (buyers). *Id.*

firms in that market" is strong indirect evidence that the merger would substantially increase supply inelasticity.[61]

41. Lastly, a post-merger firm's share of the relevant market is relevant to its monopsony power in two respects. First, if an input purchaser controls a substantial share of an input market, such that alternative purchasers are few and small, that is indirect evidence that residual demand is inelastic. Second, and more significantly, for a firm to credibly threaten or reduce input purchases, it must purchase enough inputs at the sub-competitive price to offset any profits it stands to lose from forgone sales in the output market. While the share of an input market needed for a monopsonist to recoup lost profits in the output market depends on the output product's unit margin and the size of the input's price decrease, in general, a higher market share improves a monopsonist's power by spreading its recoupment across more input units. For this reason, evidence that a merger would substantially increase a firm's share of an already concentrated market is strong indirect evidence that the merger will enhance the merging parties' monopsony power.

42. In accordance with these factors, enforcement actions have focused on industries characterized by both inelastic residual demand and supply. For example, 50% (six of 12) of monopsony merger challenges involved mergers between purchasers of agricultural products (e.g., dairy processors,[62] meat packers,[63] and grain processors).[64] The agricultural sector is prone to residual demand and supply inelasticity because agricultural products must be processed locally within a narrow window of time due to their seasonal nature and risk of spoilage. Similarly, 36% (four of 12) of monopsony challenges were brought against health insurance mergers,[65] a sector prone to monopsony because physicians sell their services in local geographic markets to a small number of payors and, due to their highly specialized training, cannot find equally profitable employment in other sectors. Additionally, most agricultural and healthcare sectors are concentrated.

43. Starting with the introduction of unilateral effects in the 1992 Guidelines, the Agencies have also relied on evidence of close competition between the merging firms, modeling the extent of a merger's effect on monopsony power.[66] Indeed, eight of the 12 merger challenges initiated by the Agencies

---

61 *Id.* (quoting *Phila. Nat'l Bank*, 34 U.S. at 363).

62 Complaint, *Danone*, 2017 WL 3172888 (raw organic milk processors).

63 Complaint, *Tyson Foods*, 2014 WL 4249929 (sow processors); Complaint, *George's Foods*, No. 5:11-cv-00043 (chicken processors); Complaint, *JBS*, No. 08-CV-5992 (beef packers).

64 Complaint, *Cargill*, 2000 WL 1475752 (grain purchasers); *Rice Growers*, 1986 WL 12562 (rice millers).

65 Final Judgement, *UnitedHealth Group*, 71 Fed. Reg. 13991 (health insurers); Complaint, *Aetna*, 1999 WL 1419046 (health insurers); U.S. Dep't. of Justice Press Release, *supra* note 31; *Anthem*, 2017 WL 527923 (health insurer).

66 *See* 1992 Guidelines, *supra* note 28, at §§ 2.1–2.22; 1997 Guidelines, *supra* note 28, at §§ 2.2–2.212; 2010 Guidelines, *supra* note 28, at § 6.

since 1992 alleged the merger would harm sellers by substantially lessening competition between the merging parties.[67]

44. The Agencies have also assessed mergers between buyers for their ability to cause coordinated effects since their introduction in the 1982 Guidelines.[68] In particular, Agencies assess mergers between buyers to determine if the transaction will increase market participants' ability or incentive to mutually decrease competition, either through agreement or parallel accommodating conduct. To date, the Agencies have challenged two mergers based on coordinated effects. In *Bertelsmann*, the DOJ alleged, and the district court ultimately concluded, that coordinated effects were likely because the market for purchasing anticipated top-selling books was already prone to collusion, as evidenced by publishers' participation in an audiobook cartel.[69] In *Danone/WhiteWave*, the DOJ based a coordinated effects case on evidence the market for purchasing raw organic milk was highly transparent and that the merger would reduce processors' incentive to compete by increasing the opportunity for illicit information sharing.[70]

45. In assessing mergers between buyers, the Agencies tend not to place significant credence on a merger's effect on prices in the upstream input market. As a preliminary matter, this type of evidence is rarely available outside of non-consummated mergers. But even if available, the Agencies do not treat evidence indicating a transaction will lower prices as definitive proof the transaction will enhance monopsony power because lower prices often result from procompetitive forces.[71] For example, a merger between purchasers may cause prices to fall if the purchaser and seller are able to reduce transaction costs and enable cost-reducing to achieve efficiencies (e.g., more efficient distribution). Alternatively, lower prices may result from the purchaser's ability to negotiate lower prices through volume-based discounts.

46. Similarly, the Agencies tend not to rely on evidence of the merger's likely effect on output when assessing a transaction's likely effect on competition. This is because, as discussed above, monopsony power can be exercised without a reduction in output.[72] For this reason, "Agencies do

---

67 *Aetna*, 1999 WL 1419046; Final Judgement, *UnitedHealth Group*, 71 Fed. Reg. 13991; *Grifols,* FTC File No. C-4654; Complaint, *Danone*, 2017 WL 3172888; Complaint, *Tyson Foods*, 2014 WL 4249929; Complaint, *George's Foods*, No. 5:11-cv-0004; *Anthem*, 2017 WL 527923; *Bertelsmann*, 646 F. Supp. 3d 1.

68 Although the Merger Guidelines did not refer to Coordinated Effects by name until the 2010 Guidelines, prior Guidelines instructed that mergers in industries prone to coordination were suspect, especially when the merger eliminated a unique impediment to coordination. *See* 1982 Guidelines, *supra* note 26, at §§ 1.D; 1984 Guidelines, *supra* note 27, at § 3.4; 1992 Guidelines, *supra* note 28, at § 2.1; 1997 Guidelines, *supra* note 28, at § 2.1.

69 *Bertelsmann*, 646 F. Supp. at 45 (citing United States v. Apple, Inc., 791 F.3d 290, 339 (2d Cir. 2015)).

70 *Danone*, 2017 WL 3172888 at *9.

71 *See* 2010 Guidelines, *supra* note 28, at § 12 ("A merger that does not enhance market power on the buying side of the market can nevertheless lead to a reduction in prices paid by the merged firm, for example, by reducing transactions costs or allowing the merged firm to take advantage of volume-based discounts. Reduction in prices paid by the merging firms not arising from the enhancement of market power can be significant in the evaluation of efficiencies from a merger.")

72 *See* Section II (2.) *supra* at 7.

not view a short-run reduction in the quantity purchased as the only, or best, indicator of whether a merger enhances buyer market power."[73]

47. Courts have been similarly inclined to adopt precedents from buyer-side cases. For example, in *Pennzoil, Rice Growers of America*, and *Bertelsmann,* all three district courts held that the transaction was presumptively unlawful based on *Philadelphia National Bank*.[74] Similarly, in determining that the government's prima facie case was buttressed by evidence of unilateral and coordinated effects, the *Bertelsmann* court cited *FTC v. H.J. Heinz Co.*,[75] *United States v. Anthem*,[76] *FTC v. Staples, Inc.*,[77] *FTC v. Wilhelmsen Holding ASA*,[78] *FTC v. CCC Holdings*,[79] and *United States v. H & R Block*,[80] despite those cases all concerning sell-side markets.

48. Courts have hewed to established practices even when analytical approaches from buyer-side markets are inapplicable in the seller-side context. For example, courts have adopted the hypothetical *monopsonist* test when defining relevant seller markets, as applied through the "small but significant and non-transitory *decrease* in price" (SSNDP) test.[81] In other monopsony cases brought under the Sherman Act, courts have simply opted to swap "buyer" for "seller" and "increase" for "decrease" to align precedent to seller-side markets.[82] The key takeaway is this: courts and the Agencies analyze mergers between buyers using existing techniques and analytical frameworks unless those techniques are demonstrably inapplicable, in which case they will adopt the existing practice to reflect market realities.

4. The Agencies have been Inconsistent in their Requirement of Evidence of Consumer Harm

49. The DOJ initiated 11 of the 12 challenges to transactions based on buyer power concerns.[83] Undoubtedly, the FTC investigates mergers for monopsony issues. Indeed, since the publication of the 1997 Guidelines, the FTC has

---

73 2010 Guidelines, *supra* note 28, at § 12.

74 *Pennzoil*, 252 F. Supp. at 985; *Rice Growers,* 1986 WL 12562 at *12; *Bertelsmann*, 646 F. Supp. 3d at 37–38.

75 246 F.3d 708 (D.C. Cir. 2001).

76 236 F. Supp. 3d 171 (D.D.C. 2017).

77 970 F. Supp. 1066 (D.D.C. 1997).

78 341 F. Supp. 3d 27 (D.D.C. 2018).

79 605 F. Supp. 2d 26 (D.D.C. 2009).

80 833 F. Supp. 2d 36 (D.D.C. 2011).

81 *Bertelsmann,* 646 F. Supp. 3d at 34–35 (adopting a relevant market based on evidence a hypothetical monopsonist could profitably impose a "small but significant and non-transitory decrease" in advances paid for anticipated top-selling books.")

82 Todd v. Exxon Corp., 275 F.3d 191 (2d Cir. 2001) (Sotomayor, J.); W. Penn Allegheny Health Sys., Inc. v. UPMC, 627 F.3d 85, 105 (3d Cir. 2010); *Khan,* 93 F.3d at 1361; O'Bannon v. National Collegiate Athletic Association, 7 F. Supp. 3d 955, 993 (9th Cir. 2014).

83 In *Grifols/Biotest*, the one case initiated by the Federal Trade Commission, the parties settled the FTC's concerns the transaction would eliminate competition in the market for the collection of human blood plasma by divesting blood collection facilities in three cities. *See* Decision and Order, *Grifols,* FTC File No. C-4654.

publicly investigated at least three transactions for monopsony concerns.[84] But the FTC has historically declined to bring enforcement actions in cases where there is no evidence of downstream harm to consumers.

50. The FTC first announced its consumer harm policy in a statement on its decision not to challenge *Caremark/AdvancePCS*.[85] That case concerned a merger between two pharmacy benefit managers (PBMs), or brokers that negotiate with pharmacies and pharmaceutical manufacturers on behalf of insurers to secure lower drug prices. PBMs secure discounts and rebates on prescription drugs based on guaranteed patient volumes and redirect purchases to lower cost, more efficient sources. These buying practices are generally procompetitive because they tend to increase competition between sellers, lower the price of drugs, and expand output. Retail pharmacy groups, however, complained to the FTC that the merger would harm sellers by creating a firm with sufficient size to force sellers to accept lower prices without increasing efficiency. In response to these complaints, the FTC investigated whether *Caremark/AdvancePCS* would result in monopsony.

51. To ascertain whether lower prices resulting from the merger would result from more efficient purchasing (procompetitive) or monopsony power (anticompetitive), the FTC evaluated whether the merged firm could exercise *classical monopsony*.[86] Specifically, the FTC analyzed whether the merged firm could profitably reduce pharmaceutical prices "below the competitive levels by curtailing purchases of [its] relevant product or service," either by "shift[ing] some purchases to a less efficient source, supply[ing] too little output to the downstream market, or [] both."[87] Based on evidence that the pharmaceutical reimbursement rates were set though individually negotiate contracts (rather than an open market) and that the post-acquisition market share of the merged firm would be below the level at which classical monopsony would be profitable, the FTC determined that the market was not conductive to classical monopsony and declined to bring an enforcement challenge.[88]

52. In reaching its enforcement decision, the FTC appears not to have seriously considered the risk that the merged firm could exercise *monopsony power*. While individually negotiated contracts can be a barrier to classical monopsony, they are not an impediment to monopsony power. Quite the opposite – in the Nash bargaining model of monopsony leverage, bilateral

---

84 *Caremark Rx, Inc./AdvancePCS*; *Express Scripts/Medco Health Solutions*; and *Lifespan/Care New England Health System.*

85 *Statement of the Federal Trade Commission in the Matter of Caremark Rx, Inc./AdvancePCS*, File No. 031 0239 (Feb. 11, 2004).

86 *Id.* ("At most, the acquisition is likely to increase the bargaining power of the merged PBM and to increase its shares (and correspondingly reduce the pharmacies' shares) of the gains flowing from contracts between the PBM and the pharmacies .... Although retail pharmacies might be concerned about this outcome, a reduction in dispensing fees following the merger could benefit consumers.")

87 *Id.* at 2 (The FTC investigated whether the combined firm could "profitably reduce prices in a market below competitive levels by curtailing purchases of the relevant product or service.")

88 *Id.* at 2–3, 3 n.4.

negotiations are a necessary precondition for and multiply the degree of monopsony power.[89] Likewise, as with the relationship between market power and monopoly, the market share needed for a firm to exercise monopsony power is substantially less than the share needed to impose classical monopsony.

53. The FTC's narrow focus on classical monopsony and its ultimate decision not to prosecute a monopsony case should not be understood as a mistake or misunderstanding of monopsony power. Rather, it reflects a policy decision to minimize the risk of false positives by declining to challenge mergers involving plausible efficiencies from bargaining power absent clear evidence of reduced downstream output or other evidence of consumer harm.

54. The DOJ has taken a different approach. As Marius Schwartz, then the DOJ's Economics Director of Enforcement, explained during a discussion of the DOJ's enforcement actions in *Aetna* and *Cargill*, "if a merger increases market power and thereby harms the firm's trading partners – customers or suppliers – by more than it benefits the firm, antitrust concern is warranted ... there is little basis to oppose the exercise of market power against individuals in their capacity as buyers of products but not as sellers of their resources."[90] Put differently, the DOJ resolves the risk of false positives in the opposite direction of the FTC: whereas the FTC requires clear evidence of consumer harm to challenge a merger between buyers, the DOJ will challenge a merger that harms sellers unless there is clear evidence of countervailing consumer benefit.

55. Pursuant to this policy, the DOJ has challenged at least three mergers where the increase in buyer power could not have injured consumers.[91] In these cases, which concerned mergers between grain, chicken, and pork processors, the price of the processed agricultural commodities was determined in national or global commodity markets, where the merged firms had little to no market power. In such a circumstance, the threatened or actual exercise of monopsony power over local farmers, despite having the potential to significantly harm the farmer, could not have materially affected the quantity or price of products supplied to consumers.

56. The DOJ's approach is more consistent with the 2010 Guidelines, which instruct, in relevant part, that the Agencies do not "evaluate the competitive effects of mergers between competing buyers strictly, or even primarily, on the basis of effects in the downstream markets in which the merging firms sell."[92] The FTC co-authored those Guidelines but has not previously tried to reconcile those Guidelines with its enforcement practice.

---

89 *See* Scott Hemphill & Rose, *supra* note 4, at 2093.

90 U.S. Dep't. of Justice Antitrust Division, Marius Schwartz, Buyer Power Concerns and the Aetna-Prudential Merger, Address at the 5th Annual Health Care Antitrust Forum (Oct. 20, 1999), https://www.justice.gov/atr/speech/buyer-power-concerns-and-aetna-prudential-merger; *see also* Sharis A. Pozen, *Agriculture and Antitrust: Dispatches and Learning from the Workshops in Competition in Agriculture*, ANTITRUST Spring 2012 8, 9 (Aug. 8, 2012).

91 Complaint, *Cargill,* 2000 WL 1475752; Complaint, *Tyson Foods,* 2014 WL 4249929; Complaint, *George's Foods, LLC*, No. 5:11-cv-00043 (W.D. Va. May 10, 2011).

92 2010 Guidelines, *supra* note 28, at § 12.

III. Treatment of Monopsony Under the 2023 Guidelines: A Prospective

57. The 2023 Guidelines do not depart from the principles for assessing monopsony power established in prior guidelines. As before, the Agencies will continue assessing mergers between buyers using "the same – or analogous – tools used to assess the effects of a merger of seller."[93] While some in the post-Chicago and Neo-Brandesian schools may criticize prior enforcement as reflecting a static competitive effects analysis grounded in a transaction's immediate effect on consumers, the Agencies' enforcement record demonstrates anything but. Nevertheless, the 2023 Guidelines do materially expand on prior Guidelines in two significant respects.

58. First, the 2023 Guidelines significantly develop the Agencies' framework for analyzing the effects of monopsony power in labor markets. While Agencies have assessed mergers for their effect on labor markets since at least the DOJ's 1999 challenge to Aetna/Prudential Insurance, prior Guidelines did not formally establish the Agencies' framework for assessing monopsony in labor markets.

59. Second, the 2023 Guidelines affirm that cross-market balancing is disallowed. Agency policy has long been that purported benefits of a merger attributable to a loss of competition or other anticompetitive effects were not cognizable as efficiencies. The 2023 Guidelines confirm that purported consumer benefits in a downstream market cannot offset a loss of competition in an upmarket market. In so doing, the 2023 Guidelines repudiate any consumer harm test in monopsony cases.

1. The 2023 Guidelines Elaborate on the Agencies' Existing Approach to Assessing the Effect of Monopoly on Labor Markets

60. Mergers that reduce competition for labor have historically been subject to Agency scrutiny. Since 1990, the Agencies have challenged five mergers under a labor monopsony theory of harm: *Aetna/Prudential Insurance*,[94] *United Health Group/PacifiCare Health*,[95] *Anthem/Cigna*,[96] *Blue Cross Blue Shield of Michigan/Physicians Health Plan of Mid-Michigan*[97] and *Penguin Random House/Simon & Schuster.*[98]

61. However, until the 2023 Guidelines, the Agencies' Merger Guidelines never formally recognized that mergers that harm workers by reducing

---

93 2023 Guidelines, *supra* note 1, at § 2.10.

94 Complaint, United States v. Aetna, Inc., No. 3-99-CV-1398 (N.D. Tex. June 21, 1999).

95 Complaint, United States v. United Health Group Inc., No. 1:05-CV-02436 (D.D.C. Mar. 3, 2006).

96 United States v. Anthem, Inc., No. CV 16-1493 (ABJ), 2017 WL 527923 (D.D.C. Feb. 8, 2017)

97 U.S. Dep't. of Justice Press Release, *supra* note 31.

98 *Bertelsmann*, 646 F. Supp. 3d 1.

competition between employers violated the Clayton Act. While the Agencies' enforcement record makes clear that such mergers are, in fact, unlawful by not directly addressing the labor monopsony issue, the Guidelines left courts and market participants little guidance for how the Agencies assessed labor market competition.[99] For example, while the 2010 Guideline's adoption of the hypothetical monopsonist test clarified the Agencies' framework for defining the outer boundaries of a relevant market comprised of purchasers or goods and services, it did little to clarify how markets involving competing employers should be defined. Similarly, the 2010 Guidelines did not explain whether the Agencies considered HHIs to be an appropriate measure of concentration in labor markets or how to assess a merger's effect on non-price terms and conditions of employment (e.g., tenure, leave and illness policies, workplace safety conditions, etc.). The lack of clarity proved especially disconcerting after the Biden Administration directed the Agencies to focus on employer competition in July 2021.[100]

62. The 2023 Guidelines fill in the analytical gaps left by the 2010 Guidelines. In this way, developments in the 2023 Guidelines should not be understood as a material change in the Agencies' analysis but rather a reflection of the Agencies' actual practices and enforcement priorities.

63. The 2023 Guideline's first and most substantive development is Guideline 10, which formally recognizes that mergers likely to substantially lessen competition for workers or other types of human labor are unlawful.[101] This guideline clarifies that "labor markets are important buyer markets" and that the Agencies will analyze mergers to assess whether the transaction will "lower wages or slow wage growth, worsen benefits or working conditions, or result in other degradations of workplace quality."[102] Pursuant to this policy, Agencies will challenge all mergers shown to harm workers by reducing competition between employers, regardless of any benefits to downstream consumers. This is because, by the language of the Clayton Act, purported benefits in a separate downstream product market cannot be used to offset harm to workers.[103]

64. Second, the 2023 Guidelines state that "observed market characteristics" are a sufficient independent basis for identifying a relevant product

---

99 The 2010 Guidelines' hypothetical monopsonist test instructed that a relevant product market exists around a set of products if a hypothetical monopsonist that was the products' only present and future buyer could profitably decrease the price of at least one product by a small but significant amount, typically 5%. *See* 2010 Guidelines, *supra* note 28, at § 12 ("In defining relevant markets, the Agencies focus on the alternatives available to sellers in the face of a decrease in the price paid by a hypothetical monopsonist." *Id.*

100 *See Executive Order on Promoting Competition in the American Economy*, Exec. Order No. 14036, 86 FR 36987 (2021).

101 2023 Guidelines, *supra* note 1, at § 2.10.

102 *Id*, at 26–27.

103 *Id.* at 27 ("Because the Clayton Act prohibits mergers that may substantially lessen competition or tend to create a monopoly in any line of commerce and in any section of the country, a merger's harm to competition among buyers is not saved by benefits to competition among sellers.")

market.[104] These observed characteristics, derived from the "practical indicia" described by the Supreme Court in *Brown Shoe*, include industry or public recognition of the products as a separate economic entity, the product's peculiar characteristics and uses, unique production facilities, distinct buyers, distinct prices, sensitivity to price changes, or specialized vendors.[105] On its face, the 2023 Guideline's adoption of the *Brown Shoe* practical indicia is substantive change in Agency policy, as no prior guidelines recognized this as a basis for defining relevant markets. However, the Agencies have regularly relied on the practical indicia to allege and define markets in court, so their adoption by the 2023 Guidelines is not a substantive deviation in Agency practice.[106] As applied to mergers between employers, the Agencies can be expected to use the practical indicia to define markets around labor services that require workers with unique or peculiar abilities (e.g., level of education or specialized training) or to distinguish a subset of workers within a labor service that the merger may uniquely injure. For example, in *Penguin Random House/Simon & Schuster*, the Agencies alleged that the court adopted a market around advances paid to authors greater than $250,000 as a proxy for assessing the merger's impact on advances paid for "anticipated top-selling books."[107]

65. Third, the 2023 Guidelines adopt a unified framework for implementing the hypothetical monopolist/monopsonist test.[108] Under the new a small but significant and non-transitory increase in price (SSNIP) or other worsening of terms (SSNIPT) test, a relevant market exists around a group of products or services if a hypothetical monopolist (or monopsonist) would impose a small but significant and non-transitory increase (or decrease) in price or worsening of terms for at least one product in the group.[109] Economically, the SSNIPT test is equivalent to the 2010 Guideline's SSNIPT in that both test whether the putative market is sufficiently broad to capture all reasonably interchangeable substitutes for the relevant product. Practically, the SSNIPT test expands on the SSNIP test to account for competition on non-price terms. This is important for labor markets because non-wage compensation and benefits are key dimensions of employer competition. Terms of employment the Agencies are likely to focus on when implementing a SSNIPT test include health benefits, retirement benefits (e.g., 401-K matching, pensions, etc.), vacation and leave policies, and travel stipends.[110]

---

104 *Id.* at § 4.3 at 41 ("A relevant market can be identified from evidence on observed market characteristics ('practical indicia.')."

105 *Brown Shoe*, 370 U.S. at 325.

106 For instance, of judicial reliance on the practical indicia, see *Bertelsmann*, 646 F. Supp. 3d at 25, *FTC v. Whole Foods Market, Inc.*, 548 F.3d 1028, 1038–39 (D.C. Cir. 2008), *FTC v. Swedish Match*, 131 F. Supp. 2d 151, 159 (D.D.C. 2000) and *FTC v. Staples, Inc.*, 970 F. Supp. 1066, 1075 (D.D.C. 1997)

107 *Bertelsmann*, 646 F. Supp. 3d at 25–29.

108 2023 Guidelines, *supra* note 1, at § 4.3.A at 41.

109 *Id.* at 41–42.

110 *See* 2023 Guidelines, *supra* note 1, at § 2.10 at 27.

The Agencies may also consider working conditions, such as the employers' willingness to invest in workplace safety and comfort.[111]

66. Lastly, the Guidelines attempt to describe what diminution in employment terms would qualify as "small but significant" for purposes of the SSNIPT, explaining that the change in terms must be competitively significant in light of the industry's nature and the merging parties' positions in the market.[112] Typically, the Agencies will use a 5% SSNIPT if the worsening can be represented as an explicit or implicit price. However, in labor markets, the Agencies will ultimately adopt a threshold corresponding to the workers' willingness to switch. For example, the Agencies will set lower thresholds for and define narrower labor markets in industries characterized by high switching costs or matching frictions.[113] For this reason, although not formally stated in the 2023 Guidelines, Agencies should be expected to define narrow labor markets around workers facing only a small number of employers willing to pay a premium for their specialized knowledge, such as engineers, physicians, or other workers.

2. The 2023 Guidelines Prohibit Cross-Market Balancing and Disallow Using Benefits to Downstream Consumers to Offset Harm to Upstream Harm Sellers

67. Whether a merger that reduces seller welfare while plausibly expanding consumer welfare is unlawful under the Clayton Act has historically divided the Agencies. As discussed in Section II.4, the FTC has historically required clear evidence of consumer harm to challenge a merger between buyers. In contrast, the DOJ has required clear evidence of countervailing and consumer benefit *not* to challenge mergers that lessened buyer competition and threatened to increase monopsony power. The 2023 Guidelines resolve the Agency split by adopting a new, total competition standard. Under this approach, all mergers that may substantially lessen competition in any market are presumptively unlawful and will be challenged, regardless of their effect in another market.[114] This standard is more aggressive than either Agency's prior approach in two key respects.

68. First, the 2023 Guidelines generally reject using consumer welfare as the primary basis for assessing a transaction's competitive effects. Since 1984, the Guidelines' "unifying theme" has been to prevent mergers that create or facilitate the exercise of market power to protect consumers from higher prices, reduced output, diminished innovation, or other forms of

---

111 *Id.*

112 *Id.*, § 4.3.B at 43.

113 *Id.*, § 2.10 at 27 (The Agencies will define "relatively narrow" labor markets where in markets with "characteristics that can exacerbate the competitive effects of a merger between competing employers," such as switching costs and matching frictions.)

114 2023 Guidelines, *supra* note 1, at § 1 at 1 ("To show that a merger is unlawful, a plaintiff need only prove that its effect 'may be substantially to lessen competition'" or to tend to create a monopoly.").

harm.[115] The 2023 Guidelines, however, make preserving "open and fair" competition the primary object of merger enforcement policy.[116] Under this approach, competitive effects are no longer an end in themselves but rather a tool for assessing the transaction's effect on competition. The practical effect of this evolution in enforcement priority is that the Agencies are no longer concerned with "attempt[ing] to predict" whether a merger that lessens competition between buyers will result in lower prices as a result of anticompetitive monopsony power or procompetitive bargaining power.[117] Instead, the Agencies will treat the loss of competition itself as an independent and sufficient basis to challenge a transaction.

69. Second, the 2023 Guidelines reject cross-market balancing. Cross-market balancing refers to the question of whether a merger that reduces competition in one market can be offset by a greater increase in competition in a different market. Despite stated policies that disfavored such balancing, both Agencies have historically tolerated cross-market balancing when assessing transactions that plausibly increase consumer welfare at the expense of sellers, only disagreeing about the strength of evidence and magnitude of consumer benefit needed to offset harm to sellers. Where the DOJ required the merging parties to introduce clear evidence of countervailing consumer benefit to engage in cross-market balancing, the FTC was willing to offset a loss of competition between buyers based on only plausible consumer benefits.

70. The 2023 Guidelines now interpret the Clayton Act as categorically prohibiting cross-market balancing.[118] In a repudiation of their prior positions, the Agencies now take the position that "harm to competition among buyers [cannot be] saved by benefits to competition among sellers," even in the face of significant and certain consumer benefits.

71. Under the 2023 Guidelines, merging parties should be prepared to demonstrate that their transaction will not reduce competition in any upstream or downstream market in which the parties compete. If the transaction will reduce some degree of competition, the parties must be prepared to show the loss of competition will not be substantial. Parties should no longer expect to the Agencies to credit evidence showing the loss of competition will be offset by a countervailing benefit to consumers in another market.

---

115 *See* 1984 Guidelines, *supra* note 27, at § 0.1 ("The unifying theme of the Guidelines is that mergers should not be permitted to create or enhance market power or to facilitate its exercise. Market power to a seller is the ability profitably to maintain prices above competitive levels for a significant period of time."); 2010 Guidelines, *supra* note 28, at § 1 ("The unifying theme of these Guidelines is that mergers should not be permitted to create, enhance, or entrench market power or to facilitate its exercise .... A merger enhances market power if it is likely to encourage one or more firms to raise price, reduce output, diminish innovation, or otherwise harm customers as a result of diminished competitive constraints or incentives.").

116 2023 Guidelines, *supra* note 1, at § 1 at 1.

117 *Id.* at 1–2.

118 2023 Guidelines, § 2.10, at 27 ("Because the Clayton Act prohibits mergers that may substantially lessen competition or tend to create a monopoly in any line of commerce and any section of the country, a merger's harm to competition among buyers is not saved by benefits to competition among sellers."

Mergers That Increase Buyer Power and the Function of Presumptions: Two Key Issues in the Revision of the Merger Guidelines

PETER C. CARSTENSEN*
University of Wisconsin Law School

* Fred W. & Vi Miller Chair in Law Emeritus

72. The latest iteration of the Merger Guidelines has some positive features but leaves a number of unanswered or undeveloped issues that may reduce the effectiveness of the guidance offered. This chapter focuses on two of those issues: the analysis of mergers that increase buyer power and the meaning of the presumption of illegality in merger law.[1]

73. The 2023 Guidelines retain the explicit recognition of the 2010 Guidelines that buyer power is a significant concern of merger law.[2] However, the exposition is less robust than the 2010 version. These limitations are likely to reduce the effectiveness of this guideline to encourage and justify stronger enforcement on this side of the market. The 2023 Guidelines continue the failure to articulate the definition of the presumption of illegality created by the *Philadelphia Nation Bank* decision and explicated in subsequent Supreme Court decisions.[3] While the resulting ambiguity is consistent with the Agencies own limited conception of that presumption, ignoring those Supreme Court precedents has weakened one of the most effective doctrines in the enforcers' toolbox.

74. The next section will focus on Guideline 10 concerning mergers that create unreasonable buyer power. This requires a review of the competitive risks that such power can create after which it is then possible to identify the weaknesses and omissions in Guideline 10. The second part focuses on the failure of the 2023 Guidelines as well as its predecessors to define the presumption of illegality in line with the Supreme Court's definition.

I. The Importance of Controlling Buyer Power for Workable Competition[4]

75. Before examining Guideline 10, it is necessary to summarize the range of competitive risks that undue buyer power creates as well as describe when buyer power can arise in terms of market structure. This background provides the basis for an informed critique of the new guideline.

1 I have written on both of these topics, and this chapter draws shamelessly on that prior work: Peter C. Carstensen, Competition Policy and Buyer Power: A Global Issue (2017); *Buyer Power and the Horizontal Merger Guidelines: Minor Progress on an Important Issue*, 14 U. Penn. Bus. L.J. 775 (2012); *Buyer Cartels versus Buying Groups: Legal Distinctions, Competitive Realities, and Antitrust Policy*, 1 William & Mary Bus. L. Rev. 1 (2010); *The Philadelphia National Bank Presumption: Merger Analysis in a Dynamic Economy*, 80 Antitrust L.J. 219 (2015); *The Merger Incipiency Doctrine and the Importance of "Redundant" Competitors,* 2018 Wis. L. Rev. 780 (with Robert Lande).

2 *Compare* Fed. Trade Comm'n and U.S. Dep't. of Justice, *Horizontal Merger Guidelines* (2010) ("2010 Guidelines"), https://www.justice.gov/atr/file/810276/dl?inline, *with Merger Guidelines* (2023) ("2023 Guidelines"), https://www.ftc.gov/system/files/ftc_gov/pdf/2023_merger_guidelines_final_12.18.2023.pdf.

3 United States v. Phila. Nat'l Bank, 374 U.S. 321 (1963).

4 This Part draws significantly from my article on buyer power and merger analysis, *supra* note 1.

1. The Competitive Risks Buyer Power Creates and the Structural Indicia of Such Power

A. *The Competitive Risks Buyer Power Creates*

76. Buyers can employ their power over their suppliers both to exploit them by obtaining inputs at prices below those that would prevail in a workably competitive market and by using their power to exclude their competitors from access to necessary inputs. Moreover, both of these effects create further indirect harms to competition. The scope of this indirect harm is one feature of buyer power that differentiates its harms from those associated with seller power.

77. A firm with buyer power can exercise that power to exploit its suppliers through lower prices. There have been conspiracies among blueberry buyers and tobacco buyers.[5] Buyer cartels have existed in various employment markets including high-tech, nurses, and doctors as well as poultry growers and employees in poultry processing.[6]

78. Unilateral buyer conduct can also produce lower input prices. Walmart has a long-standing history of compelling its suppliers to give it lower and lower prices.[7] The end result is that a number of these suppliers were forced into bankruptcy.[8] Walmart's response was to move to another supplier.[9]

79. If there is a public market or a publicly reported price, large buyers have an incentive to engage in manipulation of that price. By manipulating the price downward, the buyer gains the advantage of lower input costs.[10] For example, most cattle are sold under contracts that rely on prices set in the residual public trading market. Packers have a manifest incentive to limit the cash prices on which they base substantial

---

5 *See* Deloach v. Philip Morris Cos., Memorandum Opinion, Case No. 1:00CV01235, 2003 WL 23094907 (M.D.N.C. Dec. 19, 2003); Nathan Assocs., *Blueberries Price Fixing Class Action Finally Ends*, 2 Proceedings: Litigation, Regulatory & Other News 1 (May 13, 2005).

6 *See, e.g.*, Final Judgment, United States v. Adobe, Complaint, Case No. 1:10-cv-01629 (D.D.C. Oct. 1, 2010) (condemning a no poaching agreement in high-tech industry), see also Jean-Christophe Roda, *Agreements banning cold calling of employees: The US DOJ settles with six high tech companies to stop entering into anticompetitive employee non solicitation agreements (United States/Adobe Systems, Apple, Google, Intel Corporation, Intuit, and Pixar)*, Concurrences No. 1-2011, art. No. 34396, pp. 230–231; United States v. Arizona Hosp. and Healthcare Ass'n, Complaint, Case No. CV07-1030-PHX-JAT (D. Ariz. Sept. 12, 2007) (no poaching agreement in the healthcare industry); Cason-Merenda v. Detroit Med. Ctr., 862 F. Supp. 2d 603 (E.D. Mich. 2012) (denying summary judgement with respect to an information exchange among hospitals to limit wages for nurses); Complaint United States v. Cargill (alleging an unlawful agreement to exchange information about poultry workers' wages and compensation for poultry growers) https://www.justice.gov/atr/case/usv-cargill-meat-solutions-corp-et-al.

7 *See* Timothy Richards & Geoffrey Pofahl, *Pricing Power by Supermarket Retailers: A Ghost in the Machine?*, 25 Choices: The Magazine of Food, Farm, and Resource Issues (2010).

8 Barry C. Lynn, *Breaking the Chain: The Antitrust Case Against Wal-Mart*, Harper's Bazaar 29, July 1, 2006.

9 Robert. A. Schultz, Contemporary Issues in Ethics and Information Technology 80 (2006).

10 In public markets, if most of the relevant commodity is traded, there are offsetting interests. Hence, when there are numerous parties on both sides of such a market there should be a shared interest in neutrality. This interest is greater as the number of both buyers and sellers increases.

contracts.[11] The price of milk rests largely on the price of cheese as set in public markets and there was well documented manipulation of the cheese market located in Green Bay.[12] Such manipulative use of public market prices is an old story.[13]

80. Two other uses of buyer power can create serious competitive concerns. First, buyers often have the incentive and capacity to engage in geographic price discrimination among their suppliers. Whenever suppliers are geographically constrained, the buyer buying in several regions can adjust its price depending on the level of local competition. Other limits can be the result of buyer-imposed allocation of sellers precluding competing bids, or a consequence of significant switching costs.[14] Hence, just as in selling markets so too on the buying side the potential to discriminate among classes of producers exists.

81. Second, buyers' markets have greater potential to develop anticompetitive, linked oligopolies than is likely in seller markets.[15] Because of the shared interest in retaining the lowest input prices possible, buyers will find it attractive to avoid competition for inputs in so far as possible. Moreover, the risk of retaliation across markets when firms compete in the purchase of multiple inputs at multiple locations provides a context in which tacit understandings become more enforceable.[16] Each firm will have an incentive to develop its own sources of supply and not engage in vigorous competition with rival buyers. In agricultural markets such as poultry, processors tend to avoid building facilities that compete very directly.[17] Another form is for a buyer to buy and then close plants that are "too competitive" with those of other buyers.[18] By doing so, the new

11 In the case of beef cattle, such contracts are called alternative marketing agreements. The use of such contracts when based on a cash market price result in an aggregate reduction in prices for cattle. *See* Francisco Garrido et al., *Buyer Power in the Beef Packing Industry: An Update on Research in Progress* (Apr. 13, 2022), http://www.nathanhmiller.org/cattlemarkets.pdf; *see generally* Peter C. Carstensen, *Dr. Pangloss as an Agricultural Economist: The Analytic Failures of the U.S. Beef Supply Chain: Issues and Challenges*, 68 S.D.L. Rev. 458 (2023).

12 *See* Willard F. Mueller et al., *Cheese Pricing: A Study of the National Cheese Exchange*, Dep't of Agric. Econ., Univ. of Wis.-Madison (Mar. 1996).

13 *See* Peter Carstensen, *The Content of the Hollow Core of Antitrust: The Chicago Board of Trade Case and the Meaning of the "Rule of Reason" in Restraint of Trade Analysis*, 15 Res. L. & Econ. 42–43 (1992) (discussing early market manipulation cases).

14 *See* Lynn Hunnicutt et al., *Rigidity in Packer-Feedlot Relationships*, 36 J. Agric. & Applied Econ. 627 (2004) (discussing measures used to describe feedlot-packer relations).

15 *See* Elinor Harris Solomon, *Bank Merger Policies and Problems: A Linkage Theory of Oligopoly*, 2 J. Money Credit & Banking 323 (1970) (discussing market-extension mergers in banking); *see also* Cargill, Inc. v. Monfort of Colo., Inc., 479 U.S. 104 (1986) (denying standing to a single-plant company challenging a multi-plant operator's purchase of a directly competing slaughterhouse).

16 It was the risk of predatory buying (raising cattle prices) that motivated Monfort's effort to block the merger creating Cargill's massive, multi-market beef packing operation. *Cargill*, 479 U.S. at 104 (denying standing because plaintiff would not suffer an antitrust injury as result of higher prices to input suppliers). Having lost the case, Monfort sold out to another multi-regional packer. *Company News: Conagra Deal for Monfort*, N.Y. Times, Mar. 6, 1987, at D4.

17 James M. MacDonald, U.S. Dep't of Agric., The Economic Organization of U.S. Broiler Production 4–5 (2008).

18 A possible example is the decision of Smithfield to close the Farmland plant in Dubuque, Iowa, after buying the company. *Dubuque Packing Company*, Wikipedia, https://en.wikipedia.org/wiki/Dubuque_Packing_Company.

owner reduces competitive pressure on its rival within the rival's sphere of influence expecting that the rival would reciprocate by focusing their buying interests away from other areas of potential overlap.

82. Buyer power is also used to impose constraints on suppliers that cause other buyers to have higher prices for or even no access to an important input. In one case, the buyer got all the major suppliers of the key input to agree to exclusive dealing contracts fencing out its competitors.[19] Other examples include toy and appliance markets.[20]

83. Another indirect exclusionary consequence of imposing a low price, especially if below that firm's average cost per unit, is that the producer is likely to be compelled to raise its prices to its other customers. This is the waterbed effect.[21] Assuming that the product at issue is somewhat differentiated, the seller can raise its price to its other customers in order to recover its losses.[22] This is a sub-optimal result because otherwise the supplier would already have been charging those prices. But if at least short-run demand is relatively inelastic, it would be feasible to extract additional income from the other buyers, even if the longer run implications are negative in terms of lost sales or buyer failure. If those customers, in turn, compete with the favored buyer, they will face a cost disadvantage. Indeed, the favored buyer will have effectively made its supplier's other customers subsidize its purchases.[23]

84. In standard merger analysis concerning seller power, the impact on the immediate downstream market is the primary focus. This is sensible because if the merger will result in higher prices to that market, then the effects further downstream are predictable. While in general the same can be said of buyer power, there is more ambiguity as to the explanation for lower input prices that might result from a merger. On their face, such "cost savings" appear to promise an efficiency gain.[24] But the capacity of the upstream supplier to provide further price discounts to

---

19 FTC v. Mylan Labs., Inc., 62 F. Supp. 2d 25 (D.D.C. 1999) on reconsideration in part sub nom. FTC v. Mylan Labs., Inc., 99 F. Supp. 2d 1 (D.D.C. 1999).

20 Klor's, Inc. v. Broadway-Hale Stores, Inc., 359 U.S. 207 (1959); Toys "R" Us, Inc. v. FTC, 221 F.3d 928 (7th Cir. 2000).

21 *See generally*, Paul W. Dobson & Roman Inderst, *The Waterbed Effect: Where Buying and Selling Power Come Together*, 2008 Wis. L. Rev. 331 (2008).

22 The producer of a differentiate good has some capacity to vary its prices because its product or location allow that. As a rational actor it will locate the optimal price/output combination. *See generally*, Edward H. Chamberlain, The Theory of Monopolistic Competition (8th ed. 1962).

23 There is an illustrative historical case study of this process. Standard Oil used its power as a buyer of rail services to require the railroads both to give it discounts and to pay it a percentage of the freight charges levied on its competitors. Thus, it both raised its rivals' costs and got a piece of the overcharge. *See* Elizabeth Granitz & Benjamin Klein, *Monopolization by "Raising Rivals' Costs": The Standard Oil Case*, 39 J.L. & Econ. 1 (1996).

24 *See e.g.*, Fee & Thomas, *Sources of Gains in Horizontal Mergers: Evidence from Customer, Supplier, and Rival Firms*, 74 J. Fin. Econ. 423 (2004) (finding reduced input costs as clear evidence of increased efficiency, but to the extent that the cost savings are the result of buyer power exploitation of upstream suppliers, that characterization would be incorrect); s*ee also*, 2010 Guidelines, *supra* note 2, at § 12 (excluding wealth transfers from inclusion as a part of an efficiency defense).

a consolidated buyer may reflect only the ability of that supplier, given its increased volume of purchases resulting from the downstream merger, to exert its own increased monopsony power against its upstream input providers. Thus, the adverse effect of a consolidation in grocery retailing or the manufacture of food products may primarily impact farmers and ranchers who see the price for the basic ingredients driven down.[25] Thus, as the downstream buyer consolidates its purchases, it endows its upstream supplier with greater buyer power derivatively.

85. Another example of this phenomenon is the manipulation of cheese prices.[26] The direct goal of such manipulation was to lower the price of cheese for the advantage of major cheese buyers. By selling small amounts of cheese on the old Green Bay cheese exchange, the major buyers of cheese could manipulate the price downward or retard its increase. This allowed them to buy cheese directly from producers based on the manipulated exchange prices. Milk converts to cheese on a relatively fixed ratio, and so when the price of their product declined, cheese makers reduced the price paid for milk. While the cheese makers may have absorbed a small amount of the price reduction, the great bulk of this buyer power was passed on to the dairy farmers.[27]

86. The point is that the impact of anticompetitive conduct on the buyer side of the market is often at one or two stages prior to the party bearing the immediate impact of the lower price. A full analysis of the effects of a merger that increases buying power needs to trace out the potential for such indirect impacts if it is to provide a comprehensive evaluation of the potential competitive harms from a transaction.

87. In the standard economic models of monopsony, the effect of lower prices is to reduce output even if supply is price inelastic. This assumes that there is an upward sloping cost curve for the producer. But, given those standard assumptions, a powerful buyer can use an "all or nothing" buying strategy to demand that the supplier provide the quantity that it would have provided at a competitive (i.e., higher) price if it wants to make any sale at all.[28] The price ought to approximate the average cost of producing the set quantity of goods. Given an increasing marginal cost, this means that the seller loses money on some part of the order, but that loss is offset by the lower costs of the infra-marginal production. In substance, the buyer has appropriated the efficiency gains that would otherwise accrue to the producer and left it in a breakeven position.

---

25 *See generally* United Food and Commercial Workers Int'l Union, Ending Walmart's Rural Stranglehold (2010) (offering evidence of the ways in which Walmart, the nation's largest food retailer, exploits its buyer power).

26 Mueller et al., *supra* note 12.

27 Dairy farms are very price inelastic. A herd of cows, every day, seven days a week, produces a relatively set quantity of milk, depending on the season of the year. Until the herd is liquidated, the dairy farmer has to sell that output at whatever price the market provides.

28 Carstensen, Buyer Power, *supra* note 1, at 42–43; Roger D. Blair & Jeffrey L. Harrison, Monopsony in Law and Economics 83–85 (2010).

88. Although output remains constant and the buyer has a lower cost for the input, the result is allocatively inefficient because the cost of the marginal unit exceeds the price paid for it. Moreover, the producer surplus transferred to the buyer reflects the extent to which the specific producer has achieved lower costs of production than the market price. Thus, this part of the surplus, sometimes called Ricardian Rents, is the reward for efficient production. Taking that reward from the producer, therefore, reduces the incentives of innovate or to pursue greater efficiency.

B. *The Structural Criteria for Buyer Power*

89. The capacity to choose among potential suppliers can create a great deal of power even when the buyer's market share is modest by seller side measures.[29] Indeed, the reason that fairly high market shares are used in assessing when seller combinations create risks of competitive harm is because buyers have the discretion to switch suppliers and thus de-stabilize the potential market power effects of a selling side merger.

90. In the UK single firm market shares of less than 10% of all of some class groceries purchased in the country have produced unilateral buyer power effects.[30] In *Toys R Us*, the market share that allowed the firm to impose anticompetitive restraints on its suppliers was about 20% of the national market for toys. While no market share is reported in the *Klors* case, it is unlikely that Broadway-Hale dominated the retail appliance market in California or nationally, but it still had the power to coerce its suppliers into agreeing to cut off Klors. These cases suggest that unilateral effects are possible from mergers resulting in control of 10% to 20% of the buying market. The EU found in a study of grocery manufacturers that when a buyer took 20% or more of the product, it had significant buyer power.[31] Several EU Member States as well as the UK and Japan have adopted regulations controlling buying practices by large retailers.[32]

91. Economies and diseconomies in supplier production affect the unilateral market power of buyers. A plausible reason for the power of a 10% buyer

29 A buyer able to affect 10% or more of producer's output assuming any kind of economies of scale has the potential for considerable leverage over that seller. Another relevant condition is whether there is another outlet for this production that is easily accessible. The Blair–Harrison Index of Buyer Power predicts that under some conditions, i.e., elasticity of supply and fringe demand equal to one, such a firm can impose an 5% decrease on its suppliers' prices. Blair & Harrison, *supra* note 28, at 59. Manifestly, in most industrial situations, a change in output for a producer in the 10% or greater range is likely to result in significant short-term impact at the very least. With longer term impact uncertain, under such circumstances every major buyer has significant leverage over such a producer. When the buyer takes a much higher percentage of a specific sellers output, the dislocation resulting from the lost sales opportunity will be even greater assuming the seller has relatively few alternative outlets readily available.

30 Paul Dobson, *Exploiting Buyer Power: Lessons from the British Grocery Trade*, 72 Antitrust L.J. 529, 535 (2005). One might question whether there is any reason to think that smaller markets in terms to total sales volume may result in buyer power at smaller market shares than would be the case in markets with larger total volumes. This is the kind of question that ought to be under consideration in rethinking the merger guidelines, but to date has received no noticeable attention.

31 Carstensen, Buyer Power, *supra* note 1, at 64 n.58.

32 *Id.* at 140–149.

in the retail grocery business is that a threatened reduction in volume of 10% could cause a firm significant diseconomies of scale especially if it will be difficult to find an alternative outlet for that quantity of production.[33] Thus, if two of customers of a supplier combine so that their combined purchases would significantly affect the volume of sales for the producer, then the producer will become dependent on the merged buyer's continued patronage.[34] This in turn can confer on such a buyer a great deal of buyer power with respect to that seller.[35]

92. A second context where buyer power may arise at relatively low market shares occurs if the buyer takes all or most of the output of the seller and the merger eliminates the next best alternative outlet for such a seller.[36] Switching totally from one buyer to another involves greater transition costs and risks. If the switch does not work out, the supplier may now be without any market for its output. For example, no one cattle feedlot is essential to the packer's volume, but each feedlot needs to make sales regularly. Hence, the ability of a regular buyer to refuse to deal or impose lower prices is quite substantial as the number of alternative buyers decline.[37] Thus, in such contexts mergers among such buyers will be likely to have significant effect on the power of all buyers in the market because of the reduction in alternative outlets.

93. The implication of these studies and examples is that mergers that create buyer control over 15% of an input market create significant potential for unilateral effects. As Blair and Harrison have shown, the relative levels of elasticity on both the supply and demand side affect the level of power that will result.[38] Supply side market structure may also be relevant as a concentrated supply side may produce countervailing power, but such power may result in higher consumer prices as the concentrated buyers and sellers collectively raise input prices and find ways to share the overcharge even if the downstream market appears competitive.[39]

---

33 The potential lack of alternative outlets either in the market as a whole or in a regional segment important to achieving efficient use of national advertising makes retail buyer power analysis an especially important focal point.

34 This effect is most likely in contexts such as grocery retailing where the seller already is selling to other major outlets. Hence, the lost sales cannot easily or readily be recouped by adding other outlets.

35 The extent of that power will be a function of the diseconomies that might result from reduction in output as well as the potential that the producer can find other outlets for its products. This is the converse of the committed and uncommitted entrant analysis in the 2010 Guidelines, but now framed in terms of committed and uncommitted buyers. *See* 2010 Merger Guidelines, *supra* note 2, at 15–16 (discussing "rapid entrants"), 27–29 (discussing entry conditions).

36 This is in part the explanation for why the Antitrust Division challenged mergers among health insurers where the market shares were below the safe harbor levels that the Division's own guidelines set for health care buying groups. See Mark J. Botti, *Observations on and from the Antitrust Division's Buyer-Side Cases: How Can "Lower" Prices Violate the Antitrust Laws*?, (Paper presented at the ABA Antitrust Section Spring Meeting, Apr. 17, 2007).

37 *See* Hunnicutt et al., *supra* note 14; *see generally* Jeremy Sandford, *Competition and Endogenous Impatience in Credence-Good Markets*, 169 J. Isti. Theo. Econ. 531 (2013) (showing that seven or options are necessary when the counter party faces problems of returning to a former partner).

38 Roger D. Blair & Jeffrey L. Harrison, Antitrust Laws and Economics 36–42 (1993).

39 *See* Chris Doyle & Martijn A. Han, *Cartelization Through Buyer Groups*, 44 Rev. Ind. Org. 265 (2014).

94. Second, as *Todd* teaches, it is possible for a more dispersed set of buyers to find it rational to coordinate their buying activities than would be the likely case on selling side of the market.[40] This occurs for a couple of interrelated reasons. Buyers generally share an interest in reducing input prices, especially when lower prices, e.g., wages, do not trigger a significant decrease in supply. Closely related, the benefit of cheating on a price reducing understanding is minimal. The immediate effect is to increase the costs of the deviant. If that deviant is selling into a competitive output market, its costs will go up and so its margin will decrease. The deviant can expect to gain only if any resulting output increase were substantial and durable. Such results are unlikely. This means that buyer collusion will be more self-policing and so can accommodate many more parties than would output collusion.[41] Hence, again, lower levels of concentration create risks of coordinated effects. Put in somewhat different terms, a reduction from six to five substantial buyers should be a cause for concern and a presumption of illegality.

2. The 2023 Guideline Compared to 2010 – Not as Good

95. While the 2010 Guidelines did not mention labor markets, the 2023 Guidelines gives a disproportionate emphasis to labor markets (five of the eight paragraphs focus on this market context) relative to the other markets in which such power can be and is abused.[42] Labor markets are very important domains in which monopsonistic and oligopsonistic harms can and do result. Moreover, the significance of the competitive risks more clearly emerged after 2010, and a clear recognition of that risk is an important addition. But the text of the 2023 Guidelines should have recognized more fully that many producers of inputs face similar risks and incur comparable harms. Such a more balanced exposition of the competitive risks resulting from mergers creating increased buyer power would be helpful in providing greater credibility to the 2023 Guidelines.

96. A second problem with the new Guidelines is that they omit the statement from the 2010 Guidelines that claims of no reduction in the volume of buying were not sufficient to disprove that resulting buyer power was likely to have adverse competitive effects.[43] This is an important point because although conventional monopsony analysis rests on a theory that exploitation of buyer power will result in reduced input volume, this is not necessarily the case.[44] Because the 2023 Guideline do not repeat that caution, this may implicitly suggest that if the parties can credibly claim

40 Todd v. Exxon, 275 F.3d 191 (2nd Cir. 2001).

41 This analysis is developed by Robert Marshall & Michael James Meurer, *Bidder Collusion and Antitrust Law: Refining the Analysis of Price Fixing to Account for the Special Features of Auction Markets*, 72 ANTITRUST L.J. 83 (2004).

42 2023 Guidelines, *supra* note 2, at 26–27.

43 *See* 2010 Guidelines, *supra* note 2, at 27.

44 See text, *supra*, at note 28 (describing the all-or-nothing buying strategy).

that volume will not be affected that somehow disproves the potential for any risk to competition.

97. The draft of the 2023 Guidelines included the statement that: "The level of concentration at which competition concerns arise may be lower in a buyer market than in seller markets, given the unique features of certain buyer markets."[45] However, in the final version, this sentence was changed and moved: "The level of concentration at which competition concerns arise may be *lower in labor markets than in product markets*, given the unique features of certain buyer markets."[46] This revised sentence is followed by the statement that: "In light of their characteristics, labor markets can be relatively narrow."[47] Now labor markets are subject to two modifications: 1) lower market shares in; 2) narrowly drawn markets. The double limitation may be appropriate in the analysis of labor markets, but that market power arises at lower levels of concentration is relevant to many buyer markets.[48] Indeed, there are good reasons to think that narrowly defined buyer markets are also appropriate in a variety of contexts involving products as well as labor. These modifications further unbalance the resulting guidelines to make them even more labor centric.

98. Another omission from the 2023 Guidelines is any express recognition of the unique indirect competitive harms that exploitation of buyer power can create. It does identify generally how market power can result in control over market access (Guideline 5) and entrench a firm's market dominance (Guideline 6). The textual explanations of those guidelines ought to have more explicitly highlighted how buyer power resulting from mergers is one of the primary sources of such potential harms.

99. Lastly, it is unclear whether the presumption of illegality that is set forth in Guideline 1 for horizontal mergers that increase concentration in markets at least moderately concentrated will apply to the buyer side of the market as well. Even if it did, the problem discussed earlier is that buyer side power arises at lower market shares than on the selling side of the market. The revisions of Guideline 10 with respect to lower levels of market concentration apparently only with respect to labor markets further undermines the potential to have buying side presumptions that reflect the empirical realities of buyer power generally.

A. *Conclusion on Buyer Power*

100. Despite these problems, Guideline 10 does continue an important move in antitrust enforcement to recognize that the buyer side of the market merits antitrust focus and concern.

---

45 2023 Draft Merger Guidelines ("2023 Draft Guidelines"), at 25, https://www.ftc.gov/system/files/ftc_gov/pdf/p859910draftmergerguidelines2023.pdf

46 2023 Guidelines, supra note 2, at 27 (emphasis added).

47 *Id.*

48 As discussed, *supra*, text at notes 29–41, buyer power arises at relatively modest market shares.

II. The Meaning of the Presumption of Illegality in Merger Law[49]

101. The *Philadelphia Bank* decision established a presumption of illegality for mergers in concentrated markets which involve a significant increase in concentration.[50] Over the following years, the revisions of the Merger Guidelines have weakened the strength of that presumption. The 2023 Guidelines continue that process of attenuation. The term is used many times in the 2023 Guidelines, but its content is never explicated. Specifically, what is presumed and what will rebut that presumption.

102. The presumption, even in its current application, is still a useful element of merger law, but its capacity to provide resolution to those merger cases most likely to harm competition is significantly impaired. First, this section sets forth the original, strong version of this presumption and its rebuttal based on the key Supreme Court decisions. Second, the changes in the Merger Guidelines over the years illustrate the weakening of the presumption. Third, a strong presumption is likely to prohibit some mergers that, if allowed, would not cause significant competitive harms, and might indeed have positive economic effects. Such "false positives" are, however, almost certain to be few and nearly impossible to identify even with a detailed search. A review of both empirical and theoretical work confirms that conclusion. Finally, the Agencies can restore the presumption to its full vigor by employing it strategically.

1. The Original Presumption and its Rebuttal

103. Section 7 of the Clayton Act condemns mergers which either "may … substantially lessen competition" or "tend to create a monopoly." The first clause aims at the risk of harmful conduct, without regard to the size of the firm in the market, while the second has an explicit structural focus. That clause should be read to condemn all mergers that move a market closer to monopoly regardless of whether specific competitive risks are shown. The Supreme Court in a series of decisions in the 1960s and early 1970s explicated what the presumption meant and how it could be rebutted.

104. The presumption is that any merger in concentrated markets that results in increasing concentration and involves one or more of the leading firms in that market is illegal because of the structural fact that it has increased concentration. This structural premise means that the only rebuttals that are cognizable must focus on rebutting the inference

49 This section draws heavily on my earlier article about the presumption, Carstensen, *The Philadelphia Nation Bank Presumption, supra* note 1.

50 United States v. Phila. Nat'l Bank, 374 U.S. 321 (1963).

that the merger would produce a firm with greater market dominance. This presumption is rebuttable only if the combination is shown to have little or no future relevance to competition in the market.[51] Such rebuttals include proof that the acquired firm would not have remained a significant competitor in the market, that the market itself included additional products or geographic areas with the result that the level of concentration was lower than initially appeared, or that for some other reason the inference that the acquisition constituted a significant change in the market was wrong.

105. The presumption removes the need to prove specific competitive effects. It focuses on the basic fact that one competitor would now control the capacity of its rival to compete in the market as well as the probability of further concentration of the industry structure. This takes account of static and dynamic implications for competition and includes all possible adverse effects whether unilateral, collusive, exclusionary, or exploitive. Therefore, the presumption is that any merger between competing firms with combined substantial market shares is sufficiently likely to result in a "substantial lessening of competition" or "tend to create a monopoly"[52] that it should be presumed to be illegal.

106. The procedural implications of the presumptive framework are central to its utility in simplifying and focusing merger analysis at the Agencies and in the courts. The initial burden is on the government to establish that the proposed combination involves a significant increase in concentration in an already moderately to substantially concentrated market. Thus, the focus in litigation is on the current state of competition and not predictions of the specific kinds of future conduct. Once the market is established, the presumption applies and the merging parties bear the burden of rebuttal except for the basic market definition. Moreover, any rebuttal is narrowly focused on the current market context. The primary defense is that the merger lacks the capacity to make a significant change in the market. Considerations such as failing firm status or the continuation of an existing control relationship would also be relevant.[53] Thus, the presumptive framework properly understood implements a manageable review and evaluation process that focuses on the kind of factual issues that Agencies and courts are able to resolve without undue speculation.

---

51 This is a strict standard and would preclude other claims of justification. In particular, it implies that putative efficiency gains achievable only by a presumptively illegal merger are irrelevant to the analysis.

52 Currently in draft is an article arguing from a textualist perspective that increased concentration is explicitly condemned regardless of competitive effect by this clause of the statute. Robert H. Lande et al., *The Forgotten Half of the Antimerger Statute.* forthcoming in the Texas Law Review.

53 Unexplored is the role of barriers to entry into identifiable markets. If two dominant firms in a market could credibly show that entry was easy and likely if the market became attractive for entry, would that rebut the presumption? Certainly, subsequent developments in the law of mergers have identified this as a potential rebuttal. But in context of the presumption of illegality this consideration goes more appropriately to the definition of the market itself. *See* Darren Bush & Salvatore Massa, *Rethinking the Potential Competition Doctrine*, 2004 Wis. L. Rev. 1035 (2004).

2. The Development of the Presumption

107. The Cellar-Kefauver amendment to Section 7 clarified that the anti-merger provision applied to asset acquisitions as well as stock acquisitions, thereby removing a technical problem with enforcement.[54] However, the amendment did not clarify what constituted a potential "substantial" lessening of competition or a tendency to monopoly? In the 1950s both the Antitrust Division and the FTC wrestled with those questions, as did the scholarly community.[55] Two conflicting approaches emerged. One focused on changes in market structure as the key factor in answering the forward-looking questions of potential effects on competition. The other was a case-specific prediction based on extensive evaluation of the likely future conduct of the resulting firm. With respect to the later method of analysis Derek Bok observed:

> An unwillingness to recognize the limits of our understanding hardens resistance to simple rules because of the false hope that more information can somehow dispel doubts about the consequences of a disputed merger. Similarly, the virtues of clarity and simplicity are foregone, for it is thought that rules that embody these characteristics are needlessly arbitrary when in fact they are no more so than their more complicated counterparts.[56]

108. The first merger case after the 1950 amendment to reach the Supreme Court was *Brown Shoe*.[57] The case involved both a vertical claim based on foreclosure of other shoemakers from the acquired firm's retail outlets and a horizontal claim based on the consolidation of the two firms' retailing operations. Because the Antitrust Division won the *Brown Shoe* case at trial, the defendants had the option under the Expediting Act to appeal and they did. The opinion in *Brown Shoe* started with market definition in both geographic and product terms followed by measuring market shares and the change in market shares. The legal analysis focused on an evaluation of the vertical aspect of a merger that involved low, national market shares.[58] The decision acknowledged that the resulting market share was too low to be presumed illegal,[59] as the Court had done in the *DuPont-GM* case,[60] but too significant to warrant dismissal, as it had

54 For examples of these problems, *see* Arrow-Hart & Hegeman Elec. Co. v. FTC, 291 U.S. 587 (1934); FTC v. W. Meat Co., 272 U.S. 554 (1926).

55 *See, e.g.*, Derek C. Bok, *Section 7 of the Clayton Act and the Merging of Law and Economics*, 74 Harv. L. Rev. 226 (1960) (reviewing the contending methods of merger analysis).

56 *Id.* at 349.

57 Brown Shoe Co., Inc. v. United States, 370 U.S. 294 (1962).

58 Brown Shoe produced about 4.9% to 6.5% of different types of shoes, while Kenny sold between 1.5% and 3.1% of those same categories. *Id.* at 327.

59 *Id.* at 328–29.

60 United States. v. E.I. du Pont de Nemours & Co, 353 U.S. 586 (157).

done in the *Tampa Electric* case.[61] Hence, the Court needed to find some factors that justified the condemnation of the merger.[62]

109. The *Philadelphia National Bank* decision came only a year after *Brown Shoe* and featured a stronger set of structural facts for finding a violation.[63] The primary issue in *Philadelphia National Bank* was whether Section 7 applied to bank mergers.[64] In the part of the opinion devoted to the merits of the merger, the Court focused first on market definition, which in the case of banking was problematic in both its product and geographic elements.[65] Having satisfied itself that the primary competitive impact would be in commercial banking in localized markets, the Court faced the question of this merger's effect on competition. Each bank had a significant market share in a relatively concentrated market. As a result, concentration would increase substantially. The trial court had evaluated the evidence concerning the present competitiveness of the Philadelphia market and its prospects which in turn led it to the conclusion that the merger would not decrease competition.[66]

110. The presumption model from *Brown Shoe* offered a method to reverse the trial court decision without excessively rejecting its fact findings. If the merger created concentration that exceeded the level necessary to trigger that presumption, then the burden of persuasion shifted to the defendants who had to identify relevant factual proof that rebutted the presumption. The opinion considered the merging parties rebuttals, but failed to develop a coherent theory of the factors that might justify rebutting the presumption. Instead, it rejected specific rebuttals based on claims that competition was robust or that there were positive justifications for the merger.[67]

111. A year later, *United States v. Continental Can Co.*,[68] refined and clarified the presumptive model by identifying the basis for the presumption and thus defining the nature of the relevant rebuttal. The Continental Can–Hazel-Atlas merger combined one of the largest metal can producers with one of the largest glass container manufacturers. The merger reduced the major competitors in the combined bottle and can market from five to four and gave the merged firms about 25% of the sales of glass and

61 Tampa Electric Co. v. Nashville Coal Co., 365 U.S. 320 (1961).

62 370 U.S. at 329.

63 United States v. Phila. Nat'l Bank, 374 U.S. 321 (1963).

64 *Id.* at 335–354.

65 *Id.* at 334–335.

66 *Id.* at 365–69.

67 Phila. Nat'l Bank, 374 U.S. at 367–371 (bankers are not economic experts and so their opinions were not relevant; the number of banks was not relevant; banking is consistent with competition; increased entry to suburban markets was not compelling because both banks were already branching; increased lending limits making the new bank more competitive with other large banks would still harm smaller customers despite arguably helping the Philadelphia market overall).

68 378 U.S. 441 (1964).

metal containers.[69] The Court addressed the question of whether, assuming the market included both glass and metal containers,[70] the *Philadelphia National Bank* presumption would apply and whether any of the defendants' suggested rebuttals would overcome that presumption. Although the combined market share was lower than in *Philadelphia National Bank*, the presumption applied since there was an undue increase in concentration in the glass-metal container market.[71]

112. The Court framed the basis for the presumption around characteristics that inhere in a merger. The opinion identified four "important matters" that refuted the trial court's conclusion that the "the merger could have no effect on competition."[72] The first basis was that after the merger the firms would not compete with each other.[73] Second, "when a dominant firm in a line of commerce in which market power is already concentrated among a few firms makes an acquisition which enhances its market power and the vigor and effectiveness of its own competitive efforts," this does not strengthen overall competition in the market.[74] Third, a merger of this sort has a "tendency to engender a much broader anticompetitive effect by triggering other mergers by companies seeking the same competitive advantages … ."[75] Fourth, the combined entity was likely to frustrate innovation in the market.[76] Because Continental would necessarily control the future development of Hazel-Atlas and would shape its current and potential competition, such control "may actually enhance the long-run tendency of the merger to lessen competition."[77]

113. These factors are inevitable consequences of a merger and so it may substantially lessen competition if the market shares are substantial. Only a rebuttal that established that the merger would not eliminate substantial future competition could overcome the presumption. Indeed, the *Continental Can* case was remanded for further consideration of the market definition issue because if plastic and/or paper containers were sufficiently competitive substitutes, then the narrower market was not an appropriate context within which to estimate the likely effects of the merger.

---

69 The two largest firms would have just under 50% of the total volume and the six largest in combination held slightly over 70% of the volume in the year prior to the merger. *Id.* at 461, n.11.

70 In evaluating bottle and can competition, the product market question was whether plastic or paper were also part of the relevant container market. The scope of the product market relevant to this case highlights the fact that in some merger analyses market definition, either product market or geographic market, can be quite contentious and potentially ambiguous. *Id.* at 447–48.

71 *Id.* at 461.

72 *Id.* at 462.

73 *Id.* at 463.

74 *Id.* at 464.

75 *Id.*

76 *Id.* at 465 ("It would make little sense for … Continental … to … persuad[e] the public of metal's superiority over glass … while… making plans to increase … glass container output for that same end use").

77 *Id.*

114. While the presumption announced in *Philadelphia National Bank* and clarified in *Continental Can* governed merger analysis for the succeeding decade, the element that remained uncertain was what would overcome the presumption. The *General Dynamics* case involved the acquisition of a company that exclusively mined coal underground by another mining company that specialized in open-pit mining. Despite the significant differences in the method of mining the coal, the coal itself was identical from the perspective of the buyer. Both firms operated in the Midwest and so were competitors in the sale of coal. The majority recognized that if the market were limited to coal in the Midwest region alleged by the government, then the merger involved the kind of structural change that required a presumption of illegality.[78] The central dispute in the case was whether the defendants had overcome that presumption.

115. The majority accepted two key factual claims of the defendants. First, the acquired firm had by the time of its acquisition committed all its reserves to long-term contracts.[79] Hence, given its present set of mines, it was not capable of competing significantly for future sales. The majority also accepted the finding that the target could not expand its operations either by opening new underground mines or by entering into surface mining.[80] These two factual findings meant that the acquired firm had no capacity to expand production and would have ceased to be a significant competitor. This merger, therefore, did not confer control over a significant independent competitive actor in the market.

116. In *Marine Bancorporation*, decided the same year as *General Dynamics,* the Court applied the presumption in a potential competition context.[81] The structural factors justified a presumption: the buying bank was one of the very few potential entrants into highly concentrated market.[82] However, under the applicable state law, a bank not headquartered in the county could not open additional branches in that county.[83] The Court concluded that a branch network was essential to effective competition. Hence, de novo entry was not possible and entry by acquisition froze the entrant with whatever branches it had acquired. Hence, potential entrants were neither present nor future competitive threats to the existing market participants. Based on this logic, the loss of one of the few significant potential entrants could not have the presumed effect on competition.

---

78 *Id.* at 497–98. The majority did not explicitly reject the trial court's expansive definition of the market to include other fuels. *Id.* at 415 U.S. at 491–92, 510–11.

79 *Id.* at 506–08.

80 *Id.* at 509–10. It may seem implausible that an independent firm would engage in such a self-destructive strategy, but the record before the Court including the trial court's fact findings supported that conclusion. *Id.* at 509.

81 United States v. Marine Bancorporation, 418 U.S. 602 (1974). In doing so, the Court implicitly overturned the *Penn-Olin*, open-ended process for assessing such mergers. *See* United States v. Penn-Olin Chem. Co., 378 U.S. 158 (1964).

82 *Marine Bancorporation*, 418 U.S. at 644.

83 *Id.* at 610.

117. In *Citizens & Southern*, the Court concluded that the banks sponsored and affiliated with C&S were not independent entities even though third parties held a majority of the stock in those banks.[84] Thus, there could be no present or future competition despite nominally different ownership, and their consolidation into C&S would not affect competition.

3. The Attenuation of the Presumption

118. The presumptive model's attenuation started in the early 1980s with arrival of the Reagan Administration. A number of factors beyond the changed political environment contributed to this process. The repeal of the Expediting Act largely removed Supreme Court review.[85] The adoption of the Hart–Scott–Rodino[86] (HSR) merger reporting statute ensured prior review of most major mergers. Another change of great significance was the growth of the belief that mergers, even among very large firms, were likely to have desirable economic effects. Indeed, in 2006, the Agencies declared that "mergers between competing firms ... are a significant dynamic force in the American economy. The vast majority ... pose no harm to consumers, and many produce efficiencies ... ."[87]

119. The best lens for observing the process of attenuation is the changing nature of the Merger Guidelines that purport to set the agency standards and methods of evaluating mergers. The 1968 Guidelines explicitly mirror the *Philadelphia National Bank* presumption.[88] Market concentration is central and there is no suggestion that there is a need to show any particular competitive effect:

> [A] concentrated market structure ... tends to discourage vigorous price competition ... and to encourage other kinds of conduct ... of an economically undesirable nature. Moreover ... an enforcement policy emphasizing a limited number of structural factors ... facilitates both enforcement decision-making and business planning ... .[89]

120. Thus, the 1968 Guidelines focused on changes in market structure as the key variable while recognizing that in some limited cases special characteristics of the target might justify objection even if the structural criteria were not satisfied.[90]

---

84 United States v. Citizens & S. Nat'l Bank, 422 U.S. 86 (1975).

85 Pub. L. 95-528, 88 Sta. 1706, sec. 4 (1974) (amending 15 U.S.C. 28 and 49 U.S.C. 44 to remove the right of direct appeal of government antitrust cases to the Supreme Court).

86 Pub. L. No. 94-435, 90 Stat. 1383 (1976) (codified in various sections of 15, 18, and 28 U.S.C.).

87 Fed. Trade Comm'n and U.S. Dep't. of Justice, *Commentary on the Horizontal Merger Guidelines* (2006), at v, https://www.justice.gov/d9/383663.pdf.

88 Fed. Trade Comm'n and U.S. Dep't. of Justice, *Merger Guidelines* (1968) ("1968 Guidelines"), https://www.justice.gov/archives/atr/1968-merger-guidelines.

89 *Id.* at 1–2. See Mark J. Neifer, *Donald F. Turner at the Antitrust Division: A Reconsideration of Merger Policy in the 1960s*, 29 Antitrust 53, 53 (2015) ("Turner ... conclude[d] that merger policy should focus on the formulation and enforcement of strong anti-merger rules that minimized the need for extensive fact-finding.").

90 1968 Guidelines, *supra* note 88, at 7; *see also* Neifer, *supra* note 89, at 57 ("[T]he Guidelines articulate simple, administrable rules focused on a few key factors, including, most importantly, market structure.").

121. The 1982 Merger Guidelines[91] reflect a major shift in thinking about mergers: "Although they sometimes harm competition, mergers generally play an important role in a free enterprise economy. They can penalize ineffective management and facilitate the efficient flow of investment capital and the redeployment of existing productive assets."[92] The focus of these tests is on whether or not the resulting combination would result in a "cartel."[93] The 1992 Merger Guidelines[94] dropped the explicitly pro-merger introduction of 1982 Merger Guidelines, but the framework they adopt commits the Agencies to finding a specific, identifiable likely effect before challenging a merger. The relevant inquiry in merger evaluation, they explain, is "whether the merger, in light of market concentration and other factors that characterize the market, raises concern about potential adverse competitive effects ... ." and whether there are "any efficiency gains that ... cannot be achieved ... through other means."[95]

122. The 2010 Guidelines continued this process.[96] It did add to the competitive effects concerns about exclusionary risks. This, of course, highlights the wisdom of the 1968 Guidelines recognition that concentration can lead to "other kinds of conduct ... of an economically undesirable nature." Instead, it adopted a holistic approach akin to that urged in 1955 by the Attorney General's committee to review antitrust that there can be a violation only if a "prospective adverse impact in defined markets can be shown."[97] So after a half-century, the merger review process has come full circle and returned to the pre-*Philadelphia National Bank* open-ended review process condemned by Bok in 1960 as "needlessly arbitrary."[98] The result, manifest in many of the 2006 Commentary's vignettes,[99] is that each merger must be judged on its own unique characteristics to assess the likelihood that it will have an anticompetitive effect.

123. The 2023 Guidelines try to change some of this. They reset the structural boundaries back to the pre-2010 levels. They identify a broad range of adverse competitive effects that mergers can have. They invoke the

---

91 Fed. Trade Comm'n and U.S. Dep't. of Justice, *Merger Guidelines* (1982) ("1982 Merger Guidelines"), https://www.justice.gov/archives/atr/1982-merger-guidelines.

92 *Id.* at 1–2, 7 ("[E]ven in concentrated markets, it is desirable to allow firm some scope for merger activity in order to achieve economies of scale and to permit exit from the market.").

93 *Id.* at 16–20.

94 Fed. Trade Comm'n and U.S. Dep't. of Justice, *Horizontal Merger Guidelines* (1992) ("1992 Horizontal Merger Guidelines"), 3, 17–24, 28 (1992, revised 1997) ("1992 Horizontal Merger Guidelines"), https://www.justice.gov/sites/default/files/atr/legacy/2007/07/11/11250.pdf.

95 *See Id.* at 3, 17–24, 28.

96 2010 Guidelines, *supra* note 2. Many observers have observed that these guidelines move even further away from a clear structural analysis. *See, e.g.*, Carl Shapiro, *The 2010 Horizontal Merger Guidelines: From Hedgehog to Fox in Forty Years*, 77 Antitrust L.J. 49 (2010).

97 *See* The Attorney General's National Committee to Study the Antirust Law (1955) at 122, https://babel.hathitrust.org/cgi/pt?id=umn.31951d02427803y&seq=6.

98 *See* Bok, *supra* note 55, at 349.

99 *See Commentary on the Horizontal Merger Guidelines* (2006), *supra* note 87.

presumption but do not clarify its meaning or what rebuttal is possible. Apparently, the Agencies as part of their case must identify the way or ways in which the merger is likely to be anticompetitive and the merging parties can rebut each such claim. The presumption only operates to shift the burden of persuasion to the defendants. This limited presumption makes policy sense only if there is substantial reason to believe that major mergers are in fact likely in a significant number of cases to have positive effects associated with such combinations.

4. The Limited Risk of False Positives (Error Costs)

124. The strongest argument against a strong presumption against mergers involving significant market shares is that there is likely to be a number of such mergers that either would not harm competition or would provide unique positive results with respect to innovation or efficiency or both. The empirical data and economic theory point against the likelihood of either of these effects in the vast majority of such mergers. Moreover, it is nearly impossible to determine which merger would ultimately have either a benign or positive effect.

125. Carstensen and Lande in 2018 did an extensive review of the theoretical and empirical data with respect to the risks that might result from such errors.[100] The overall evidence was that major mergers had no positive effect on innovation.[101] They do have a strong correlation with higher prices and no increase in efficiency.[102] Moreover, such mergers, when allowed, usually result in harming the economic interests of the shareholders in the acquiring firm.[103] Indeed, the merged firms often stagnated over the succeeding years.[104] This record strongly supports the conclusion that the risk that a mistaken decision to block a major merger is unlikely to have any adverse economic effect and may actually protect the shareholders of the acquiring firm from bad and costly management decisions.

126. Once recent effort to establish that mergers produce efficient results identified a number of studies.[105] The paper lists 45 studies that purport to show that mergers or acquisitions of some sort are associated with increased efficiency measured in various ways. That listing provides a summary of key elements of those studies. Only six seem to have included market share data, and in each instance increased concentration resulted in negative overall welfare results.

---

100 *See* Carstensen & Lande, *supra* note 1; see also, Carstensen, *The Philadelphia National Bank Presumption*, *supra* note 1, at 242–265.

101 Carstensen & Lande *supra* note 1, at 809–811.

102 *Id.* at 798, 800–803 (price effects); 800–801, 815–820 (no efficiency gains).

103 *Id.* at 820–821.

104 *Id.* at 820.

105 Maureen K. Ohlhausen & Taylor M. Owings, *Evidence of Efficiencies in Consummated Mergers* (June 1, 2023), https://www.uschamber.com/assets/documents/20230601-Merger-Efficiencies-White-Paper.pdf

127. The same authors published a short version of the same efficiency argument focused on two studies that they proclaimed were the "gold standard" for such work.[106] One of these studies examined mergers in the ready-mix cement industry for the period 1977 to 1992.[107] The authors correctly report that this study found that there were efficiency gains on average from such mergers. The gains were measured by the amount of input required to produce a quantity of output. Increased capital investment or changed technology did not explain the improved productivity. Moreover, the same improvements were found whether the acquired plant was in the same geographic market or a different one from the plant(s) of the buyer. The study concluded that the primary reason for increased efficiency was change in management.[108]

128. What is significant for merger enforcement is that the study of ready-mix mergers focused on a period when there was a change in merger enforcement. From 1977 to 1982, enforcement was strong, but after the 1982 Guidelines enforcement weakened. The data allowed the author to identify mergers where the parties had been competitors as well as where there was little or no competition although the mergers were "horizontal" because the buyer and seller were both in the ready-mx business. The results showed that prior to 1982, few, if any, of these mergers involved direct competitors, but after 1982 there was a significant number.[109] The key comparison was that in the post-1982 period, the mergers that eliminated direct competition while yielding efficiency gains also resulted in higher prices and reduced output.[110] Moreover, other firms in the market reciprocated on price and output resulting in a net harm to aggregate welfare despite the increased productive efficiency.[111] This study as well as the other gold standard one support rejecting efficiency claims in horizontal merger cases because improved management was the primary basis for improved efficiency and that is not a merger specific resource.[112]

129. The gold standard, ready-mix study vindicates the antitrust policy of condemning horizontal mergers regardless of putative efficiency gains because the effects are likely to be negative. It is also likely that buyers that are not direct competitions can get the same efficiency gains without the competitive harms.

---

106 Maureen K. Ohlhausen & Taylor M. Owings, *Build, Borrow, Buy: The Case for Merger Efficiencies*, 11 J. Antitrust Enforcement 242 (2023). The other "gold standard" paper studied changes in ownership of electric generation plants. It also found increased productivity following acquisition. Like the ready-mix study, the authors identified changed management as the causal explanation for the improvements. Because the authors explicitly examined the productivity of the energy input related to the electric output, they consciously avoiding any examination of buyer or seller power effects. *See*, Mert Demirer & Omer Karaduman, *Do Mergers and Acquisitions Improve Efficiency: Evidence from Power Plants* (2022), https://www.ftc.gov/system/files/ftc_gov/pdf/demirerkaraduman.pdf.

107 Robert Kulick, *Ready-to-Mix: Horizontal Mergers, Prices, and Productivity* (2017), https://www2.census.gov/ces/wp/2017/CES-WP-17-38.pdf.

108 *Id.* at 21–24 (finding efficiency gains in both mergers between direct competitors and those involving firms that were not directly competitive, but substantial prices increases, along with reduced output, when the merging firms were direct competitors).

109 *Id.* at 26–30.

110 *Id.*

111 *Id.* at 35.

112 *Id.* at 36; Demier & Karaduman, *supra* note 106, at 4, 32, 36–37, 38–40.

5. The Presumption as Set Forth in the 2023 Guidelines and Alternative Paths Forward

130. Against this backdrop, the 2023 Guidelines continue the contemporary ambiguity as to what the presumption is and how it can be rebutted. This is unfortunate because it denies the Agencies an important teaching moment. The courts and merging parties need to be reminded that the presumption that the Supreme Court created focuses on market structure and not on specific potential harms to competition. While evidence of the risk of identified harms is always relevant, cases involving major structural changes should focus on that claim and its validity.

131. As part of the program to reassert the validity of the presumption of illegality and stop the undue concentration of competitive markets, the 2023 Guidelines ought to have defined the presumption and its rebuttal based both on the Supreme Court precedents and the overall economic literature that shows that such mergers rarely result in any productivity gains but often result in competitive harms including price increases, loss of innovation, and the entrenchment of the dominant firms. These risks are also the ones identified in the *Continental Can* decision as the reason for imposing a presumption.

132. While it may well be difficult to convince courts that a robust presumption of illegality should be applied to a merger despite the fact that it falls with the framework of the presumption of illegality. Nothing precludes the Agencies from pursuing alternative theories of liability when appropriate. One theory would be the robust presumption of illegality to which there is a very limited rebuttal while the second theory would focus on which of the specific risks of harm to competition the merger at issue would be most likely to create. By careful case selection the wisdom of the robust presumption would be demonstrated and allow courts over time to be more comfortable returning to the original meaning of that standard.

III. Conclusion

133. The 2023 Guidelines are better than their recent predecessors. They continue recognition of buyer power concerns. They continue the emphasis that major mergers should be presumptively illegal and restore the prior, stricter standards for determining unacceptable levels of concentration. However, the new guidelines could and should have been better. They should have taken a broader view of the potential harms and unique market considerations on the buying side of the market. In addition, they should have explained the structural basis for the presumption of illegality which in turn defines the narrow scope of rebuttal. Merger Guidelines will continue to evolve. The hope is that in the near future both of these defects will be remedied.

What's new in the 2023 Merger Guidelines

JOSEPH FARRELL*
University of California, Berkeley

* I thank my colleague and friend Carl Shapiro for comments on a draft and for 35 years of working together on merger analysis. Neither he nor anyone else is responsible for my views nor for any errors.

134. Despite the chapter title, I can't comment here on everything new in the 2023 Merger Guidelines ("2023 Guidelines"). I'll discuss just a few topics: (a) what the Merger Guidelines say about the scope of merger control, and how they say it; (b) their approach to market definition, market shares, and concentration measures; and (c) their discussion of the risk of coordinated conduct, broadly understood.

I. Saying it Often and Saying it Loud

135. The 2023 Guidelines raise their voice more than did previous Guidelines concerning some aspects of antitrust policy or philosophy. I would pick out three aspects:

- Non-price effects of a merger, such as on quality, service, or innovation, can be the kinds of harm that merger control should prevent. It's certainly not all about (money) price in a literal sense.
- A merger can harm sellers by limiting competition among buyers, and that too is a valid topic of concern in merger control. It's not all about protecting buyers.
- Predicting the effect of a merger is difficult, and certainty is not to be expected or required. "May substantially lessen competition" really means "may."

136. All those points have been made in previous Merger Guidelines, as I illustrate below, but the 2023 Guidelines say them more often and louder, and that matters.

1. Buyer Market Power

137. The 1982 Guidelines (section I) state in a footnote that buyer-side market power is a concern analogous to seller-side power. The 1984 Guidelines (section 1) elevate the statement to a two-sentence paragraph in the text. The 1992 Merger Guidelines (section 0.1) repeated and expanded the 1982–1984 language: "the exercise of market power by buyers ("monopsony power") has adverse effects comparable to those associated with the exercise of market power by sellers … [The] Agency will apply an analytical framework analogous to the framework of these Guidelines."

138. Is it enough to offer a few sentences and describe the problem of buyer market power as "analogous" to the mainstream problem of seller power? The phrasing admits that "the framework" treats seller-side market power; buyer-side power is a bit of an afterthought. And the paragraph refers to the ability "to depress the price paid for a product to a level that is below the competitive price and thereby depress output," while no similar mention of depressing output appeared in the immediately preceding discussion of "market power [of] a seller." Perhaps it would have been fair for a concerned seller to fear that this might have signaled

less-than-analogous treatment if effects on output are lacking or not proven.

139. The 2010 Guidelines in section 1 ("Overview") and in section 12 ("Mergers of competing buyers" – for the first time the Guidelines had a section on buyer power) offer sellers protection parallel to that given to buyers. Section 12 (roughly a page, or a bit more than 2% of the document) states that the "Agencies do not view a short-run reduction in the quantity purchased as the only, or best, indicator of whether a merger enhances buyer market power." And while Example 24 posits that a merger of buyers "inefficiently reduc[es] supply," it also denies that an increase in downstream prices (as in what is sometimes called classic monopsony power) is a necessary condition for harm or for enforcement.

140. So where did this leave us as the 2023 Guidelines were being drafted? One model of a document such as the Merger Guidelines is that it is quietly authoritative: every sentence, even in an appendix or in the whispery small font of a footnote, is to be taken fully seriously and there can be no need for repetition or a raised voice. An alternative model is that of course repetition, emphasis, and decibels count, and that it would be naïve to think otherwise. Without taking a position on how much, I think the second model deserves weight.

141. On the first model, one could say that, since the 1980s but especially post-2010, the topic of buyer power and harm to sellers was raised and addressed. On that model, it wouldn't matter that the topic was dealt with rather briefly in a document largely phrased in terms of seller-side power with harm to buyers. On the second model, however, the brevity and the resort to largely drafting in seller-side terms while offering a translation key (the 2010 Guidelines used the word "analogous" regarding both non-price harms and buyer power) are a key part of the point.[1]

142. With those thoughts in one's mind, what do the 2023 Guidelines say about buyer-side power? They too resort to the word "analogous," but they also elevate competitive concern about buyer power into its own Guideline and its own section (2.10), rather on par with the 2010 Guidelines. Perhaps it matters, in terms of repetition and emphasis, that section 2.10 is a bigger portion of the MGs than section 12 was of the 2010 Guidelines, and is placed earlier in the document. Also, the Merger Guidelines take a step toward better integrating the discussion of buyer and seller victims of enhanced power than does the not-entirely-satisfying "analogous" idea, by using the phrase "trading partner" (rather than

1 As a possible analogy, people sometimes write with masculine pronouns when they do not really mean to specify gender, and try to cure the gender bias by briefly (and sometimes in a separate locus) announcing the "generic masculine," i.e., that masculine pronouns should be interpreted as also including the feminine. That is not universally viewed as adequately curing gender-biased language. *See* Chicago Manual of Style Online, "5.222 Gender bias: Consider the issue of gender-neutral language. On the one hand, it is unacceptable to a great many reasonable readers to use the generic masculine pronoun (he in reference to no one in particular). ...."

"buyer" or "customer" or "supplier") for the potential victim a dozen or so times throughout the document.

143. Substantively, much of the additional material concerns labor markets. Labor, of course, is the main thing that most people sell, so that a price effect depressing wages in a labor market has a consumer impact somewhat like elevating prices in (portions of) many product markets at once. That fact can merit a boost in emphasis whether or not there is much new to say about it.

144. When (as is normal) merging firms procure inputs, including labor inputs, and sell outputs downstream, they often argue that they will achieve procurement efficiencies. The 2010 Guidelines warned (section 10) against claiming "efficiencies" that "arise from anticompetitive reductions in output or service." The 2023 Guidelines (section 3.3) make a similar point in footnote 71 and the sentence to which it is attached, but do not mention quantity reductions. All told, as a whole the 2023 Guidelines are positioning the Agencies as more skeptical of input-cost reductions, notably those that may even threaten to harm workers.

2. Non-Price Harms

145. Some discussion around the scope of antitrust has criticized a bogeyman version of "the consumer welfare standard" that is supposedly concerned only with money-price effects. I do not recognize this as the consumer welfare standard familiar to me from decades of antitrust economics.[2] In my experience people have long been conscious that this was only to be interpreted as "synecdoche" (part for whole); as I suggested above in the context of buyer power, the time may be ripe to step away from that synecdoche because it may have confused or offended. But this is a clarification, not a change in antitrust scope or philosophy.

146. The 1982 and (identically) 1984 Guidelines already noted that "sellers with market power also may eliminate rivalry on variables other than price." This was repeated in the 1992 Merger Guidelines, slightly enriched by adding "such as product quality, service, or innovation," but now demoted from the main text and relegated to a footnote [6].

147. The 2010 Guidelines put considerably more energy and ink into the point and had more to say. They noted in section 1 that a "merger enhances market power if it is likely to encourage one or more firms to raise price, reduce output, diminish innovation, or otherwise harm customers ...." And, two paragraphs later, "Enhanced market power can also be manifested in non-price terms and conditions that adversely affect customers, including reduced product quality, reduced product variety, reduced service, or diminished innovation. Such non-price effects may coexist with price effects, or can arise in their absence." They then concisely announce

2 This point and the dispute seem to be orthogonal to the confusions reportedly created by Robert Bork's use of the phrase "consumer welfare" to mean total economic surplus or welfare.

an approach that is "analogous" to a price competition concern. The not-just-price theme recurs in section 4.0 ("Market definition") ("market definition focuses solely on ... customers' ability and willingness to substitute away from one product to another in response to ... a reduction in product quality or service"); section 4.1.2 ("Benchmark prices and SSNIP test") ("methodology is used because normally it is possible to quantify ... price effects ..., not because price effects are more important than non-price effects"); section 4.1.3 ("Changes in price or other terms and conditions"); and perhaps most substantively the entirety of section 6.4 ("Innovation and product variety").

148. The 2023 Guidelines refer to "quality" over twenty times, and to "innovation" and its cognates similarly often. They refer frequently to a "worsening of terms," meant to include an adverse change in pricing but also non-price effects. This is both in discussing effects and when it comes to market definition: see for instance section 4.3.A. There, they consider a small but significant and non-transitory increase in price (SSNIP) or other worsening of terms (SSNIPT) test, adding the word "terms" into the acronym to honor non-price analysis, although it would be good if they said more about how to undertake that. This again represents a step away from synecdoche: even the 2010 Guidelines phrased most of the discussion in price terms, explaining separately that (in market definition as well as effects) non-price terms are important.

3. 'May' Means 'May'

149. The 2023 Guidelines also comment on their standard of proof. This is a huge subject. But it makes sense that the question is not whether the Agencies prove that a merger *will* be harmful to competition; it's whether they demonstrate a reasonable *risk* that it will be. Thus the Agencies, insist the 2023 Guidelines (section 1), "do not attempt to predict the future or calculate precise effects of a merger with certainty. Rather, the Agencies examine the totality of the evidence available to *assess the risk* the merger presents" (emphasis added).

150. This is anticipated by the 2010 Guidelines, section 1: "certainty about anticompetitive effect is seldom possible and not required for a merger to be illegal."[3] But I do like the "assess the risk" phrasing, and the 2023 Guidelines again follow through more volubly, using the term "risk" dozens more times. They thus say a vigorous "no" to what has been called the CSI effect: a dangerous expectation that each step of a merger analysis will, if valid, be supported by detailed and perhaps preferably high-tech evidence. Such an expectation could make sense if such evidence were almost always available whenever the relevant step is valid, but that is surely not the case.

3 The 1984 and 1992 Guidelines had funneled recognition of this point into citing Congress' concern with "incipiency," which semantically seems to me to be a related but distinct point, although this seems like a good time to emphasize that I'm not a legal scholar.

151. Both the 1992/7 and the 2010 HMGs acknowledged (if that's the right word) particularly severe challenges in evaluating claimed efficiencies and in predicting the risk of coordinated effects. Here I will not focus on the efficiencies discussion; coordinated effects are discussed below.

152. In tabular form we have:

	1982	**1984**	**1992/7**	**2010**	**2023**
Non-price effects	A sentence in section I: "also may eliminate rivalry on variables other than price."	Same "also" sentence as 1982, now in 1.0.	Expands the "also" sentence slightly but now relegates it to footnote 6 in section 0.1.	Multiple mentions in the text, plus all section 6.4	Multiple mentions; discussion of SSNDQ, etc.
Buyer power	Footnote 5 in section I: "analogous" effects	As in 1982 but promoted to text of section 1.0	Gets its own paragraph in 0.1; "analogous" framework, but mentions decrease in output, unlike discussion of seller power.	Gets its own section. Denies that proven output reduction is key.	Gets its own Guideline; adds stress on labor markets.
Risk and proof	"interdict competitive problems in their incipiency."	As in 1982	0.1: discusses incipiency. In 2.1, "mindful of the difficulties of predicting" based on "incomplete and sometimes contradictory information."	"Necessarily predictive"; incipiency; certainty is seldom possible and not required. In 7.1, risk "not susceptible to quantification or detailed proof."	Emphasis on gauging risk of harm. Task is not to predict harm but to identify risk of harm.

II. Concentration: The Swiss Army Knife of Merger Review

153. Some expert commenters were concerned at the draft merger guidelines stage that the Agencies might have been on track to return to an older view that concentration is so closely linked to antitrust harm that, as a practical matter, a substantially concentrating merger's fate would end there. The 2023 Guidelines assuage that concern, characterizing "market concentration and the change in concentration due to the merger [as] often useful indicators of a merger's risk of substantially lessening competition." That seems a balanced and fair characterization, although sometimes, as the 2010 Guidelines point out (section 5.3), "even a highly concentrated market can be very competitive if market shares fluctuate substantially over short periods of time in response to changes in competitive offerings."

I've heard concentration and the change in concentration referred to as a "Swiss army knife" for merger review: seldom the optimal tool but capable of being helpful in a range of tasks. For example, reasonable links can be drawn between the level of concentration and the risk of coordination, and between the change in concentration and the risk of unilateral effects.[4]

154. Thresholds for presumptions of harm based on concentration are returned in the Merger Guidelines to pre-2010 levels: they were raised in 2010 to better describe actual agency practice and to prioritize enforcement against the most severe risks to competition. We have yet to see how actual practice and prioritization at the Agencies going forward will reflect the 2023 Guidelines' change.

155. But a deeper change in concentration thresholds has attracted less popular attention: the elimination of any announced "safe harbor" zones of low concentration or small change in concentration, such as had been in the guidelines at least since 1982.[5] No such zones appear in the 2023 Guidelines section 2.1, and the issue is also absent from section 3 (rebuttal evidence). What's up?

156. Surely the Agencies are not about to start bringing cases *based on concentration* in what previous guidelines would have called unconcentrated markets. Nor I presume, is it an indirect way of guarding against the parties doing market definition and market share calculations flatly "wrong," which presumably the Agencies would dispute on that level. Rather, I think at least two things may be going on.

   – First, suppose the Agencies are bringing a case *not* based on concentration. It might be based, say, on Guideline 2, direct evidence of important competition between the parties. They appear then to be taking the position that such evidence is not persuasively undermined by defining a market and showing that it is unconcentrated (and/or there is little change in concentration), even if the parties do a good job on that analysis. For instance, they might be asserting that it is enough to have Guideline 2 type evidence of risk to competition, even if all the concentration evidence points the other way.

   – Second, the Agencies might be following through on the observation in the 2010 Guidelines and in the 2023 Guidelines that there are often multiple valid antitrust markets, and setting themselves up to argue that when there is one valid market with high concentration (and/or change) and another with low concentration (and/or change), the former should be our guide. If so, then the Agencies would like to be able to

---

4 On the latter, see Volker Nocke & Michael D. Whinston, *Concentration Thresholds for Horizontal Mergers*, 112 Am. Econ. Rev. 1915–48 (2022).

5 *See* Fed. Trade Comm'n and U.S. Dep't. of Justice, *Merger Guidelines* n.15 (2023) ("2023 Guidelines"), https://www.justice.gov/d9/2023-12/2023%20Merger%20Guidelines.pdf, for a short history, although one that does not contain the word "unconcentrated." These were never in fact safe harbors, but the phrase is widely used for those zones. Perhaps a better term, and more parallel with "presumption of harm," would be "presumption of no harm."

bring a case based on concentration in the first market, in which that "useful indicator" sounds the alarm, and declare irrelevant (as distinct from incorrectly analyzed) concentration in another valid market in which it does not.

157. At a high level, one might classify such logic as part of a position that significantly mixed evidence is generically enough to prove a risk to competition. Obviously, though, that would beg the question of what mixtures of evidence are "significantly mixed," and what it takes for a mixture to favor the parties on balance. But more specifically when it comes to concentration, the working model is that there are many valid markets and that it's not informative to demonstrate low concentration in one of them: if there is high concentration in one, then there is a problem there.

III. Market Definition, the Hypothetical Monopolist Test, and A Pair of Putative Principles

158. The 2023 Guidelines discuss concentration early in the document as in the prominent Guideline 1, but postpone substantive discussion of market definition, which underlies any measure of concentration, to near the end of the document (section 4.3). For comparison, the 1992 Merger Guidelines put both topics together in section 1, and the 2010 Guidelines put them adjacent to one another, mid-document, in sections 4 and 5.

159. What do the 2023 Guidelines then say about market definition, which after all is often the chief battleground in merger litigation? I will focus here on the hypothetical monopolist test (HMT) and on what are sometimes called the "narrowest market" and "circle" principles.

1. The Hypothetical Monopolist/Monopsonist Test

160. As the 2023 Guidelines state in section 4.3.A, the HMT "evaluates whether a group of products is sufficiently broad to constitute a relevant antitrust market," or contrariwise "whether a proposed market is too narrow." Except for recognizing buyer power concerns by adding the "monopsonist" reading to the HMT term, this is a standard formulation of what has, at least since the 1984 Guidelines, been the standard approach to market definition: find a group of substitutes, perhaps satisfying some other desiderata (see below), that is broad enough that "eliminating the competition among [them] by combining them under the control of a hypothetical monopolist likely would lead to a worsening of terms."

161. Importantly, this goal is logically distinct, and often substantively quite different, from attempting to include all, or the main, substitutes for a particular product. For an extensive discussion see section 4 of the 2010 Guidelines (giving the lie, incidentally, to concerns at the time that the 2010 Guidelines were somehow abandoning or ignoring market definition).

162. The 2023 Guidelines recognize this central status of the HMT, and the question it poses, early in their market definition discussion: they flatly state in the second paragraph of section 4.3, without any nearby reference to the HMT, that: "Market definition ensures that relevant antitrust markets are sufficiently broad...." That, of course, is precisely what the HMT ensures. Thus the 2023 Guidelines there make the HMT, as in earlier Merger Guidelines, seemingly synonymous with, and at least a necessary condition for, valid antitrust market definition.

163. But then, still in section 4.3, the 2023 Guidelines seem to say otherwise. They describe four "tools to demonstrate that a market is a relevant antitrust market," and hint that these four may not exhaust their toolkit. The HMT is the fourth, characterized as "another common method." So is it now just one (not especially preeminent) option?

164. Evidently not – and after all, it would be very odd for the Agencies to state that their proposed market was "too narrow." Thus section 4.3.A, which "describes the Hypothetical Monopolist Test in greater detail," characterizes it just as above. Section 4.3.B is introduced as "address[ing] issues that may arise when defining relevant markets ..." – and then it is actually entitled "Implementing the Hypothetical Monopolist Test."

165. I read this confusing discussion as continuing to make the HMT, interpreted as *a test*, a necessary condition in principle (that doesn't dictate who has a burden of proof on it), but as authorizing the Agencies to be flexible in coming up with a candidate market, and in particular by no means requiring the use of the *algorithm* described in the 1992 Merger Guidelines, which (if actually carried out) would have involved running an HMT on each of a gradually expanding series of candidate markets. The 2010 Guidelines likewise applied the HMT as a test rather than as a strict algorithm, although some features of algorithmic thinking survived in modified form as desiderata in the 2010 version. I think the 2023 Guidelines use the phrase "hypothetical monopolist test" or "HMT" to refer sometimes to the test and sometimes to the algorithm. If true, that is confusing, especially because I believe the 2023 Guidelines embrace the test and distance themselves from the algorithm.

166. The reading that the 2023 Guidelines contain two distinct (though related) things both called the HMT draws additional support from the fourth paragraph in section 4.4 ("Second, the market ... should be broad enough ..."). While the context is a focus on cases in which the Agencies "use evidence about market shares and market concentration...," it contains what would be odd language, to say the least, if the fourth optional *method* from section 4.3 were identical to the HMT as a *test*.[6] Thus I think the fourth option in section 4.3 is the 1992 algorithm or something similar.

---

6 Specifically, the HMT was (correctly) explained in 2023 Guidelines s. 4.3.A as testing precisely what the first sentence of the paragraph requires of a market. Thus "satisfy this condition" means "satisfy the HMT." But one cannot sensibly read the second sentence of the paragraph with that awareness. The only escape I can see, consistent with the history and logic, is to read option D of 4.3, and the "HMT" in para. 4.4, as referring

167. If this is right, I think the 2023 Guidelines' treatment of the HMT as a test is sensible and not very different from that of the 2010 Guidelines. But it would be helpful if senior Agency personnel would give some public clarification.

168. The 2023 Guidelines offer, at least to the Agencies, a lot of flexibility in choosing a market. This can be seen as continuing a trend: the 1992 Merger Guidelines described an algorithm, realistic or not, with the clear worldview that there is a correctly defined market for each of the merging firms' products; thus there could be dispute over what that correct market was. The 2010 Guidelines departed from the 1992 Merger Guidelines' algorithm and the implicit view that there is one platonically correct market, and instead asserted that the Agencies could choose one: "The [HMT] ensures that markets are not defined too narrowly, but it does not lead to a single relevant market. The Agencies may evaluate a merger in any relevant market satisfying the test, ..." (section 4.1.1).

169. However, while rejecting the 1992 algorithm and the underlying view that there is one true market, the 2010 Guidelines also pointed to some desiderata in choosing such a relevant market. These desiderata are discussed, e.g., in section 4.1.1 of the 2010 Guidelines. The 2023 Guidelines have a corresponding, but different, discussion in section 4.4 "Calculating market shares and concentration." As that placement suggests, the Agencies are newly saying that these desiderata are relevant only, or at least mainly, when "the Agencies ... use evidence about market shares and market concentration as part of their analysis." Traditionally that would be more or less always, but the Agencies may be girding themselves to bring cases without the structural presumption. Economists have long argued that such a possibility makes good sense, although it would be bold. The desiderata themselves are also different, as I discuss in the next two subsections.

2. Narrowing of the Narrowest Market Principle

170. The 1992 Merger Guidelines stated that the Agency "generally will consider the relevant product market to be the smallest group of products that satisfies [the HMT]"; the algorithm stopped there. No explanation was offered. As has been noted previously, rigid adherence to such a "narrowest-market principle" can cause anomalies and errors.[7] Accordingly, the 2010 Guidelines both explained the logic and offered additional flexibility: "[because] the relative competitive significance of more distant substitutes is apt to be overstated by their share of sales, when the Agencies rely on market shares and concentration, they usually do so in the smallest relevant market satisfying the [HMT]." The word "usually" represented

not to the HM *test* but to something like a version of the 1992 Horizontal Merger Guidelines' *algorithm* for market definition, which by construction will end up with a candidate market that passes the HM test. The remark at the end of the second sentence in the paragraph is then obvious but not as painfully tautological as it would be on, I think, almost any other reading.

7 *See e.g.*, Joseph Farrell & Carl Shapiro, *The 2010 Horizontal Merger Guidelines After 10 Years*, 58 Rev. Indus. Org. 1–11 (2021).

a softening relative to "generally," and more importantly, the explanation helps one to more intelligently gauge whether an exception is appropriate in a particular case. Essentially, the problem is that including a distant substitute with significant sales often dilutes measured concentration, and/or the merging parties' shares, more than its competitive significance justifies.

171. The 2023 Guidelines follow suit, adding a helpful refinement. Specifically, in section 4.4, they observe that "the competitive significance of the parties may be understated by their share when calculated on a market that is broader than needed to satisfy [inclusion of the products that are the focus of competitive concern, and the HMT]." Systematically including the products that are the focus of concern makes good sense and is a helpful innovation, but my point here is that the 2023 Guidelines, like the 2010 Guidelines, explain their rationale for a desideratum of not needlessly or unduly expanding market boundaries. They do so rather briefly, however, and without the illustrative examples that helped enrich and clarify the 2010 Guidelines. So, just as I acknowledge above that the 2023 Guidelines do more to "say it often and say it loud" in some aspects, I would fault them for undue brevity here.

3. Withdrawal of the Circle Principle

172. The algorithm described in the 1992 Merger Guidelines also specified that, after a candidate market fails the HMT, one should as the next step "add to the product group the product that is the next-best substitute for the merging firm's product," defining the latter in a footnote as the alternative that "would account for the greatest value of diversion of demand." This prioritization of what to add next is sometimes known as the "circle principle." As was somewhat their style, the 1992 Merger Guidelines did not explain.

173. Again, the 2010 Guidelines softened this prescription to a "normally" in defining "a market around a product offered by one of the merging firms, if the market includes a second product, the Agencies will normally also include a third product if that third product is a closer substitute for the first product than is the second product." Perhaps tellingly, the 2010 Guidelines, which generally took pains to explain themselves, did not explain this recommendation or point the way to understanding when it would make less or more sense. And, strikingly, the 2023 Guidelines do not include it at all.

174. I believe the circle principle, perhaps due to a certain intuitive appeal, has received less analytical scrutiny than the narrow-market principle.[8] But the HMT concerns the inclusion of enough substitutability, in total (weighted by margins), to make substantial within-market competitive effects possible. From that point of view, it is not clear why one would prefer an approach of (first) including one big substitute over an alternative of (first)

8 *See* Kostis Hatzitaskos et al., *Aetna-Humana and Algorithmic Market Definition in the Guidelines*, Antitrust Source, Oct. 2017, and Bryan Keating et al., *The Role of the Circle Principle in Market Definition*, Antitrust Source, Apr. 2018.

including several smaller substitutes with e.g., the same total diversion: either way, one lands up with the same aggregate substitutability captured in the candidate market. A merger with a product with a higher diversion ratio is of course apt to be more problematic (other things equal) than one with a product with a lower diversion ratio, but we are presumably in the business of evaluating one proposed merger, not of ranking other possible mergers for how problematic they would be. This fact of course does not say that the circle principle is wrong or harmful, but it does caveat any intuitive appeal.

175. Meanwhile, a worrisome flaw in the principle is how much it depends on how one aggregates or separates related products, a choice that can often be somewhat arbitrary and that therefore ought ideally not to be made to matter. This arbitrariness can cause concrete problems, perhaps especially in the simultaneous presence of the narrow market principle or of the concerns that motivate the latter.

176. For example, suppose that diversion from gadgets to widgets is 40%, evenly divided between red widgets and (functionally almost identical) blue widgets, that diversion from gadgets to gizmos is 30%, and that margins are high enough that any candidate market containing two of those products (gadgets, blue widgets, red widgets, and gizmos) would pass the HMT. Then under the circle principle, starting from gadgets, one would define different two-product markets if one treats "widgets" as one product (color being almost irrelevant) than if one distinguishes red from blue widgets. If one expanded the market to include all of the products, one would potentially err in the way that the narrowest market principle tries to guard against.

177. A second flaw is that application of the circle principle can actively cause the type of problem against which the narrowest market principle seeks to protect. That problem, recall, arises if one includes in a candidate market a product whose sales (and thus share) unduly overstate its diversion from the central products. That disproportion, which might intuitively correspond to being a popular but less directly similar product, as in the 2010 Guidelines' motorcycles-and-cars examples (Examples 4 and 7),[9] can happen in at least two ways:

- One way is that the problematic product attracts only a little diversion from the central products (here, overlap products of the merging firms), but its sales would give it a substantial share if included in the market.

9 Examples 4 and 7 discuss a hypothetical motorcycle merger. "Many more cars are sold than motorcycles," posits Example 4, and this might suggest a fairly high diversion ratio from merging motorcycle brands to cars even though "motorcycle buyers see Brand B motorcycles as much more similar to Brand A motorcycles than are cars," which in turn suggests that sales of cars are not a good indicator of the competitive significance of cars to motorcycle customers. Example 7 then counsels excluding cars from the market "unless motorcycles fail the hypothetical monopolist test." If motorcycles do fail the HMT, however, the 2010 phrasing may appear (it is not entirely clear) to assume that no other products are directly relevant and, with that assumption, to concede that cars would likely be included. In contrast, if other substitutes are available whose inclusion in aggregate would cause the candidate market to pass the HMT without "lead[ing] to misleadingly small market shares for motorcycle producers," the 2023 Guidelines would not particularly recommend including cars.

  - This is the form of the problem against which the narrowest market principle can potentially protect, by refraining from including the problematic product, as discussed in the 2010 Guidelines. In doing so it can be assisted by the circle principle.
- The same fundamental problem can instead arise a bit differently if the product: (a) attracts enough diversion from the central products such that the circle principle would mandate its inclusion; but (b) is very big, such that its sales are disproportionate even to that substantial competitive significance.
  - In this case the circle principle would positively lead one astray by mandating that the product be included, and this would ensue with or without the narrowest market principle.

178. Intuitively, one approach that might help one guard against inclusion of a popular but "competitively distant" product whose share of sales much "overstates its relative competitive significance" is to be open to considering qualitative indicators of competitive closeness alongside the quantitative analysis.

IV. Coordination

179. Especially in a concentrated industry, firms routinely respond to one another's competitive moves such as price changes or product innovations. Anticipation of such responses can significantly dilute the normal competitive reward for improving a firm's offers to trading partners. For example, if firm A is considering a price cut, its calculus will be substantially affected by how it expects a major rival, firm B, to react. As the 2023 Guidelines observe in section 2.3, "in a concentrated market a firm may forego or soften an aggressive competitive action because it anticipates rivals responding in kind." Market performance can thus suffer "if a firm's prospective competitive reward from attracting customers away from its rivals will be significantly diminished by its rivals' likely responses" (2023 Guidelines, section 2.3.B). And to the extent that anticipation of such responses is stronger as a result of a concentrating merger, which is a reasonable concern or expectation, that is a competitive harm from the merger that is not captured by conventional unilateral-effect analysis.

180. Some forms of this concern have long been built into the antitrust analysis of mergers – indeed, since well before unilateral effects were considered. Firms A and B might seek to convince one another that any price cut will be matched or even met with a sharp retaliatory response. Some techniques that they might use to establish such an expectation would amount to illegal "collusion"; others might be viewed as regrettable but not illegal "tacit coordination." The term "coordination" and its cognates are well-established as describing both of those cases, and to the extent that a merger makes coordination more likely, that would constitute a "coordinated effect."

181. But firm B's response to a move by firm A need not be part of a collusive scheme or a purposive attempt to convince A that strong responses are to be expected going forward. It could simply be a natural response to the change in B's market environment brought about by the change in A's price.[10] The economic or competitive consequences would still apply, but the word "coordination" would be a much less natural one. The economic effects span illegal collusion, "tacit coordination," and also such "natural responses." This creates a semantic issue with the word "coordination" and its cognates: do they cover that last category, "natural responses"?

182. It is not clear to me that there is a fully satisfactory answer to that question. The 2010 Guidelines (section 7) introduced the phrase "parallel accommodating conduct" as a new term for those natural responses, but I fear it never caught on. The 2023 Guidelines instead sweep the topic into the broad topic of "tacit coordination." If the Agencies agree with me that it is an important topic that (partly because of the way the economics literature has developed) has been neglected, I hope they will take opportunities to make explicit – ideally, reasonably "often and loudly" – that the 2023 Guidelines are using the phrase "tacit coordination" to include competition-sapping natural responses. I can see that inclusion in the text when I read the 2023 Guidelines section 2.3, in particular the quotes above, but I would feel better with more assurance that readers in general are being guided to seeing it that way.

183. Let me now return to an earlier theme from above: difficulty of proof and precision. The 1992 Merger Guidelines stressed "the difficulties of predicting likely future behavior based on the types of incomplete and sometimes contradictory information typically generated in merger investigations." This sounds quite a lot like the 2023 Guidelines' "do not attempt to predict the future..." – but in the 2023 Guidelines that point is in the preamble to the whole document and presumably applies throughout, whereas in the 1992 Merger Guidelines it was in section 2.1 on coordinated effects, suggesting that that topic is particularly difficult to analyze with confidence. The 2010 Guidelines recognize generally in their second paragraph that "certainty about anticompetitive effect is seldom possible and not required" but also amplify the point specifically in their discussion of coordinated effects (section 7.1) "the risk that a merger will induce adverse coordinated effects may not be susceptible to quantification or detailed proof." So 1992 and 2010 agree that coordinated effects are particularly hard to pin down. The 2023 Guidelines (section 2.3.B), in contrast, approvingly quote a "normal presumption" of coordinated effects. Is coordination an especially difficult thing to predict?

---

10 This has been a focus of my recent writing. *See* Jonathan Baker & Joseph Farrell, *Oligopoly Coordination, Economic Analysis, and the Prophylactic Role of Horizontal Merger Enforcement*, 168 U. Pa. L. Rev. 1985 (2021); Joseph Farrell & Jonathan Baker, *Natural Oligopoly Responses, Repeated Games, and Coordinated Effects in Merger Analysis: A Perspective and Research Agenda*, 58 Rev. Indus. Org. 103–141 (2021); Joseph Farrell, *The Oligopoly Problem, Trigger Strategies, and "Coordinated Effects"*, CPI Antitrust Chronicle (2023), https://www.pymnts.com/cpi_posts/the-oligopoly-problem-trigger-strategies-and-coordinated-effects/.

184. I suspect that the answer is "yes" if we focus on purposive coordination, which can be notoriously unstable: indeed, one might ponder that if successful coordination were too predictable then the prospect of renegotiation following a "defection" would paradoxically weaken the prospects for success. But I like to think that we can make progress toward getting a workable handle on what the 2010 Guidelines called "parallel accommodating conduct", and perhaps thereby put meat on a "normal presumption."

V. Appendix

185. The Appendix is an organ that until relatively recently was thought to be vestigial. So it was discouraging to see a good deal of the analytical content relegated to an Appendix in the draft merger guidelines. I'm relieved to see that content resorbed into the textual body in the final 2023 Guidelines.

Common Ownership and the Merger Guidelines

MERRITT B. FOX* AND MENESH S. PATEL**
Columbia Law School
UC Davis School of Law

---

* Arthur Levitt Professor of Law, Columbia Law School.

** Professor of Law, UC Davis School of Law. Significant parts of this chapter are derived from our earlier work in Merritt B. Fox & Menesh S. Patel, *Common Ownership, Do Managers Really Compete Less*, 39 YALE J. REG. 136 (2022) and Menesh S. Patel, *Common Ownership, Institutional Investors, and Antitrust*, 82 ANTITRUST L.J. 279 (2018).

I. Introduction

186. Common ownership occurs when each of several firms in a market has shareholders who are also shareholders of other firms in the market.[1] If a market is comprised of two firms, for instance, then it would exhibit common ownership if the two firms have at least one shareholder in common. Common ownership is a form of partial ownership in the sense that each common owner has only an incomplete ownership interest in the firms in which she is invested, rather than owning all the shares of any such firm.

187. Although common ownership is not a new phenomenon in the United States, its extent has grown significantly in the past few decades. This increase can be traced in large part to the rise of mutual funds and exchange-traded funds (ETFs) that track broad-based stock indexes such as the S&P 500 or the Russell 2000. Such a fund, by its very nature, will own shares in every publicly traded firm in each industry that the index covers. Three management companies – Vanguard, BlackRock, and State Street (the "Big Three") – dominate this space and together manage funds holding in aggregate approximately 21% of the shares of a typical S&P 500 firm.[2] In a typical industry, each of the Big Three holds approximately 4 to 9% of the shares of every one of the industry's constituent publicly traded firms.[3]

188. This rise in common ownership has been the source of considerable recent academic research. Some of this research inquires, as an empirical matter, as to whether common ownership generates competitive harm.[4] Another strand of the literature interrogates, as an analytical matter, whether and under what circumstances common ownership can be expected to generate competitive harm.[5] A third strand evaluates the public policy question of how, if at all, antitrust law and agency enforcement practice should respond to the rise in common ownership and whether new regulations

1 In the academic literature, common ownership is sometimes referred to as "horizontal shareholding." *See, e.g.*, Einer Elhauge, *Horizontal Shareholding*, 129 Harv. L. Rev. 1267 (2016); Fiona Scott Morton & Herbert Hovenkamp, *Horizontal Shareholding and Antitrust Policy*, 127 Yale L.J. 2026 (2018).

2 Matthew Backus et al., *Common Ownership in America: 1980-2017*, 13 Am. Econ. J.: Microeconomics 273, 285 (2021). By dollar volume, the bulk of the funds managed by the Big Three are broad-based index funds and, in turn, the Big Three's broad-based index funds dominate this market. *Id.*

3 Each of the Big Three has some actively managed funds and specialty index funds as well, and so the proportion of shares held in aggregate by the funds it manages varies somewhat from one corporation to the next. *See id.* at 285, fig.5 (showing that each of the Big Three held approximately 4%–9% of a typical S&P 500 firm in 2017).

4 The recent scholarly interest in common ownership was sparked by two important empirical papers evaluating the competitive effects of common ownership in the airline and banking sectors. *See* José Azar et al., *Anticompetitive Effects of Common Ownership*, 73 J. Fin. 1513 (2018) ["Airline Paper"] (empirically evaluating the effects of common ownership in the airline industry); José Azar et al., *Ultimate Ownership and Bank Competition*, 2021 Fin. Mgmt. 1 ["Banking Paper"] (empirically evaluating the effects of common ownership in the banking industry).

5 Examples of this research appearing in legal journals include Edward B. Rock & Daniel L. Rubinfeld, *Antitrust for Institutional Investors*, 82 Antitrust L.J. 221 (2018); David I. Walker, *Common Ownership and Executive Incentives: The Implausibility of Compensation as an Anticompetitive Mechanism*, 99 B.U. L. Rev. 2373 (2019); and C. Scott Hemphill & Marcel Kahan, *The Strategies of Anticompetitive Common Ownership*,

are called for.[6] All aspects of this literature – from the empirical, to the theoretical, to the public policy – remain unsettled and continue to be the active focus of academic inquiry.[7]

189. Presumably inspired by this literature, the 2023 Merger Guidelines include, for the first time, reference to common ownership. Prior versions of the guidelines, such as the 2010 Horizontal Merger Guidelines, when discussing partial ownership, focused solely on the related issue of cross ownership, where it is a firm, not one of its shareholders, that acquires an interest in a rival firm.[8] But the 2023 discussion of partial ownership, set out in Guideline 11, refers to both cross ownership and common ownership.[9]

190. Guideline 11 specifies three ways that the acquisition of partial ownership can potentially generate competitive harm and thus possibly run afoul of federal antitrust law: (i) "by giving the partial owner the ability to influence the competitive conduct of the target firm;" (ii) "by giving the acquiring firm access to non-public, competitively sensitive information; and (iii) "by reducing the incentive of the acquiring firm to compete."[10]

191. The first two of these three notions provide obvious pathways for partial ownership to inflict competitive harm, even when that partial ownership is in the form of common ownership. If a common owner's equity interests in rival firms are sufficiently large, the common owner will be able to influence the conduct of the firms in which it is invested, through voting or otherwise, in a manner that causes the firms' managers to engage in conduct that benefits the common owner at the expense of consumers and competition. With interests that large, the common owner may also

---

129 Yale L.J. 1392 (2020); as well as Merritt B. Fox & Menesh S. Patel, *Common Ownership, Do Managers Really Compete Less,* 39 Yale J. Reg. 136 (2022) and Menesh S. Patel, *Common Ownership, Institutional Investors, and Antitrust*, 82 Antitrust L.J. 279 (2018). There is also a theoretical economic literature on common ownership. *See, e.g.*, *infra* note 16 and associated text.

6 Two early papers that were the focus of significant policy discussion were Elhauge, *supra* note 1, and Eric A. Posner et al., *A Proposal to Limit the Anticompetitive Power of Institutional Investors*, 81 Antitrust L.J. 669 (2017).

7 For example, the two early empirical papers on common ownership showed a positive relationship between common ownership and competitive harm in the airline and banking sectors. *See* Airline Paper, *supra* note 4; Banking Paper, *supra* note 4. Some scholars subsequently questioned the persuasiveness of those empirical studies on methodological grounds. *See, e.g.*, Matthew Backus et al., *The Common Ownership Hypothesis: Theory and Evidence*, Econ. Stud. Brookings 2–3 (Feb. 2019), https://www.brookings.edu/articles/the-common-ownership-hypothesis-theory-and-explanation/; Rock & Rubinfeld, *supra* note 5, at 240–46; Daniel P. O'Brien & Keith Waehrer, *The Competitive Effects of Common Ownership: We Know Less Than We Think*, 81 Antitrust L.J. 729, 748–58 (2017). And other scholars conducted empirical studies of common ownership's effects in the airline and banking sectors using different empirical methodology than in the two early empirical papers and, in contrast to those early papers, found no empirical relationship between common ownership and competitive harm. *See, e.g.*, Patrick J. Dennis et al., *Common Ownership Does Not Have Anti-Competitive Effects in the Airline Industry*, 77 J. Fin. 2765 (2022).

8 *See* Fed. Trade Comm'n and U.S. Dep't. of Justice, *Horizontal Merger Guidelines* (2010) ("2010 Guidelines"), § 13, https://www.justice.gov/atr/horizontal-merger-guidelines-08192010.

9 *See* Fed. Trade Comm'n and U.S. Dep't. of Justice, *Merger Guidelines* (2023) ("2023 Guidelines"), Guideline 11, https://www.justice.gov/d9/2023-12/2023%20Merger%20Guidelines.pdf ["Guideline 11"]. Guideline 11 defines "common ownership" as "occur[ring] when individual investors hold non-controlling interests in firms that have a competitive relationship that could be affected by those joint holdings." *Id.*

10 *Id.*

be able to obtain non-public information from one rival firm and pass it on to, or use it to influence the behavior of, another rival, again with anticompetitive effects.

192. However, when it comes to the third notion – the asserted reduction in the incentive to compete – it makes a big difference whether the partial ownership is in the form of cross-ownership (one firm owning the shares of a rival) or common ownership (two rival firms having one or more of the same persons as shareholders). The guidelines lump the analysis of the two together, but in fact, when the partial ownership is in the form of common ownership, the third pathway is far less obvious.[11] In essence, Guideline 11 posits that the *mere presence of common ownership* can lessen firms' incentives to compete, even in the absence of any control or communication by the common owner.[12] The 2023 Merger Guidelines, in fact, go further and state that common ownership by itself can generate competitive harm even if the common owner has no ability to influence the conduct of the firm in which it is invested.[13] They state as well that common ownership can lessen firms' incentives to compete even in the absence of any specific anticompetitive act or intent.[14]

193. The 2023 Merger Guidelines are silent, however, on exactly how common ownership without any control or communication by the common owners could disrupt these incentives. The guidelines also do not provide any guidance to courts on the factors they should consider if asked to evaluate in a given litigation whether common ownership can dampen a firm's competitive incentives. There is also no case law or other agency guidance on the issue.

194. In this chapter, we train attention on the specific theory of unilateral harm embedded in the 2023 Merger Guidelines that common ownership by itself can lessen the commonly held firms' incentives to compete, even without any control or communication by the firms' common owners. Beyond the scholarly community, our primary audience for this piece is the Justice Department and the FTC in deciding what cases to bring,

---

11 When one firm acquires an equity interest in a rival (cross-ownership), the fortunes of the firm acquiring the interest become tied in part to the profitability of the rival. Because the two firms are in the same industry, the behavior of the firm holding the interest can affect the profitability of the rival. In deciding on its own behavior, the firm acquiring the interest may thus account for the effect of that behavior on the profitability of the rival, with an anticompetitive result. When instead a person who is a shareholder in one firm acquires shares in a rival to that firm (common ownership), the person's fortunes again become tied in part to the profitability of the first firm's rival, but the person's behavior will have no direct effect on the rival's profitability.

12 *See, e.g.*, Guideline 11, *supra* note 9 ("Partial acquisitions that do not result in control may nevertheless present significant competitive concerns. The acquisition of a minority position may … change incentives so as to otherwise dampen competition"). As with other aspects of Guideline 11, the guideline's discussion of this incentive-dampening theory of competitive harm is framed in terms of a partial acquisition generally, e.g., common ownership or cross-ownership. In this chapter, we focus only on this theory of competitive harm as it relates to common ownership.

13 *See id.* ("Th[e] reduction in the incentive of the acquiring firm to compete arises even when it cannot directly influence the conduct or decision making of the target firm.").

14 *See id.* ("The Agencies recognize that … common ownership can reduce competition by softening firms' incentives to compete, even absent any specific anticompetitive act or intent.").

judges in evaluating the competitive effects of common ownership in particular cases, and practitioners who may be litigating such cases.

195. We split our analysis into three parts. Part II is a preliminary section that frames some of the chapter's more substantive analysis in its later parts. In Part II, we describe the leading economic model of common ownership and competition that is relied on by the seminal academic literature on common ownership. The model predicts that common ownership generates competitive harm without any communication or control, *but only when certain assumptions are satisfied.* The key assumption is that common ownership causes the management of a firm subject to common ownership to abandon own-firm profit maximization as its competitive polestar in favor of making competition-related decisions for the purpose of maximizing the sum of its own firm's profits *and* some portion of rival firms' profits. If this supposition does not accurately capture common ownership's effects on managerial decision-making in a given case, then the economic model of common ownership predicts no meaningful competitive harm will arise.

196. Informed in part by this discussion, Part III elucidates the most important factors relevant to a competitive effects analysis into whether a specific manifestation of common ownership can meaningfully dampen firms' incentives to compete in the manner envisioned by Guideline 11. The most important factor is the extent to which, if any, the challenged common ownership has disrupted managerial incentives to compete. This must be analyzed in the context of the specific governance structure in which those incentives are set. We also discuss two other relevant factors: the common owners' interests in adjacent markets and market structure. If a court, in a given case, is asked to conduct a competitive effects analysis of common ownership based on the theory the common ownership lessened firms' competitive incentives without any control or communication by the common owners, these would be the major factors that the court should evaluate.

197. Part IV focuses on the manifestation of common ownership that has been the near exclusive focus of the academic literature: the common ownership of publicly traded firms, predominantly through the holdings of index funds managed by the Big Three.[15] We explain why the corporate governance infrastructure in which the incentives of managers of publicly traded firms are set makes it highly unlikely that present levels of common ownership are diminishing those managers' competitive incentives. In addition to providing strong reasons to be skeptical that common ownership is generating competitive harm among publicly traded firms solely through incentive distortions, Part IV also can be used by courts as a roadmap for how to evaluate, in a given case, whether the presence of common ownership among the publicly traded firms in an industry will lessen managerial incentives to compete, which is a necessary condition for Guideline 11's incentives-only theory of competitive harm to work.

---

15 *See, e.g.*, Airline Paper, *supra* note 4; Banking Paper, *supra* note 4. We focus specifically on publicly traded firms without a control shareholder, which has been the focus in the academic literature.

II. Common Ownership and the Potential for Competitive Harm

198. The seminal academic literature on common ownership relied on a specific economic model of oligopolistic competition in common ownership environments, one we refer to as the economic model of common ownership.[16] That model predicts that common ownership can generate competitive harm even in the absence of any control or communication by the common owners, but only if certain underlying assumptions are met. The key consideration is whether common ownership modifies managerial incentives to compete.

199. The economic model of common ownership envisions a circumstance in which firms may have both common and non-common owners. Firms in the model produce homogenous goods and engage in quantity, i.e., Cournot, competition. The relevant market is assumed to have entry barriers sufficiently high to sustain persistent supra-competitive pricing. Firms in the model return profits to their shareholders through dividend payments, and shareholders are assumed to derive utility solely from these within market monetary gains.

200. The economic model of common ownership expressly does not fully specify the important assumption of how *managers* of firms with common and non-common owners make competition-related decisions – that is, the nature of managerial objectives in common ownership environments.[17] Any hypothesis of common ownership's effects on competition, either viewed through the lens of the economic model of common ownership or otherwise, requires some specification about managerial objectives in common ownership environments. After all, it is the decisions of firm managers – not shareholders – that in the first instance determine a firm's decisions, including those that would affect the extent of competition. Any plausible prediction about common ownership's competitive effects must therefore be governed, at least in part, by the assumed specification of how, if at all, common ownership influences managerial objectives.

201. If there is no common ownership, then each of the standard economic models of competition would implicitly model the objectives of firm

---

16 This model is drawn from Daniel P. O'Brien & Steven C. Salop, *Competitive Effects and Partial Ownership: Financial Interest and Corporate Control*, 67 ANTITRUST L.J. 559 (2000). This model, or a generalization of it, was used, for instance, in the Airline Paper and the Banking Paper, among others. *See* Airline Paper, *supra* note 4, at 1521–22; Banking Paper, *supra* note 4, at 244–45. O'Brien and Salop's article builds on the work of Timothy F. Bresnahan & Steven C. Salop, *Quantifying the Competitive Effects of Production Joint Ventures*, 4 INT'L J. INDUS. ORG. 155 (1986). There are other models of common ownership in the literature. *See, e.g.*, O'Brien & Salop, *supra*, at 611 (common ownership model in which firms compete on price, rather than quantity).

17 More precisely, the common ownership model specifies that a firm's managers maximize a weighted sum of shareholders' returns. *See* O'Brien & Salop, *supra* note 16, at 609. The weights are intended to represent shareholders' control interests in the firm but are left generalized and unspecified in the model. *See id.* In other words, the common ownership model expressly leaves unspecified how managers weigh the competing preferences of a firm's common and non-common owners. The model is agnostic on that point because, as the model's originators correctly explain, managerial objectives in the face of conflicting shareholder preferences are determined by "the corporate-control structure of the firm, which determines each shareholder's influence over decision-making within the firm." *See id.*

managers as maximizing own-firm profits.[18] These managerial objectives would result in some equilibrium level of price and output in the relevant market, which would serve as the benchmark to evaluate whether common ownership would have any effect on competition in that market.

202. When a firm instead has both common and non-common owners, an issue arises as to the nature of managerial objectives, in large part because the two shareholder groups will have conflicting preferences about the objective that managers should strive for when making competition-related decisions. Because the firm's non-common owners' within-market pecuniary gains and losses are determined solely by the profits of the firm in which they are invested, their preference is that, despite the presence of common ownership, their firm's managers remain focused on maximizing own-firm profit when making competition-related decisions. This conclusion concerning the interests of the non-common shareholders is not undermined by the fact that if managers of all firms in the market decided to pursue some objective other than own-firm maximization, it would result in a lessening of competition and an increase in firms' profitability relative to the baseline where there is no common ownership. This is because any given firm's non-common owners would want their managers to instead pursue own-firm profit maximization in order to exploit the diminished competition by rival firms, holding fixed those rivals' decisions.

203. The firm's common owners see things differently. When the firm's managers make a competition-affecting decision, that decision affects the wellbeing of the common owners through two channels: the effect of the managers' decision on the firm's profits and the effect of that decision on the profits of the rival firms in which the common owners are invested. For this reason, a firm's common owners prefer that when the firm's managers make competition-related decisions, the managers take into consideration how the decision affects the firm's profitability *and also*, to some extent, how the decision affects the profitability of the rival firms in which the common owners are invested.[19]

204. The economic model of common ownership takes no position on the nature of managerial objectives in the face of these heterogeneous shareholder preferences, an approach that reflects an understanding that the nature of those objectives will depend on the governance structure in which managers operate.[20] One possibility is that common ownership generates no modification to managerial objectives, in that firm managers,

---

18 For instance, the Cournot model on which the common ownership model is based assumes each firm maximizes its own profits (taking as given the profits of other firms).

19 The specific weight that a firm's common owner would like the firm's managers to place on the profits of rival firms depends on the extent of the common owner's equity interests in those rival firms, relative to its equity interest in the current firm. For instance, suppose there are two firms in the relevant market, A and B, and suppose that there is a common owner. Holding fixed the common owner's interest in Firm A, the common owner will want the managers of Firm A to place a greater weight on the profits of Firm B if the common owner has a high interest in Firm B than if the common owner instead had a low interest in Firm B.

20 *See supra* note 17.

putting aside any agency cost considerations, remain focused just on own-firm profit maximization in common ownership environments, exactly as they would have if there were no common ownership. If this were the case, then the economic model of common ownership would predict no competitive effects from common ownership. Firm managers would have the same objective, and therefore compete equally as vigorously, whether there is common ownership or no common ownership.

205. If, instead, common ownership causes firm managers to abandon own-firm profit maximization in favor of making competition-related decisions in a manner more favored by the firm's common owners, then common ownership may generate competitive harm purely through the sort of incentive modification envisioned by Guideline 11.[21] To see this, suppose that in response to common ownership, firm managers started making competition-related decisions with the aim of maximizing the sum of their own firm's profits plus, to some extent, the profits of the rival firms in which the firm's common owners are also invested. This modification of managerial objectives would result in the firm dampening its level of competition relative to the benchmark, where there is no common ownership and in which the firm's managers make competition-related decisions with the goal of maximizing own-firm profits alone. The reasoning is that if a firm's managers make competition-related decisions with a partial eye focused on the profits of rival firms, then the managers would be willing to curtail competition more than if they were solely guided by the maximization of own-firm profits, because that competition reduction, while injurious to the managers' own firm, would increase the profitability of the rival firms in which the common owners have an interest.[22]

206. This discussion highlights an important point pertinent to the discussion below and the common ownership issue generally: while common ownership, as a matter of economic theory, has the potential to generate competitive harm, whether common ownership actually generates competitive harm in a specific instance depends on how the at-issue common ownership affects managerial incentives to compete. In a litigated challenge to common ownership predicated on pure incentives effects, the relevant antitrust question cannot be answered by reliance on an

21 A modification of managerial incentives is a necessary, but not a sufficient condition, for common ownership to generate competitive harm. For instance, depending on the nature of common owners' interests in adjacent markets, common ownership may not generate competitive harm even if the common ownership had caused managers to make competition-related decisions in a manner more favored by the firm's common owners. *See infra* Part III.B.

22 The early academic research on common ownership critical of common ownership's effect on competition postulated that managers of commonly-owned firms abandon own-firm profit maximization in favor of an objective function favored by a common owner – that is, an objective that places some weight on the profitability of rival firms when making competition-related decision. *See* Fox & Patel, *supra* note 5, at 154–60 (explicating the underlying model of managerial decision-making used in the early common ownership literature). The weight that the manager was assumed in that research to place on rival firms is that preferred by a hypothetical "blended shareholder," who represents a particular averaging of the interests of the firm's common and non-common shareholders. *See id.*

assumption of changed managerial objectives. Rather it requires actual determinations about whether the common ownership at issue in the case in fact modified managerial incentives in a way that lessened competition.

III. Primary Factors Bearing on Common Ownership's Actual Competitive Effects

207. In any antitrust challenge to common ownership based on a theory that common ownership may substantially affect competition by lessening the commonly held firms' competitive incentives as envisioned by Guideline 11, the court will be required to conduct a competitive effects analysis. What primary factors should a court evaluate when conducting that analysis? This part of the chapter addresses that question, guided in part by the discussion above, and examines the three primary factors germane to the competitive effects analysis: common ownership's modifications to managerial incentives to compete, common owners' interests in adjacent markets, and the structure of the relevant market.

1. Modifications to Managerial Incentives to Compete

208. As reflected by the discussion in Part II, the issue most relevant to an assessment of whether common ownership in a specific relevant market is generating competitive harm through the incentives-only mechanism envisioned by Guideline 11 is the extent to which it has modified *managerial* incentives to compete. If the challenged common ownership caused no change in the managers' competitive incentives, then the challenged common ownership would not be generating competitive harm, at least through the incentives-only mechanism envisioned in Guideline 11.

209. The specifics of this assessment in any given case will depend on the particular circumstances involved. To take a particularly clear example, suppose that in the relevant market, a firm with one or more common owners has a profit-minded controlling shareholder who does not herself maintain a meaningful interest in any rival firms. Absent additional evidence suggesting otherwise, the assessment in this case needs to be that the presence of common ownership has had *no* anticompetitive effects. The controlling shareholder, acting in her own interest, would be expected to continue to apply significant pressure on the firm's managers to maximize own-firm profits alone.

210. More generally, despite the particularities in any given case, some considerations relating to managerial incentives will sweep across all cases.

A. *Evaluation of the Applicable Governance Structure*

211. First, an assessment into the incentives question will involve an evaluation of the overall governance structure in which the managerial incentives at issue in the case are set. If the governance structure is such that there are strong forces pushing managers to continue to maximize own-firm profits

despite the presence of common ownership, then the associated common ownership is likely to have little or no competitive effects.

212. Evaluation of the overall governance structure in which managerial incentives are set is a non-discretionary component of the competitive effects analysis of a case based on Guideline 11's incentives-only theory. This is true regardless of the nature of the firms at issue – e.g., whether they are publicly traded firms with dispersed shareholders, publicly traded firms with a controlling shareholder, or privately held firms. The necessity of a governance-centered analysis arises because, as previously noted, a firm's competition decisions are made by the firm's managers, and not directly by its shareholders. And firm managers operate within a specific governance infrastructure.

213. Any plausible assessment of common ownership's effects on a given firm's competition decisions therefore must inquire how, if at all, common ownership has altered managerial incentives to compete, making reference to the specific governance infrastructure in which those managers operate. In other words, if common ownership influences the extent of competition in a particular relevant market through altering managerial incentives to compete as envisioned by the incentives-only theory of Guideline 11, it can only do so by operating through the specific governance framework pertinent to the litigated case. We provide an example of this governance-centered analysis and further discussion in Part IV.

214. In analyzing the potential for common ownership's effect on managerial incentives to compete, it is important for the analysis to take as given any diminished competitive incentive that existed without common ownership and not to attribute that preexisting diminution in competition to common ownership. In particular, if, in the absence of common ownership, managers were deviating from own-firm profit maximization because of agency cost considerations that drove a wedge between managerial conduct and the firm's non-common owners' objective of own-firm profit maximization, then it would be improper to attribute that deviation from own-firm profit maximization to common ownership. In other words, the managerial incentives analysis should evaluate the extent to which common ownership generated *any additional* deterioration in managers' incentives to compete relative to what may have already existed in the absence of common ownership.

B. *Assessment of Managers' Apprehension of Common Owners' Competition Preferences*

215. Second, the analysis should inquire as to whether the managers of the firms in the relevant market sufficiently apprehended the existence of the firm's common owners and the extent of those common owners' competition-lessening preferences. If firm managers did not apprehend these things to one extent or another, this would make the incentives theory in Guideline 11 less plausible, all else being equal.

216. One kind of evidence that managers did apprehend these things is active communication by the common owners urging firm managers to undertake competition-constraining actions. It should be noted, though, that the very existence of such communications can support an entirely separate theory of antitrust liability, rendering unnecessary the incentives-only theory. The common shareholders sending such communications could be regarded as the hub in a "hub and spoke" conspiracy in violation of Section 1 of the Sherman Act.[23]

C. *The Extent of Common Owner Heterogeneity*

217. Relatedly, significant differences in common owners' equity interests in firms in the relevant market may disincentivize firm's managers from deviating from own-firm profit maximization. The specific extent to which a given common owner will want a firm's managers to take rivals' profits into account when making competition decisions depends on the common owner's relative equity interests in rival firms.[24] If a firm has many common owners such that a given common owner's interests in rival firms significantly differs from other common owners' interests in rival firms, then the firm's managers may not be able to readily ascertain the specific extent to which they should take rivals' profits into account when making competition-related decisions. This is because each common owner would have a different preference as to the specific weight that they want managers to place on rivals' profits. If the preferred weight of another common shareholder is used instead, the first common shareholder may be worse off than if the firm simply pursued an own-firm profit maximizing strategy. Thus, firm managers may find it impossible or impractical to identify an objective that places weight on the profit of rival firms that balances the common owners' competing competition-related preferences, in which case they may find it easier to remain focused on own-firm profit maximization.[25]

D. *Analysis of the Relevant Decision-Makers*

218. Finally, the incentive modification question should focus on the specific decision-makers in the firm responsible for competition-related decisions. While the analysis should start with an evaluation of how, if at all, the common ownership modifies the incentives of top level decision-makers such as the company's board and officers, a complete analysis may also

---

23 *See, e.g.*, United States v. Apple, Inc., 791 F.3d 290, 314 (2d Cir. 2015) ("[C]ourts have long recognized the existence of 'hub and spoke' conspiracies in which an entity at one level of the market structure, the 'hub,' coordinates an agreement among competitors at a different level, the 'spokes.'"). See also Thomas D. Nevins, *The US Court of Appeals for the 2nd Circuit affirms ruling condemning masterminding the creation, organization and implementation of a conspiracy by five e-book publishers (Apple)*, e-Competitions June 2015, art. No. 75774.

24 *See supra* note 19.

25 As noted, the early academic research on common ownership critical of common ownership's effect on competition postulated that managers of commonly owned firm make competition-related decisions to maximize the wellbeing of a hypothetical blended shareholder who represents a particular amalgam of the firm's common and non-common shareholders. *See supra* note 22. It is not entirely clear that firm managers would be able to apprehend the competition-related preferences of this hypothetical shareholder.

necessitate an inquiry into how the common ownership affects the incentives of decision-makers lower on the firm's organizational chart, such as those employees who are the ones who actually set price or quantity or who are responsible for other competition-related decisions.

2. Common Owners' Interests in Adjacent Markets

219. In addition to their equity interests in the relevant market, the common owners may also have equity interests in adjacent markets. This is especially likely with respect to the broad-based index funds managed by the Big Three, which have meaningful equity holdings in all market segments. This is important because it is the increase in the holdings of these funds that has been the primary motivator of the literature expressing concern about common ownership.

220. Where a common owner of firms in one industry also has shares in one or more firms in an adjacent industry, the common-ownership-induced interest that it might otherwise have had in limiting competition in the first industry may be attenuated or even fully eliminated.[26] For example, if the common owner in one industry has shares in a firm downstream from that industry, these shares become less valuable when the firms in the first industry raise prices on what they supply the downstream firm. Thus, while an abatement of competition in the first industry would benefit the common owner through increases in the profitability of those firms, there would be an offsetting cost to the common owner because of the diminished value of its interest in the downstream firm.

221. Similar logic applies to other adjacent markets, such as input markets and markets for products complementary to those in the relevant market. Firms in these other markets do better when the initial industry's quantity of output is higher (or prices are lower), exactly the opposite of what happens when competition in that industry is limited. Thus, again, a common owner's shares in one of these types of adjacent industries will cancel out in part or in whole any common ownership-induced interest that it might otherwise have had in limiting competition in the initial industry.[27]

222. The key point is that the mere fact that firms in an industry have common owners as shareholders does not automatically lead to the conclusion that these persons have any greater interest in limiting competition in the industry than if they each invested in only one firm in the industry. Where the common owners do not have any greater interest, the idea that their common ownership will lead to diminished competition can be dismissed

---

26 Others have made this point. *See, e.g.*, Jonathan B. Baker, *Overlapping Financial Investor Ownership, Market Power, and Antitrust Enforcement: My Qualified Agreement with Professor Elhauge*, 129 HARV. L. REV. F. 212, 217 (2016); John R. Woodbury, *Paper Trail: Working Papers and Recent Scholarship*, ANTITRUST SOURCE 6 (Dec. 2014), https://www.americanbar.org/content/dam/aba/publishing/antitrust-magazine-online/dec14_paper_trail_12_16f.pdf.

27 Common owners' divergent interests in adjacent markets would amplify the observation above concerning how differences in common owners' equity interests could disincentivize firm's managers from deviating from own-firm profit maximization. *See supra* Part III.A.3.

before we even get to the analysis of whether, if the common owners in fact did have a greater interest, management would change behavior. In sum, in any antitrust challenge based on common ownership in an industry, the competitive effects analysis must include an assessment of the common owners' out-of-market interests and of whether these interests largely cancel out any interests that they have in curtailing competition in the industry.[28]

3. Market Structure

223. Market structure also has a bearing on the extent to which common ownership can generate competitive harm in an industry and thus should also be a component of the competitive effects analysis. As an example, consider the issue of demand-side substitutability. If there is little substitutability between the products sold by the commonly owned firms in the industry, common ownership may not generate substantial competitive harm. The underlying reasoning parallels the reason why a merger among firms selling weak substitutes may not generate substantial unilateral price effects. If two commonly owned firms' products are poor substitutes, then even if the managers of the firms adhered to the competition-related preference of the common owners, the fact that the shareholders of one of the firms had concurrent ownership interests in another firm in the same industry would not strongly incentivize the managers of either firm to compete less, since only a small proportion of the sales that one of the commonly owned firms forgoes would accrue to the other firm.[29] In other words, an assessment of common ownership's potential for competitive harm in a given case necessities an inquiry into the structure of the relevant market pertinent to the competition question, such as demand-side substitutability.[30]

IV. Common Ownership's Effects on the Competitive Incentives of the Managers of Publicly Traded Firms

224. While common ownership can arise among any types of firms, the literature concerning it has peered most closely at the common ownership of publicly traded firms. As discussed, this is because focus on the

---

28 This issue does not arise in the economic model of common ownership discussed above, *see supra* Part II, because the model does not take into consideration any ownership interests that shareholders may have in adjacent markets such as input markets, downstream markets, or markets for complementary products. This is not a shortcoming of the model but simply an assumption needed to make the model tractable.

29 If the goods sold by commonly owned firms are especially poor substitutes, then those goods may be in different relevant markets, which itself may be grounds for concluding there is no antitrust issue with the common ownership of those firms.

30 Of course, other aspects of market structure beyond demand-side substitutability will be relevant to the competitive effects analysis. For instance, if market entry is easy, then this would serve to lessen or eliminate any competitive harm that could potentially be generated by common ownership. Common ownership also has the potential to generate within-market efficiencies. *See, e.g.*, Jie He & Jiekun Huang, *Product Market Competition in a World of Cross-Ownership: Evidence from Institutional Blockholdings*, 30 Rev. Fin. Stud. 2674 (2017) (empirically finding that commonly held firms experience market growth, greater product market collaboration, and improved innovation productivity and operating profitability). Such efficiencies may arise even if common ownership does not modify managerial incentives to compete because they may make both common and non-common owners better off.

matter has been motivated in large part by the growth in the broad-based index funds managed by the Big Three. In this part, we assess the plausibility that common ownership of firms of this type impairs their managers' incentives to compete.[31] Consistent with the discussion of managerial incentives above, we frame our discussion with necessary reference to the overall governance structure in which the managerial incentives in such firms are set.[32]

1. Managerial Preferences: Higher Own-Firm Profit

225. Before analyzing whether the growth in common ownership of publicly traded firms without a control shareholder lessens the competitive incentives of those firms' managers, it is worth first considering the managers' own preferences concerning their firms' profit objectives. There is much that can be said about managerial preferences, but the important point developed here is that the managers of any given publicly traded firm would want their firm to focus on own-firm profit maximization, as the firm's non-common owners would want, rather than trading off their own firm's profits with the profits of rival firms, as the common owners prefer.

226. To see why, start with the observation that the managers' positions in their firm are likely to give them, to one extent or another, a variety of benefits that most people desire: compensation, perquisites, power, prestige, the pleasure of benefiting their associates in the firm, a sense of doing social good, and so on. The extent to which the firm can provide the managers with these desired benefits depends on its residuals: the difference between what it can sell its output for and the cost of producing that output, the maximization of which is achieved by the firm maximizing its own profits. The profits of a firm's rivals provide its managers with none of these benefits. And, as noted above, if all firms were abiding by

31 As noted, we focus attention in this Part on publicly traded firms without a controlling shareholder. *See supra* note 15. Because a controlling shareholder has determinative or near-determinative influence over a firm's decisions, the issue of common ownership's influence on managerial incentives raises special considerations. These considerations are not explored in this Part beyond a few simple observations. First, only a small portion of publicly traded corporations have a control shareholder. They constitute only 3.6% of S&P 500 and 8.4% of the entire Russell 3000 and, as of 2015, only represented approximately 10% of the total capitalization of S&P 1500 companies. *See* Kosmas Papadopoulos, *CEO Ownership, Corporate Governance, and Company Performance*, Harvard Law School Forum on Corporate Governance (2019), https://corpgov.law.harvard.edu/2019/05/13/ceo-ownership-corporate-governance-and-company-performance/ (based on ISS data, reporting the percentage of S&P 500 and Russell 3000 firms that have controlling shareholders); Edward Kamonjoh, *Controlled Companies in the Standard & Poor's 1500*, IRRC Institute (March, 2016), at 9, https://bpb-us-w2.wpmucdn.com/sites.udel.edu/dist/8/12944/files/2022/08/Controlled-Companies-IRRCI-2015-FINAL-3-16-16.pdf (based on 2015 data, reporting that the average market capitalization of the 105 firms in the S&P 1500 with a controlling shareholder was $20.6 billion, while the average market capitalization of all firms in the S&P 1500 was $14.3 billion). Second, among public firms that do have a control shareholder, in many cases she is the entrepreneur founder and thus is very unlikely to be a common shareholder. In any firm where the control shareholder is not a common owner, whether the founding entrepreneur or otherwise, it is implausible that the firm would deviate from own-profit oriented decisions with regard to competitive matters even if some of the other shareholders are common owners. Finally, if instead the control shareholder is a common owner, the fact of its common ownership does raise the likelihood, all else equal, that the firm's managers will be influenced to act less competitively. This is nothing new, however, and has been a concern of the antitrust laws for many decades. It is the growth in broad-based index funds that has sparked the recent literature expressing a concern with common ownership, but these funds never act as controlling shareholders.

32 For additional details of the analysis below, see Fox & Patel, *supra* note 5.

the common owners' desired objectives, the managers of any given firm could further increase their own firm's residuals by taking advantage of the other firms' suppressed competition and reverting back to own-firm profit maximization, holding fixed the decisions of those other firms.[33]

2. Modification of Managerial Incentives to Compete Through the Applicable Governance Framework

227. Next, turn to the primary question of whether common ownership of firms in an industry will dampen managerial incentives to compete.[34] The forces that shape managerial incentives have been the central focus of the study of corporate governance over the last few decades, a study usually characterized as concerning the agency costs of management. If common ownership were to alter managerial decision-making, it would be through this already familiar incentive structure, one that consists of a number of sticks and carrots.

228. The sticks involve a variety of threats: (i) A proxy fight (the threat of management being voted out of office by its existing shareholders); (ii) a hostile tender (the threat that some person will purchase enough shares to be able itself to vote management out of office); (iii) an activist campaign (the threat that some person purchases a foothold stake in the firm and then persuades a sufficient number of existing shareholders to vote to replace management); (iv) sale of a share position (the threat of a shareholder with a significant block of shares selling and thereby depressing share price to the disadvantage of the managers); and (v) fiduciary duties (the threat of a derivative suit against the firm's directors and officers claiming that they are not acting in the best interests of the corporation and its shareholders). Students of the role played by block shareholders often list "jawboning" as an additional influence on management, but this will only be effective if backed up by one of the foregoing threats. The carrots are the design of the managers' compensation packages and the managers' own shareholdings in the firm.[35]

229. As we have explained in some detail elsewhere, the kind of common ownership that has led to its significant growth over the past several decades – the rise in the holdings of broad-based index funds – is unlikely to have altered managerial incentives to compete through any of relevant features of the corporate governance infrastructure in which those incentives are set. Rather, these features continue to exert strong pressures on

33 In other words, from the managers' perspective, sacrificing own-firm profits is not a best response to rival firms sacrificing own-firm profits.

34 For expositional ease, in the remainder of this subpart we remove the modifier "dispersed ownership" and "publicly traded," with an understanding that the discussion, including discussion of the incentive structure below, pertains to publicly traded firms (without a controlling shareholder) and the managers of those firms.

35 These various components of the corporate governance framework identified in the text above are not intended to be exhaustive. Other factors may also determine the shape of managerial incentives in a given case. *See, e.g.*, Dorothy S. Lund & Elizabeth Pollman, *The Corporate Governance Machine*, 121 COLUM. L. REV. 2563, 2578–609 (2021) (discussing other aspects of the corporate governance framework).

managers to focus on maximizing own-firm profits.[36] We summarize that discussion here.

230. ***Proxy Fights***. Because today, common ownership arising from the nation's mutual funds and ETFs rarely exceeds about 20% of all the firms in an oligopolistic industry, the threat of a proxy fight to remove a firm's managers who refuse to trade off the firm's profits for the profits of rival firms is entirely empty.[37] The non-common shareholders constitute a very substantial majority and are unlikely to vote for a change in management that, contrary to their interests, would abandon the pursuit of own-firm profits.

231. ***Hostile Tender Offer***. The threat of a hostile tender offer to remove a firm's managers because they refuse to sacrifice own-firm profits seems similarly empty. Mutual funds and ETFs are not organized to pursue such an activity, and so any potential hostile tender offer acquirer would need to be some other kind of common owner. To profit, this other common owner's gain from reducing the output level must be greater than the considerable transaction costs and significant share price premium needed to acquire the high percentage of the target's shares, sufficient for the acquiring common owner to be able to squeeze out the remaining minority who fail to tender.[38] For the gain to exceed these costs, the potential acquirer's percentage stake in competing firms in the industry would likely need to be large enough that the acquisition of the target's shares would disrupt competitive incentives and violate antitrust law. And, even more to the point, there is little reason to think that this calculation would be in any way affected by whether there are or are not mutual funds and ETFs that also hold shares in both the target and other firms in the industry.

232. ***Activist Investors***. It is also very unlikely that an activist investor will target a firm to force its managers to abide by the preferences of the firm's common owners and forego own-firm profits in favor of rival firms' profits, which is necessary for lessening of competition. Suppose that Firm A's managers are making competition-related decisions with the goal of maximizing own-firm profits. The question, then, is whether, given the standard business model for activist investors, it is likely that such an investor would intervene to force Firm A's managers to abandon own-firm profit maximization.

---

36 *See* Fox & Patel, *supra* note 5. The discussion in that other work also conducts the analysis with specific reference to the economic model of common ownership discussed above, in which firms engage in Cournot competition, and with specific reference to the relevant choice variable in that model, i.e., firms' output decisions.

37 To simplify the discussion, we assume that a firm's shareholders are either non-common owners or one of the Big Three, who, in any given market, will maintain an equity interest in all relevant competitors and at present collectively hold approximately 21% of the shares of a typical S&P 500 firm. *See supra* note 2 and associated text. In actual markets, a firm's shareholders may also include other shareholder types, such as shareholders who maintain an equity interest in just some of the relevant competitors in the market. The presence of these and other shareholder types does not significantly alter the conclusions in this subpart. *See* Fox & Patel, *supra* note 5, at 165–66, 181–85.

38 *See, e.g.*, Sandra Betton & B. Espen Eckbo, *Toeholds, Bid Jumps, and Expected Payoffs in Takeovers*, 13 Rev. Fin. Studs. 841, 853 (2000) (for all single-bid takeovers opposed by management between 1971 to 1990, bidder offered a 40% average initial premium).

233. The standard business model for such an intervention involves the activist undertaking four steps: (i) identify a firm where a change in the way it is run would increase its share price; (ii) acquire a foothold stake in the target firm of perhaps 5–7% of its outstanding shares; (iii) persuade enough of the other target's shareholders of the desirability of the change to constitute a majority vote to oust the incumbent managers if they do not adopt the change; and (iv) sell the shares at a profit after the change is adopted and the share price increases to reflect the improvement. The standard financial economics model of an issuer's share price is that it reflects the market's best estimate of the issuer's expected future dividends and other distributions to shareholders discounted to present value,[23] which in turn depend solely on the firm's own net cash flow. Accordingly, an activist pursuing this business model would not push for trading the issuer's profits for the profits of rival firms, because to do so would lower, not increase the issuer's share price.[39]

234. ***Sales of Share Blocks***. It is also very unlikely that a threat by a common owner to depress share price by selling a substantive block of shares would result in managers abandoning own-firm profit maximization. This is because the threat that the price will in fact stay depressed beyond a very short period of time as a result of the sale of the position is not credible. Microstructure economics teaches us that the reason that a share sale can depress price is because the market infers from the seller's order the possibility that the seller has negative nonpublic information not reflected in the price prior to the sale.[40] If, however, nothing comes out subsequently to suggest the existence of any negative news, the price will regain what it lost. Again, the price reflects the market's best estimate of the issuer's expected future dividends and other distributions to shareholders discounted to present value. The sale by the common holder does not change what the future dividends and other distributions will be. So, as soon as the market perceives that there was no negative nonpublic information driving the sale, the price should be no different than if the sale had not occurred. Where the price dip is short lived, management is unlikely to suffer significantly.

235. ***Fiduciary Duties***. An officer or director of a corporation has fiduciary duties to the corporation of care and of loyalty, the breach of either of which can subject her to suits seeking injunctive relief or monetary damages. The duty of care requires the director or officer, even where no conflict of interests exists, to exercise an appropriate standard of care that the actions she takes are in the best interests of the corporation.[41]

---

39 Consistent with this reasoning, Rock and Rubinfeld observe, "[a]lthough there have been dozens of activist hedge fund engagements, we are not aware of any in which the fight was over whether target management engaged in excessive competition." Rock & Rubinfeld, *supra* note 5, at 250.

40 *See, e.g.*, Lawrence R. Glosten & Paul R. Milgrom, *Bid, Ask, and Transaction Prices in a Specialist Market with Heterogeneously Informed Traders*, 14 J. Fin. Econ. 71, 72 (1985); Larry Harris, Trading and Exchanges: Market Microstructure for Practitioners 300 (2002).

41 *See, e.g.*, Principles of the Law, Corporate Governance: Analysis and Recommendations § 4.01(a) (Am. L. Inst. 2005).

The duty of loyalty requires a director or officer that has an interest in a proposed corporate action to behave fairly toward the corporation,[42] in essence she is prohibited from participating in any decision by the corporation to take the action unless she can affirmatively show that the action is in the best interests of the corporation. It is extremely unlikely that the threat of a suit claiming the violation of one of these duties will result in managers foregoing own-firm profits to amplify rivals' profits as the firm's common owners would want.

236. As the above description of these two duties indicates, understanding each of them depends on the concept of the "best interests of the corporation." Suppose, as is typical, about 20% of a corporation's shares are owned by funds managed by the Big Three and that most of the other shareholders are non-common. The question is whether a court would interpret the concept of best interest in such a way that it would intervene to find a violation of the duty of either care or loyalty if a firm's managers pursued the objective that is preferred by the clear majority of the corporation's shareholders, i.e., the non-common owners, who prefer that managers act with the aim of maximizing own-firm profits. The answer seems obvious: the court would interpret the objective preferred by the clear majority as more in the interests of the corporation than the objective preferred by the about 20%, i.e., the common owners, because the latter objective generates less profit than the former and is preferred by only a minority of the shareholders.[43]

237. The business judgment rule is a further, monumental roadblock to the success of duty of care cases based on the failure of management to abide by the preferences of the common owners and abandon own-firm profit maximization. The rule is based on the idea that judges are not business experts and so, as a general matter, a judge should not substitute her judgment for that of a firm's directors or officers. The only exceptions are in instances where the director or officer is interested in the transaction, the procedures used for approving a corporate action are totally flawed, or it is self-evident that the decision lacks any reasonable basis for being in the best interests of the corporation and its shareholders.[44] Moreover, the party challenging the director or officer's conduct bears the burden of establishing the duty of care breach,[45] a rule which in essence creates a presumption of compliance.

---

42 *See id.* at ch. V, Introductory Note.

43 To the extent that the concept of the best interests of the corporation relates to the interests of individual shareholders, rather than what generates the most profit for the corporation, an argument could be made that the best interest of the corporation is the decision that maximizes the aggregate wealth of the shareholders as a group. However, we can find no legal precedent that a corporate action shown to be in the best interests of a majority and to maximize the corporation's cash flow is a violation of either the duty of care or loyalty on the grounds that the best interests of the corporation are really those of a blended shareholder of the sort relied on in the literature critical of common ownership's effects on competition. *See supra* note 22.

44 *See, e.g.*, Principles of the Law, *supra* note 41, at § 4.01(c).

45 *Id.* at § 4.01(d).

238. ***Managerial compensation and shareholdings.*** There is also nothing in the carrots – managerial compensation packages and shareholdings – that would incentivize a firm's managers to sacrifice own-firm profits in the manner preferred by the firm's common owners. The ways that a manager's decisions influence the value of her compensation package relate to her firm's profitability. This is because her compensation package, to the extent that it deviates from straight salary, is typically tied in some way to the firm's profitability or the value of its shares. The package will not reward her for any positive effect that her decisions have on the profits of the firm's competitors. So, her compensation package will create no incentive for her to trade the firm's profits for rivals' profits. Her shareholdings in her firm work the same way since, as noted, she is unlikely to have significant holdings in the shares of her firm's competitors.

239. The remaining issue is whether common ownership can cause firms to *alter* their executive compensation schemes such that managers are less incentivized to compete.[46] For instance, if common ownership were to cause firms to adopt compensation schemes that were less tethered to the profits or share price of managers' own firms, this could reduce the incentives managers to compete vigorously. However, this is implausible. Common owners have no means of directly dictating executive compensation, because it is the board, not shareholders, that sets executive compensation.[47] Nor would the existence of common owners among the firm's shareholders likely affect those who actually do dictate executive compensation schemes. If the board, for instance, were to modify the CEO's compensation in response to common owners' preferences, such that the CEO's incentive to compete was reduced, this would disadvantage the much larger group of non-common owners, who would seek the board's removal. A board that modified executive compensation in a manner that incentivizes managers to compete less also increases the risk of an activist campaign seeking to turn around the firm's drop in profitability.

V. Summary and Implications

240. Some of the recent academic research in common ownership has raised alarm bells that common ownership by itself is impairing publicly traded firms' incentives to compete. Missing in that conversation was an answer to the mechanism question: precisely how can common ownership disrupt managerial incentives to compete in the absence of any control or communication by the common owners? The analysis above shows why

46 This observation reflects the more general point that in addition to evaluating whether common ownership can modify managerial competitive incentives by working through the governance regime in which those incentives are set, the competitive effects analysis should also evaluate whether common ownership can modify that governance regime.

47 Shareholders do have an opportunity to vote on executive compensation, but only in certain circumstances. For example, stock exchange rules require shareholder approval of equity compensation plans. *See, e.g.*, NASDAQ, Inc., The NASDAQ Stock Market LLC Rules, Rule 5635, https://listingcenter.nasdaq.com/rulebook/nasdaq/rules/Nasdaq%205600%20Series.

there is no such plausible mechanism, at least at common ownership levels at or congruent with current levels.

241. Managerial incentives are not formed in the abstract but instead are formed through and by a multifaceted corporate governance framework that has developed over the years to mitigate the agency costs of management. When, as here, that framework is dissected and each constituent part is analyzed to inquire whether common ownership, operating through that particular constituent part, can plausibly lessen public firm managerial incentives to compete, the analysis yields a clear negative response. This conclusion suggests that courts should be very skeptical of claims that, for a publicly traded corporation with no control shareholder, its current level of common ownership is generating competitive harm though the pure-incentives theory articulated in Guideline 11.[48]

242. The analysis above also provides a roadmap for how courts should assess claims that the current level of common ownership of any given such firm is generating competitive harm solely through a distortion of competitive incentives. The paramount question is whether the common ownership involved in fact reduced managerial incentives to compete, i.e., that the presence of the firm's common owners caused firm managers to focus less on the maximization of their own firms' profits in favor of making competition-related decisions with a greater emphasis on the effects of those decisions on rivals' profits. As reflected by the analysis above, to answer this paramount question, the court should systematically work through each of the various components of the corporate governance framework and any other particular features of the firm's corporate governance, and inquire whether common ownership can plausibly be expected to distort the incentives of the firm's managers to compete.

VI. Conclusion

243. Common ownership has the potential to generate harm to competition in a manner that violates antitrust law. Guideline 11 identifies two plausible pathways to competitive harm: common owners' control of, or communication with, the firms in which they are invested. Guideline 11 also articulates a third more contested theory of competitive harm – the theory that common ownership can generate competitive harm purely by reducing incentives to compete even in the absence of any control or communication by the firms' common owners.

244. While common ownership has the *potential* to inflict competitive harm by distorting competitive incentives, it will *actually* distort these incentives only in certain circumstances. The 2023 Guidelines do not articulate what these circumstances might be, a gap that this chapter has sought to fill. As discussed above, while considerations such as the common owners'

48 We take no position on whether common owners are exercising any control of or are communicating with the firms in which they are invested in a way that is generating competitive harm.

interests in adjacent markets and the structure of the relevant market are essential to the competitive effects analysis, the most important factor pertinent to the incentives-only theory of harm in Guideline 11 is whether the challenged common ownership modified a firm's managerial incentives to compete. Unless common ownership causes firm managers to focus less on the maximization of own-firm profits than they would if there were no common ownership, competition will not be lessened.

245. In evaluating whether the challenged common ownership modified managerial incentives to compete, which is a precondition to an incentives-only theory of competitive harm, the analysis must be undertaken with express reference to, and framed by, the specific governance structure in which those managerial incentives are set. The chapter's evaluation of common ownership's ability to modify the incentives of the managers of publicly traded firms embodies the broad contours of that approach.

Awakening Merger Control: The New U.S. Merger Guidelines

ELEANOR M. FOX*

New York University School of Law

* Eleanor Fox is Walter J. Derenberg Professor of Trade Regulation Emerita at New York University School of Law. She thanks Sean Sullivan for his helpful comments. This chapter is based on Eleanor Fox, A Slice of Forgotten History and Its Light on the Future – Changing the Lens on Antitrust, ProMarket Merger Guidelines Symposium Round I, Aug. 14, 2023, https://www.promarket.org/2023/08/14/eleanor-fox-a-slice-of-forgotten-history-and-its-light-on-the-future-changing-the-lens-on-antitrust/; Eleanor Fox, Tackling the Critics of the Draft Merger Guidelines, ProMarket Merger Guidelines Symposium Round II, Sept. 5, 2023, https://www.promarket.org/2023/09/05/eleanor-fox-tackling-the-critics-of-the-draft-merger-guidelines/; and Comment from Eleanor Fox on draft guidelines to DOJ and FTC, Public Submissions posted Sept. 18, 2023, https://www.regulations.gov/comment/FTC-2023-0043-1424.

I. Introduction

246. The Biden Administration antitrust authorities have published new merger guidelines that nicely accord with the Administration's efforts to put teeth back into U.S. antitrust. Frontally addressing what the Administration repeatedly identifies as a serious problem of the past, the new Guidelines ("2023 Guidelines") move away from the previous merger guidelines and start on a fresh page.

247. The serious problem is the extreme laissez faire lens that has shaped the perspective of U.S. antitrust law for 44 years, creating a growing gap between U.S. antitrust and that of most of the rest of the world. The problem can be traced in part to the US Department of Justice (DOJ) Merger Guidelines of 1982. Revolutionary at its time, the 1982 Guidelines redefined the merger problem as (almost) only cartels – i.e., mergers should be scrutinized because they might increase the likelihood that the firms in a concentrated market would fix prices or facilitate collaboration.

248. The guidelines were incrementally amended after 1982, most importantly by the 2010 Horizontal Merger Guidelines. While the 2010 document featured important amendments, the string of guidelines emanating from the 1982 touchstone is part of the problem. Judges adopted or were guided by them. They served to entrench the laissez faire premises in U.S. antitrust case law. Those premises give excessive deference to firms with significant market power and to stories of how their acquisitions are good for the market. It was, therefore, in the eyes of the Administration and its supporters, time for a very different-looking document.

249. The Agencies have now given us a very different-looking document. They return our gaze to whether the merger will soften competition, rather than whether it will lower output. They return us to the task of examining and appreciating the quality of competition that is likely to be lost by the merger – consistent with the language of the statute, which asks whether the effect of the merger "may be substantially to lessen competition." They revive the significance of market structure as a major predictor of the health of markets.

250. This chapter begins with history. It focuses on the dramatic inflection point: The 1982 Merger Guidelines, which decisively changed the course of antitrust for two score years. The 1982 Guidelines wiped out from U.S. antitrust a worldview of dynamic competition. The 2023 Guidelines aim to resuscitate the original, statutory focus, compatible with sound modern economics.

251. I first make a brief comment on 1950s, '60s and '70s antitrust law including the first set of U.S. Agency Merger Guidelines in 1968, which synthesized the then Supreme Court caselaw. Second, I turn to the change ushered in by the (Reagan) 1982 Merger Guidelines, and note in particular what these guidelines left on the cutting floor. Third, I comment on how the new 2023 Guidelines promise to restore the best of the earlier vision while incorporating modern realities. Fourth, I attempt to answer the critics.

252. The revised Guidelines give good guidance on how the antitrust Agencies approach antitrust merger analysis. The Agencies, of course, also want to win their cases in court, and it remains to be seen whether the Guidelines are likely to gain the sympathy of the judiciary – a particular challenge given the excessive deference to business that is entrenched in Supreme Court caselaw.

II. The 1950s to 70s

253. *The 1950 statute, the 1960s caselaw, and the 1968 Guidelines.* The Celler-Kefauver amendment to the Clayton Act of 1950 is – still – the current U.S. statutory merger law. By enacting this law, Congress meant to stop economic concentration in its incipiency. The main goal was a political-economy goal – to preserve democracy.[1] The Act was a post-World War II law, driven by the specter of how Hitler used concentrated corporate power in the service of fascism. The amendment also had economic ends. At mid-century, the U.S. had high trade barriers, as did most nations. Most major U.S. industries were highly concentrated, the industry leaders were only weakly challenged by competition, and the few big players had become both chummy and sleepy. Steel and cars were exhibits A and B. It took Ralph Nader's Unsafe At Any Speed[2] to alert the public to the scandalously low safety standards of Big Auto. High concentration accompanied by poor performance were laboratory facts that gave birth to the Harvard School of antitrust economics and the structure–conduct–performance paradigm that informed antitrust economics for years to come. In 1968, Harvard professor Donald Turner was Assistant Attorney General in Charge of Antitrust. Reportedly with the guidance of his Harvard colleague Carl Kaysen, Turner and his staff wrote the 1968 Merger Guidelines, which were more conservative than the caselaw, giving it boundaries. (Even so, by today's standards, it was very aggressive against mergers.)

254. The 1970s was a critical decade. The trading nations concluded the Tokyo Round of the General Agreement on Tariffs and Trade in 1979. Trade barriers went down dramatically. Strong and efficient German and Japanese firms threatened the complacent U.S. giants. As the world became more global, the United States became concerned with global competitiveness, and the public, and policymakers, began to attack over-regulation in all segments of life and economy. Overbreadth of antitrust law came into the crosshairs. Ronald Reagan won the Presidential election of 1980 on the promise to get government off the back of business. The Chicago School of economics (trust the market, not the government) got major traction. Reagan appointed distinguished Stanford Professor William Baxter as Assistant Attorney General in Charge of Antitrust,

---

1 Eleanor Fox, *The Modernization of Antitrust: A New Equilibrium*, 66 Cornell L. Rev. 1140 (1981), at 1150–51.

2 Ralph Nader, Unsafe at Any Speed: The Designed-In Dangers of the American Automobile (1965).

and Baxter and team set out to change the course of antitrust. Two of the most powerful tools to do so were to be: A program of filing amicus briefs in favor of antitrust defendants, and revised merger guidelines.[3] Also, 1974 was the first year of the business-friendly Supreme Court led by Chief Justice Warren Burger.[4]

III. The Reagan Revolution

255. By the mid to end 1970s, antitrust laws needed a course correction. The caselaw had become excessively prohibitive and the economy required more business flexibility. One logical corrective would have been a limiting principle, capping antitrust where it had gone too far. This corrective would mean listening to defendants' and merging parties' claims about why their conduct and transactions were good for the market and accepting them when they made sense.[5] But that was not the course chosen.

256. The course chosen was a U-turn: Neo-classically trained economists would become king. Antitrust would be driven by price/output theory embellished with the presumptions that market power sufficient to reduce output was rare, and that business acts were efficient. Under the new paradigm, antitrust law would prohibit conduct and transactions only if they impaired the efficient allocation of resources, and it was presumed that they would not. This was a wrenching change from a worldview suspicious of industry concentration and wary of big business strategies that strangled small business.

257. The only significant concern of the 1982 Merger Guidelines was: Mergers could facilitate collusion.[6] While the Reagan Administration labeled the 1982 Guidelines "evolutionary, not revolutionary," antitrust experts understood. Professor Louis Schwartz declared the 1982 Guidelines a device for "smuggling" Chicago School into antitrust.[7]

258. In summer/fall 1982 I published a special supplement to my merger book[8] describing the then Merger Guidelines in some detail for practitioners, and ending with this caveat:

> "The Justice Department's merger policy is confined to mergers that are 'inefficient' because they tend to produce lower output and higher

3 Fox, *supra* note 1.

4 *Id.*, at 1152. *See*, for the increasing pro-business stance of the U.S. Supreme Court, Adam Liptak, *The Roberts Court has distinguished itself as the most pro-business in decades*, N.Y. Times, May 5, 2013, Sunday Business at 1; Jeffrey Toobin, *The Conservative Pipeline to the Supreme Court*, New Yorker Magazine, Apr. 10, 2017; Filippo Lancieri, Eric Andrew Posner, and Luigi Zingales, *The Political Economy of the Decline of Antitrust Enforcement in the United States,* 85 ANTITRUST L.J. 441 (2023).

5 Fox, *supra* note 1.

6 *See* 1982 Merger Guidelines, https://www.justice.gov/archives/atr/1982-merger-guidelines.

7 *See* Eleanor Fox, *Introduction: The 1982 Merger Guidelines: When Economists Are Kings?*, 71 Cal. L. Rev. 281, 293–94 (1983), and Louis Schwartz, *The New Merger Guidelines: Guide to Government Discretion and Private Counseling or Propaganda for Revision of the Antitrust Laws?*, 71 Cal. L. Rev. 575, 576–77 (1983).

8 B. Fox & E. Fox, Corporate Acquisitions and Mergers (Matthew Bender, Lexis/Nexis, last revised 2023).

prices relative to costs. The concern of the Congress that enacted the principal antimerger law, as reflected in numerous Supreme Court opinions, is broader. Congress was concerned with preserving, for social, political, and economic reasons, a dispersion of centers of decision-making, diversity, ease of access and freedom of choice, as well as price near cost. Congress wished to fulfill these ends by preserving a dynamic process of rivalry, always protecting opportunities for change by a maverick…."[9]

259. This 1982 supplement advised business managers and antitrust counsellors to be cognizant not just of the risks of collusion, as instructed in the new guidelines, but also the risks identified by the caselaw for mergers that blocked opportunities to deconcentrate markets in which firms already held market power, that removed important innovative forces, that substantially increased concentration among top firms in concentrated markets, and that significantly foreclosed competitors from access to scarce inputs or to a substantial share of the business in a concentrated high-barrier market. The then current Supreme Court law was particularly concerned with mergers between major firms that were important competitors of one another and would take off the market the dynamic force of the rivalry between them.

260. As it turned out, the caveat to be alert to the risks spelled out in the caselaw and disregarded by the 1982 Guidelines was not important for too long, for these were the days when the judiciary was deferent to the expert Agencies, and hundreds of new judges were appointed by Reagan[10] and were largely sympathetic to his laissez faire views. The 1982 Guidelines were soon absorbed into the law.

261. It was wise and inevitable that antitrust would become more economically sophisticated. But it was never inevitable that its bite would become almost undetectable because of ideological premises that defied market realities and would make the law a paper tiger in the face of new waves of business consolidation; a phenomenon especially palpable in markets of necessities such as food, health care, energy, transportation, communications, and information.

IV. Picking up Pieces and Recognizing New Realities

262. In the years following 1982, periodic revisions of the merger guidelines addressed some of their shortcomings. Eventually, the guidelines recognized harm based on the lost competition between leading firms, which

---

9 *Id.* Supplement of June 18, 1982 (on file with author).

10 President Reagan appointed 402 judges. *See* Ballotpedia, https://ballotpedia.org/Federal_judges_nominated_by_Ronald_Reagan; Elliott Ash et al., *Ideas Have Consequences: The Impact of Law and Economics on American Justice* (Nat'l Bureau of Econ. Rsch., Working Paper No. 29788, Feb. 2022), https://users.nber.org/~dlchen/papers/Ideas_Have_Consequences.pdf (showing effect of neoliberal judge-training on decisions of judges). See, for business capture of antitrust, including effect on judiciary, Lancieri *et al.*, *supra* note 4.

the Agencies dubbed "unilateral effects" – as if this phenomenon were just discovered. The harm from loss of direct rivalry had been recognized from at least 1960 as a basic, common-sense ground for concluding that a merger may lessen competition. Antitrust practitioners in the 1960s and 70s – as I then was – would flag this scenario as the one at the forefront of the Agencies and the law. But it was dropped from the radar screen in 1982.

263. The new 2023 Guidelines show clear concern about the loss of competition between leading firms, while also reviving other major concerns that the 1982 Guidelines dropped, embellishing collusion concerns to include AI influences, and adding new issues that are now a common part of the discourse, such as multi-sided platform competition, serial acquisitions, cross shareholding and partial acquisitions, and mergers that create buyer power. The strongest guidance is provided in the first six guidelines: Mergers that significantly increase concentration in a highly concentrated market raise a presumption of illegality. Red flags are raised for mergers that eliminate substantial competition between firms, for mergers that increase the risk of coordination, for mergers that eliminate a potential entrant in a concentrated market, for mergers that create a firm that may limit access to products or services that its rivals use to compete, and for mergers that entrench or extend a dominant position.

264. The tried-and-true concern that mergers may facilitate coordination has survived through the years. As noted, it was at the heart of the 1982 Guidelines. Collusion among rivals is a conduct feared by liberals, conservatives, and neo-liberals alike. Indeed, many conservatives and neoliberals would limit antitrust interventions entirely to stopping cartels and mergers that are basically understandable as cartels. (Thus, the 1982 Guidelines.) The ground of controversy is the level of concentration at which risk of collusion is a threat. The 1982 Guidelines introduced a benchmark measured by the Herfindahl–Hirschman Index. The thresholds for antitrust scrutiny crept up through the years. The new Guidelines would revert to the 1982 level, while also expressing a benchmark for concern in market shares: Greater than 30%, along with a significant increase in concentration, thus matching the guidance of *Philadelphia National Bank,*[11] which remains good law. The lower threshold accords with increasing possibilities for collusion through use of artificial intelligence, and, for unilateral power concerns, it adjusts to the reality of new forms of market power that do not fit classic monopoly or oligopoly.

265. After identifying the ways in which a merger may soften or eliminate competition and explaining their application in specific settings, the 2023 Guidelines invite rebuttal evidence showing that no substantial lessening of competition or tendency to create monopoly is threatened by the merger.

11 United States v. Phila. Nat'l Bank, 374 U.S. 321 (1963).

V. Answering the Critics

266. There is misplaced alarm that the 2023 Guidelines abandon reason, economics, and consumers. The argument comes in different forms and intensities; for example: That the Guidelines disavow consumer welfare and output limitation as the goal and metric for analysis. That they are inherently hostile to mergers. That they wage a war against business concentration. That they disregard pro-competitive, pro-consumer effects. That they are political and will destroy the integrity of guidelines and the Agencies.[12]

267. I examine these arguments in four points: 1) The concern that the 2023 Guidelines forsake consumer welfare as the goal and output limitation as the metric, and that this is problematic; 2) The concern that economics is being demoted; 3) The concern that the 2023 Guidelines are hostile to mergers, which are generally good for society, and that therefore their implementation will hurt consumers; and 4) The concern that the 2023 Guidelines are political, tainting the whole enterprise.

268. 1) The claim that the 2023 draft guidelines forsake consumer welfare. Yes, the new 2023 Guidelines change the music play-sheet. They step away from the mantra of consumer welfare and the methodology of outcome/result analysis and they return to the language of the statute – "competition." In the overly quoted language of *Brown Shoe*, "It is COMPETITION ... that the law protects."[13] Not competitors, but also not incumbents. The apparent motivating force of this move by the Guidelines is two-fold. First, "consumer welfare" has become a chameleon. Second, the concepts of consumer welfare and output limitation are static, result-oriented, and one-way-directed (downstream only), and the draft guidelines try to revive a perspective much closer to original intent – to preserve a process and environment that is valuable both as process and as a methodology likely to provide the best results for consumers and the other stakeholders in markets. Workers, farmers, and other upstream suppliers are recognized as stakeholders who have a right not to be anticompetitively exploited and excluded by market power.

269. As for the chameleon character of "consumer welfare," the phrase has baggage, as Assistant Attorney General Jonathan Kanter observes.[14] It means different things to different people. To Professor Carl Shapiro, it includes the welfare of workers and anyone in the supply chain who is

---

12 *See e.g.*, Dennis Carlton, *Have the Draft Guidelines Demoted Economics?*, PROMARKET (Aug. 4, 2023), https://www.promarket.org/2023/08/04/have-the-draft-guidelines-demoted-economics/; Herbert Hovenkamp, *Competitive Harm and the 2023 Draft Merger Guidelines*, PROMARKET (July 27, 2023), https://www.promarket.org/2023/07/27/herbert-hovenkamp-competitive-harm-and-the-2023-draft-merger-guidelines/; Carl Shapiro, *Why Dropping Market Power from the Merger Guidelines Matters*, PROMARKET (Aug. 7, 2023), https://www.promarket.org/2023/08/07/carl-shapiro-why-dropping-market-power-from-the-merger-guidelines-matters/; all in Promarket Merger Guidelines Symposium, https://www.promarket.org/2023/07/26/announcing-the-promarket-merger-guidelines-symposium/.

13 Brown Shoe Co. v. United States, 370 U.S. 294, 344 (1962) (emphasis added).

14 AAG Jonathan Kanter, Milton Handler Lecture, New York City Bar Association (May 18, 2022), https://www.justice.gov/opa/speech/assistant-attorney-general-jonathan-kanter-delivers-remarks-new-york-city-bar-association.

the target of creation or abuse of market power.[15] To Professor Herbert Hovenkamp, it means that antitrust enforcement is not appropriate unless the conduct or transaction limits output of a good or service.[16]

270. Federal Trade Commission Chair Lina Khan correctly observes:[17] We have gone down a decades-long path of hinging violations to output-limiting results, and although this may be the economists' metric for identifying inefficiency, it does not capture the dynamic work of antitrust. Preserving the dynamic of modern markets defies output analysis. The powerful, perfect discriminator can reap unimagined profits without lessening output. The digital platform gatekeepers, while vacuuming up budding competitors, demoting rivals, and controlling gateways, are not dreaming of less output; they are hoping for more. The concept "competition" lifts our gaze from results – which we are at peril to engineer – to a *process*, which the law commands us to preserve. The 2023 Guidelines helpfully refocus on competition. Mergers may soften competition in significant ways, chilling incentives of firms to do better, to be more creative, to anticipate the needs of buyers and suppliers; and, when they do, they raise red flags of violation.

271. This does not mean that effects are irrelevant. Expected effects are totally relevant. It does not mean that consumers are not important or that harming consumers is fair game. A negative effect on consumers continues to be the most likely result of harm to competition. Consumer harm is still the major harm alleged in U.S. Agency antitrust complaints. As AAG Kanter has said,[18] and the Supreme Court has said through time,[19] competition, like free speech, has a multitude of positive effects – better and more goods and services at lower costs, economic opportunity, resiliency, less inequality, and more democracy. That does not mean that we use inequality or democracy as the metric to decide if a merger is anticompetitive.[20] But neither do we have to ignore the cluster of values that preservation of competition promotes.

272. 2) The claim that the 2023 Guidelines demote economics. Three points should be made: First, the draft guidelines do demote *neoclassical* economics. In fact, they jettison it. Second, they do not forsake economics.

---

15 *See* Shapiro, *supra* note 12.

16 *See* Hovenkamp, *supra* note 12.

17 *See* Lina Khan, *The New Brandeis Movement: America's Antimonopoly Debate*, 9 J. Eur. Comp. L. & Pract. 131–132 (2018); Lina Khan, Remarks before Economic Club of New York (July 24, 2023), https://www.ftc.gov/news-events/news/speeches/remarks-chair-lina-m-khan-economic-club-new-york.

18 AAG Jonathan Kanter, Remarks at the Fordham Competition Law Institute's International Antitrust Law and Policy Conference (Sept. 22, 2023).

19 *See e.g.,* No. Carolina State Bd. of Dental Examiners v. FTC, 574 U.S. 494, 502 (2015) (quoting United States v. Topco Associates, Inc., 405 U.S. 596, 610 (1972)), see also Christopher Sagers, *The US Supreme Court decides on whether nominally public body must show "active supervision" by the state government to enjoy antitrust immunity (North Carolina State Board of Dental Examiners)*, e-Competitions Feb. 2015, art. No. 72018. Cf. Bates v. State Bar of Arizona, 433 U.S. 350 (1977).

20 *See* Lina Khan & Sandeep Vaheesan, *Market Power and Inequality: The Antitrust Counterrevolution and Its Discontents*, 11 Harv. L. & Pol'y Rev. 235, 237 (2017).

They engage with modern progressive economics built on realistic market assumptions given current market realities. Third, the 2023 Guidelines reassert the obvious fact that antitrust law is LAW.

273. Antitrust law is deeply informed by economics. Antitrust economics is a generalized form of economics, generalized both to fit the values of the law and to fit the need for administrability of the law. In many situations, especially mergers, economists are partners, but the law is the senior partner. *Philadelphia National Bank*[21] is a good example. If a leading firm in a concentrated market acquires a significant competitor, significantly increasing concentration, in litigation, these facts make a prima facie case and the burden falls to the merging parties to show that the merger is not anticompetitive. Economists have debated for years and still debate whether, on the skeletal facts given, the *Philadelphia National Bank* presumption is warranted by economics. Some experts agree;[22] some do not.[23] In court, it doesn't matter. There is a sufficiently large chance that such a merger will harm competition, the merging parties have access to the facts, and, for efficiency in litigation, it is convenient and wise to shift the burden.

274. The wisdom of a burden shift to the merging parties in appropriate cases (significant threatened harm) is confirmed by modern research and market facts. Mounting evidence shows the high costs of mergers, their common inefficiencies, the exaggeration of their hope-for efficiencies, and their failure to achieve the efficiencies they expect. Big mergers are prone to fail. High financial rewards from the big transactions go to a handful of executives and advisors[24] regardless of post-merger performance. Quoting lyrics from Taylor Swift's *Blank Space*, United States Senator Mike Lee described the Ticketmaster/Live Nation merger in the aftermath of the ERAs monopoly ticketing debacle as a "nightmare dressed like a daydream."[25] So it is with so many big mergers. While the high social costs of a large percentage of mergers may not be a reason to declare a particular merger anticompetitive, it does seem that the high regard for mergers and the hopes placed on them in the Reagan era forward in hopes of making America globally competitive have been deeply undermined by the revealed facts.

275. 3) The concern that the 2023 Guidelines are hostile to mergers and that implementation of the Guidelines will hurt consumers. The Guidelines are

---

21 *Phila. Nat'l Bank*, 374 U.S. at 321.

22 *See* Herbert Hovenkamp & Carl Shapiro, *Horizontal Mergers, Market Structure, and Burdens of Proof*, 127 YALE L.J. 1996 (2018).

23 *See* Douglas Ginsburg & Joshua Wright, *Philadelphia National Bank: Bad Economics, Bad Law, Good Riddance*, 80 ANTITRUST L.J. 377 (2015).

24 *See* Jeff Gordon, *Too Many Mergers? The Golden Parachute as a Driver of M&A Activity in the 21st Century* (on file with author).

25 *See* Palak Jayswal, *Mike Lee quotes Taylor Swift at Senate hearing, and gets the Internet's attention*, SALT LAKE TRIBUNE, Jan. 24, 2023.

aggressive, compared with the conservative state of U.S. antitrust law. For most of the last half century, the law has shown excessive hospitality to mergers. Whatever Congress meant in passing the Celler-Kefauver Act in 1950, it did not mean hospitality to mergers. While trying to move the goalposts from conservative to progressive, the Guidelines do not suggest that consumer-benefiting mergers will be blocked. They invite the parties to bring forward evidence of pro-competition, pro-consumer benefits. The Agencies want not just to bring cases; they want to win them; and protecting consumers from loss of competition is both traditional and high on the agenda.

276. 4) The concern that the 2023 Guidelines are political. Antitrust law is a phase of political economy. As political economy, antitrust has always been political policy. The most political merger guidelines were the Reagan Guidelines of 1982, for those guidelines incorporated an ideology at war with the statute; they disavowed the will of Congress to be skeptical of mergers and to stop increases in concentrations in their incipiency. The 2023 Guidelines, in contrast, would return the merger law to compatibility with congressional intent, consistent with modern economics.

277. Much of the charge of politicization is directed toward Federal Trade Commission (FTC's) Chair Khan, who wrote now-famous articles challenging hyper-concentration of business in America and the corporate power of Big Tech. Khan has been labeled "antimarket," but she presents her views as pro-market and especially pro-open market. Moreover, personalizing Chair Khan and highlighting her student scholarship is a poor way to assess how the 2023 Guidelines will be applied. The Guidelines are pro-competition; and the FTC and the DOJ are strongly anchored democratic institutions.

278. But what if I am wrong? What if the Guidelines are a way to bring (one view of) Neo-Brandeisian philosophy into the mainstream? To privilege workers and small businesses at the expense of consumers? To protect inefficient small business, rather than protect competition? To revive *Brown Shoe*[26] and *Vons Grocery*[27] as the paragons of U.S. merger law?

279. It is difficult to imagine that this will be the result of guidelines that speak so clearly of protecting competition from elimination or erosion. An anti-market vision would not be accepted by the courts, which are charged with protecting competition. Such a dramatic shift could not be accomplished without legislative amendment. The Guidelines shift merger policy from: "Don't challenge a merger unless it is output-limiting," to: "Intervene to protect competition." Critics characterize the shift as: "This is all about protecting inefficient competitors at the expense of consumers." It just isn't.

---

26 *Brown Shoe Co.*, 370 U.S. at 294. While parts of the decision continue to be robust, I refer here to the parts that protect competitors from changing trends, and to the holding, which condemns a merger of firms with low market shares in fragmented markets.

27 United States v. Vons Grocery Co., 384 U.S. 270 (1966).

280. The claim that the 2023 Guidelines abandon reason, economics and consumers is wrong. To the contrary, the Guidelines have the potential to lead us out of a reductionist cul-de-sac, and to hitch our sight to a dynamic competition perspective.

VI. Conclusion

281. The 2023 Guidelines are a progressive document for modern merger control. They are in service of the aim to make markets work; to prevent mergers from compromising important forces that keep firms responsive, innovative, and resilient. The spirit of the Guidelines, if appreciated by the judiciary, could help turn the corner by shifting merger control from the reductionist paradigm of 1982 to a dynamic vision: Merger law should safeguard the forces of competition, and mergers should not be allowed to compromise them. If the new Guidelines make headway in shifting the perspective and in taking the neoliberal worldview and presumptions out of the merger law, that will be success.

Antitrust Ideology and the 2023 U.S. Merger Guidelines

Diana L. Moss*
Progressive Policy Institute

* Vice President & Director of Competition Policy, Progressive Policy Institute.

I. Introduction

282. In late December 2023, the U.S. antitrust agencies jointly issued new merger guidelines.[1] The 2023 Merger Guidelines ("2023 Guidelines") are the seventh substantive version since they were first issued 55 years ago by the U.S. Department of Justice (DOJ) and Federal Trade Commission (FTC). Promoting competition in the U.S. economy is a priority for the Biden Administration, as reflected in a 2021 executive order that set forth an ambitious plan to harness a "whole of government" approach.[2] An uptick in resolving challenged mergers through injunctions, restructurings, and forced abandonments is visible evidence of this commitment. The same is true of a surge in monopolization cases, limited thus far to the digital sector, the outcomes of which will likely be determined by a future administration.

283. As part of the broader competition mandate under the current administration, the DOJ and FTC issued a draft of revised merger guidelines in mid-July 2023.[3] After collecting comments and holding public workshops, the Agencies turned a final version of the guidelines six months later, which will replace the 2010 Horizontal Merger Guidelines.[4] The changes to the draft guidelines, which presumably reflected public input, were far from cosmetic. Indeed, they reflect pressure to move the draft version away from the far left of the ideological spectrum and towards the center. This tells us a lot about the debate over antitrust ideology in the U.S. is today.

284. The Agencies received feedback on the draft guidelines from all sides. These include Chicago School advocates of laissez faire conservatism and Neo-Brandeisian advocates of "bright line" tests that are the foundation of a broader anti-monopoly approach. The Agencies also received comments from center-left, post-Chicago School, advocates focused on promoting more vigorous enforcement through strong presumptions, a broad interpretation of the consumer welfare standard, and a skeptical view of merger efficiencies. As the originators of the pro-enforcement movement 25 years ago, the center-left has held significant ground in promoting stronger merger enforcement. The influence of center-left commentary on final guidelines speaks to its appeal and durability.

285. Less ideologically polarized merger guidelines avoid operationalizing the goals of perspectives at the ends of the spectrum, which risks the pull-back of agency guidance by future administrations. It also avoids creating poor caselaw if the government does not prevail in blocking mergers on the

1 Fed. Trade Comm'n and U.S. Dep't. of Justice, *Merger Guidelines* (2023) ("2023 Guidelines").

2 *Executive Order on Promoting Competition in the American Economy*, The White House (July 9, 2021), at § 1.

3 Fed. Trade Comm'n and U.S. Dep't. of Justice, *Draft Merger Guidelines* (2023) ("2023 Draft Guidelines").

4 Fed. Trade Comm'n and U.S. Dep't. of Justice, *Horizontal Merger Guidelines* (2010) ("2010 Guidelines").

basis of novel, or poorly supported, theories of competitive harm.[5] Both of these factors work against the goal of stronger enforcement. The final guidelines responded to a number of such concerns, especially as they relate to the transparency of the guidelines for the business community, practitioners, and the public; and their administrability in federal courts.[6] At the same time, material in the final guidelines that was the subject of center-left commentary, but remained unaltered from the draft, could potentially work against stronger enforcement moving forward.

286. The final version of the 2023 Guidelines clearly represents a compromise document that attempts to balance and resolve strong feedback. This article explains major themes that are apparent in the 2023 Guidelines. The first section provides a brief overview of the new structure of "frameworks" and "applications" guidelines. The second section turns to an analysis of changes that make the final guidelines a less ideologically polarized document than the draft version. The third section looks at features that could reduce the transparency and administrability of the guidelines and pose risks to more vigorous enforcement.

II. The "Frameworks" and "Applications" Approach to Guidelines

287. The revised guidelines come at a critical time. Concern over declining competition in the U.S. economy continues to rise in the pro-enforcement community. This is reflected in high levels of market concentration, growing gaps in wealth and income, high margins for the top firms, and a loss of worker bargaining power.[7] The "incipiency" standard embedded in U.S. merger law – or stopping harmful transactions before they happen – makes enforcement a first line of defense to the emergence of durable monopolies and oligopolies that inflict lasting damage on consumers, workers, and smaller businesses.[8]

288. The government and private antitrust plaintiffs face a high bar in bringing monopolization and collusion cases under the Sherman Act.[9] The incipiency standard thus draws attention back to the importance of merger control under Section 7 of the Clayton Act in promoting competition in

---

5 *Federal Trade Commission Withdraws Vertical Merger Guidelines and Commentary*, Fed. Trade Comm'n. (Sept. 15, 2021), https://www.ftc.gov/news-events/news/press-releases/2021/09/federal-trade-commission-withdraws-vertical-merger-guidelines-commentary.

6 Unlike the 2010 Guidelines, the 2023 Guidelines do not explain their importance to the business community, practitioners, and the public. The 2010 Guidelines state "These Guidelines are intended to assist the business community and antitrust practitioners by increasing the transparency of the analytical process underlying the Agencies' enforcement decisions. They may also assist the courts in developing an appropriate framework for interpreting and applying the antitrust laws in the horizontal merger context." 2010 Guidelines, *supra* note 4, at § 1.

7 *See, e.g.*, Council of Economic Advisers, Benefits of Competition and Indicators of Market Power, The White House (Apr. 2016), at 4.

8 15 U.S.C. §§ 18.

9 15 U.S.C. §§ 1 and 2.

a market economy. As such, it elevates the importance of transparency and administrability in agency guidance and gives balance to the roles of legal doctrine and economic and business analysis that improves merger review.

289. The 2023 Guidelines support the incipiency standard with an expanded set of theories of harm for evaluating how a merger is likely to substantially lessen competition. These are referred to as "frameworks" guidelines. The 2010 Guidelines articulate four major theories of harm around mergers that are: (1) highly concentrative, (2) eliminate head-to-head competition, (3) enhance incentives to engage in anticompetitive coordination, and (4) eliminate a potential entrant. The 2023 Guidelines reiterate these four theories of harm and extend coverage to a fifth theory, vertical mergers, which supersede the guidance in the 2020 Vertical Merger Guidelines issued by the Trump administration and withdrawn by the FTC in 2021.[10]

290. The 2023 Guidelines add a sixth theory of harm – mergers that entrench or expand a dominant position. This is a needed response to expansion, for example, in business models that feature platforms, ecosystems, and that grow largely through acquisition, versus organically.[11] The 2023 Guidelines also introduce the "applications" guidelines, or settings in which the frameworks guidelines are applied. These five guidelines cover: (1) trends toward concentration, (2) serial acquisitions, and mergers involving (3) multi-sided platforms, (4) buyers of inputs, and (5) partial ownership acquisitions.[12]

291. As in the case of the frameworks guidelines, the applications guidelines are not all that novel. For example, mergers that raise concerns over powerful buyers and partial ownership shares are addressed in the 2010 Guidelines. This leaves three new settings covered in the applications guidelines in the 2023 revision: trends toward consolidation (revised from "concentration"), serial acquisitions, and multi-sided platforms.[13] A guideline on multi-sided platforms provides important clarity on complex market definition questions. In doing so, the Agencies helpfully cabin problematic market definition in *Ohio v. Amex* and *Sabre-Fare Logix*.[14]

292. The 2023 Guidelines also introduce the "trends" applications guideline, which recognizes three major dynamics: a trend toward higher concentration in horizontal mergers, a trend toward vertical integration, and "arms race" mergers motivated by incentives to gain bargaining power

10 *Id.* Guideline 5.

11 2023 Guidelines, *supra* note 1, Guideline 6.

12 *Id.* Guidelines 7–11.

13 2010 Guidelines, *supra* note 4, at § 8 and § 13.

14 138 S. Ct. 2274 (2018); United States v. Sabre Corp., 452 F. Supp. 3d 97 (D. Del. 2020). *See also,* Randy Stutz, *We've Seen Enough: It Is Time to Abandon Amex and Start Over on Two-Sided Markets* (Apr. 21, 2020), https://www.antitrustinstitute.org/work-product/aai-says-its-time-to-cancel-amex-sabre-farelogix-opinion-makes-a-mockery-of-market-definition/. See also, Irving Scher, *The US Supreme Court rules that "anti-steering" clauses are not anticompetitive on the two-sided credit card market (American Express)*, E-COMPETITIONS June 2018, art. No. 96404.

over inputs suppliers or distributors. Finally, the applications guideline for serial acquisitions holds promise to address concerns involving business models that grow primarily through acquisition and acquisitions of smaller rivals that fly below the Hart-Scott-Rodino merger filing requirements thresholds.[15]

293. The 2023 Guidelines' larger universe of theories of harm and settings in which they can be applied is an intentional feature. It creates more combinations of potential anticompetitive scenarios and applications in horizontal and vertical mergers. Indeed, the guidelines are clear in stating that "...for any given transaction the Agencies may limit their analysis to any one guideline or subset of guidelines that most readily demonstrates the risks to competition from the transaction."[16] The reality, however, is that the Agencies have never limited themselves to alleging any single theory of harm. For example, mergers that eliminate head-to-head competition and leave a fringe of smaller rivals can also increase the risk of post-merger coordination. In these cases, the Agencies allege harm from unilateral and coordinated effects, such as in a number of pharmaceutical mergers.[17]

294. In sum, the 2023 Guidelines establish a new two-part structure of "frameworks" and "applications" guidelines. Many of these are not new, but some innovations are important in light of experience from past mergers, new business models and expansion strategies, and incentives for strategic competition. A major takeaway, however, is that the major thrust of the 2023 Guidelines is to provide the Agencies with more "options" to pursue potentially anticompetitive mergers.

III. Repositioning the 2023 Guidelines from the Far-Left Toward the Center-Left

295. The evolution of the 2023 Guidelines from draft to final form reveals a number of fundamental changes, some more obvious and others more nuanced. Together, they reflect a repositioning of the document from the far-left, toward the center-left of the ideological spectrum. The major issues that prompted reaction to the more polarized approach taken in the draft are most visible in Sections 1 and 2.[18] This section examines these features, including converting quasi-bright line tests to rebuttable presumptions and expanding citations from "binding" legal precedent to

15 *See Premerger Notification and the Merger Review Process*, Fed. Trade Comm'n. https://www.ftc.gov/advice-guidance/competition-guidance/guide-antitrust-laws/mergers/premerger-notification-merger-review-process.

16 2023 Guidelines, *supra* note 1, at 3.

17 *See e.g.*, Diana L. Moss, *From Competition to Conspiracy: Assessing the Federal Trade Commission's Merger Policy in the Pharmaceutical Sector*, American Antitrust Institute (Sept. 3, 2020), at 13, https://www.antitrustinstitute.org/wp-content/uploads/2020/09/AAI_PharmaReport2020_9-11-20.pdf.

18 Section 1 of the 2023 Guidelines provides an overview of the document and section 2 explains the frameworks and applications guidelines in detail.

"applicable" legal precedent. Both of these changes improve the transparency and administrability of the 2023 Guidelines, which works to strengthen stronger enforcement.

1. Converting Quasi-Bright Line Tests to Rebuttable Presumptions

296. The draft guidelines presented what appeared to be quasi-bright line tests for determining whether a merger is illegal under Section 7. The standout feature of the original frameworks guidelines was the wording "a merger *should not*" result in an outcome likely to substantially lessen competition. This syntax lent a commandment-style flavor, fortified by little, if any, reference to "effects-based" analysis under the consumer welfare standard. Other features reinforced these concerns, including relocating economics and rebuttal evidence discussion away from the guidelines and to remote sections and appendices.[19]

297. Center-left commentators worried about the impact of the foregoing shift on enforcement. To be sure, the Agencies intended the guidelines to be rebuttable. But for non-experts, it was far from clear and fueled concern that the guidelines reflected polarized ideology and sacrificed transparency and administrability. For example, Section 1 of the draft guidelines did not include the important explanation of *how* a merger can substantially lessen competition. That is, how does eliminating a rival increase a firm's ability and/or incentive to exercise enhanced market power, for example, by controlling the terms of exchanges, or by frustrating the ability of rivals to compete?

298. Moreover, the draft guidelines did not discuss how the exercise of market power harms consumers, workers, and rival businesses. This analysis was clear in the 2010 Guidelines.[20] Absent an explicit departure from the consumer welfare standard in the 2023 Draft Guidelines, quasi-bright line tests appeared to depart from effects-based analysis under the consumer welfare standard, demoting the role of economic analysis and evidence and impeding stronger enforcement.

299. The final guidelines contain modifications that, to some extent, address the foregoing problems. Section 1 provides new context for what the guidelines are designed to do. For example, the final guidelines explain that competition is a process that "…incentivizes businesses to offer lower prices, improve wages and working conditions, enhance quality and resiliency, innovate, and expand choice..."[21] They also explain that a merger can "increase, extend, or entrench" market power that can harm

---

19 *See, e.g.*, Comments of the Progressive Policy Institute on the Draft Merger Guidelines for Public Comment (Docket FTC-2023-0043), Progressive Policy Institute (Sept. 18, 2023), https://www.progressivepolicy.org/wp-content/uploads/2023/09/PPI_Merger-Guidelines_Comments_9.18.23.pdf.

20 2010 Horizontal Merger Guidelines, *supra* note 4, at § 1.

21 2023 Guidelines, *supra* note 1, at § 1, 1.

competition and market participants.[22] These explanations did not appear in the draft guidelines.

300. The final frameworks guidelines revise the controversial language "mergers should not" result in a substantially lessening of competition, to mergers that "raise the presumption" or "can violate the law."[23] The language backs away from a quasi-bright line test for illegality and makes clear that the presumptions embedded in the frameworks guidelines are rebuttable. For example, the text of the final guidelines states that "the agencies will also examine relevant evidence to determine if it disproves or rebuts the prima facie case..."[24]

301. In sum, the quasi-bright line tests and scant reference to effects-based analysis under the consumer welfare standard positioned the 2023 Draft Guidelines on the far-left end of the ideological spectrum. These optics were magnified by relegation of economic analysis and rebuttal evidence to distant sections and appendices. The practical implication of the draft guidelines was, therefore, to make them less transparent and administrable, and therefore potentially less effective in promoting stronger enforcement. In addressing commenters' concerns with the draft guidelines, the Agencies moved the final version of the guidelines toward the ideological center, which improves their transparency and administrability.

2. Converting "Binding" Legal Precedent to "Applicable" Legal Precedent

302. A second major feature of the draft guidelines is citation to legal precedent for a select body of caselaw.[25] The draft explained that the 50 unique citations to cases were "binding," 60% of which were decided earlier than 1980s.[26] To be sure, citation to strong legal precedent supports stronger enforcement but elevating the importance of certain cases highlights the dangers of "selective" citations in promoting stronger enforcement. For example, it is widely recognized that merger enforcement weakened dramatically after the 1980s as the Chicago School conservatism ascended.[27] However, there is post-1980 caselaw that supports stronger enforcement on a wider variety of important merger issues. A reluctance to give credit to more recent administrations for stronger merger enforcement telegraphed a more polarized ideology.

---

22 *Id.* at § 1 and § 2.

23 *Id.*

24 *Id.*

25 2023 Draft Guidelines, *supra* note 3, at § 1, 5.

26 The unique citation count omits multiple references to a single case, including in different courts (*e.g.*, district vs. appellate).

27 *See, e.g.*, statement of former FTC Chair Robert Pitofsky, *Fair Fight in the Marketplace*, AMERICAN ANTITRUST INSTITUTE https://vimeo.com/151190144. ["...antitrust enforcement was almost asleep during the 1980s," at minute 6:07–6:20]. https://vimeo.com/151190144.

303. For example, merger enforcement under the Obama administration featured a historical shift toward a higher rate of merger abandonments, restructurings, and injunctions.[28] A number of these cases support the draft guidelines' citations to highly concentrative mergers or the elimination of head-to-head competitors. DOJ's success in forcing the abandonment of the 4–3 merger of wireless facilities-based carriers AT&T and T-Mobile in 2011 illustrates the importance of enforcement against highly concentrative mergers.[29] The FTC's successful block of the merger of broadline food distributors Sysco and U.S. Foods in 2015 is another leading example of how vigorous enforcement prevented the elimination of a head-to-head competitor.[30] The same is true of the DOJ's case against H&R Block and Tax Act, which would have led to a duopoly in tax preparation software.[31]

304. Other Obama-era cases not mentioned in the draft guidelines took up issues that were not present in pre-1980 cases. In 2015, for example, the DOJ also prevailed in blocking the merger of commercial health insurers Anthem and Cigna, setting pro-enforcement precedent on the treatment of merger efficiencies.[32] The final version of the guidelines makes a number of changes that responds to the foregoing concerns, moving them further to the center. Reference to "binding" legal precedent is replaced with "applicable legal precedent." There are fewer citations to pre-1980 caselaw and more citations to recent merger law. The final guidelines double the number of citations to cases during the Obama administration and include references to both anticompetitive effects and efficiencies defenses.[33]

305. These modifications in the final guidelines widen the aperture for recognizing, per center-left ideology, the importance of rebuttable presumptions while significantly raising the bar on efficiencies claims. In revising

---

28 Rates are based on merger challenge outcomes as a percentage of clearances. Data collected from Fed. Trade Comm'n. and U.S. Dep't of Justice, Hart-Scott-Rodino Annual Reports, (fiscal years 1993–2021), https://www.ftc.gov/policy/reports/annual-competition-reports.

29 U.S. v. AT&T, Inc. and T-Mobile USA, Inc., et al, Complaint, Case No. 1:11-cv-01560 (D.D.C. Aug. 31, 2011), https://www.justice.gov/d9/atr/case-documents/attachments/2011/08/31/274613.pdf, see Jeffrey May, *The US DoJ joins seven States to block the proposed merger between two of the four largest national providers in the mobile wireless telecommunication services (AT&T / T-Mobile)*, e-Competitions September 2011, art. No. 38573.

30 Fed. Trade Comm'n. v. Sysco Corp., Memorandum Opinion, Case No. 1:15-cv-00256-APM (D.D.C. June 26, 2015), at 98, https://www.oag.state.va.us/consumer-protection/files/Lawsuits/Sysco-RedactedOpinion.pdf.

31 U.S. v. H&R Block Inc., et al, Memorandum Opinion, Case No. 1:11-cv-00948-BAH (D.D.C. Nov. 10, 2011), https://www.justice.gov/d9/atr/case-documents/attachments/2011/11/10/277287.pdf, see James A. Keyte, *The US District Court for the District of Columbia blocks a merger between two digital do-it-yourself tax preparation software providers giving insight on an S. 7 challenge of the Clayton Act (H&R Block / TaxAct)*, e-Competitions November 2011, art. No. 45926.

32 U.S. v. Anthem Inc. and Cigna Corp., Memorandum Opinion, Case No. 17-5024 (D.D.C. Apr. 28, 2017), https://www.justice.gov/atr/case-document/file/971316/dl?inline. The case sets legal precedent on the treatment of merger efficiencies, namely, that lower reimbursement rates to providers resulting from the larger insurer's enhanced buying power do not equate to cost savings for health plan subscribers. See Clifford H. Aronson et al., *The US District Court for the District of Columbia blocks two proposed mergers in the insurance sector brought and litigated under the Obama administration (Aetna / Humana and Anthem / Cigna)*, e-Competitions February 2017, art. No. 83761.

33 *Id.* at § 3.3, n.68, citing to U.S. v. Anthem.

"binding" to "applicable" legal precedent, the final guidelines reduce the costs of a narrower body of potentially incomplete caselaw and increase the benefits from a larger body of more inclusive and comprehensive merger caselaw.

IV. Ongoing Risks to Transparency and Administrability in the 2023 Merger Guidelines

306. Despite revisions to the 2023 Draft Guidelines, there are still features of the final guidelines that pose challenges to stronger enforcement. This section examines these features, including the inherent riskiness of the "applications" guidelines and questions raised by guidelines that assess dynamic scenarios, such as trends toward consolidation and serial acquisitions.

1. Inherent Riskiness of the "Applications" Guideline

307. The "applications" guidelines describe specific settings in which one or more of the frameworks guidelines can be applied. It is clear that the applications guidelines largely draw attention to successful cases brought by the Biden agencies. These include the merger of book publishers Penguin Random House and Simon & Shuster, where the DOJ's complaint alleged harm in a labor market for authors.[34] A serial acquisition is currently the subject of the FTC's case against private equity firm Anesthesia Partners.[35] Likewise, the vertical merger of UnitedHealthcare and Change Health involved a platform market where DOJ alleged that the anticompetitive exchange of sensitive information could stifle competition and innovation.[36]

308. The applications guidelines provide useful and important context to aid the agencies and courts in promoting stronger enforcement. But there are other applications that are equally important but *not* included in the guidelines. Other candidate settings for application guidelines come to mind. For example, some markets are dominated by only a few vertically integrated, multi-level "systems," such as in agricultural biotechnology and healthcare. In this setting, further horizontal or vertical consolidation exacerbates barriers to entry to smaller rivals[37] but merger reviews should also be concerned competitive paradigms, or the importance of competition *within* a system versus *between* systems.[38]

---

34 U.S. v. Bertlesmann SE & Co. KGaA, Penguin Random House, LLC, Viacom CBS, Inc. and Simon & Shuster, Inc., Memorandum Opinion, Case No. 1:21-cv-02886-FYP (D.D.C. Nov. 7, 2022).

35 Fed. Trade Comm'n. v. Anesthesia Partners, Inc., et al., Complaint for Injunctive and Other Equitable Relief (S.D. Tex. Sept. 21, 2023), https://www.ftc.gov/system/files/ftc_gov/pdf/2010031usapcomplaintpublic.pdf.

36 U.S., et al. v. UnitedHealth Group Inc. and Change Healthcare, Inc., Complaint, Case No. 1:22-cv-00481 (D.D.C. Feb. 24, 2022), https://www.justice.gov/atr/case-document/file/1476901/dl?inline.

37 The 2023 Guidelines discuss multi-level entry in the context of vertical mergers but do not reference markets dominated by just a few vertically integrated systems. *See*, 2023 Guidelines, *supra* note 1, at 14.

38 Letter from the American Antitrust Inst., Food & Water Watch, and National Farmers Union, to AAAG Andrew Finch Re: Proposed Merger of Monsanto and Bayer, (July 26, 2017), https://www.antitrustinstitute.org/wp-content/uploads/2018/08/White-Paper_Monsanto-Bayer_7.26.17_0.pdf.

309. Another candidate for an application guideline is the "ecosystem" merger, where acquisitions in a platform market, applications markets, or cloud computing market, could make it easier for the merged firm to leverage market power into another market.[39] For example, the DOJ noted in Google's 2011 acquisition of Admeld that the acquisition would enable Google to extend its market power in Internet search to the display advertising market.[40]

310. These examples highlight the concern that a selective list of applications could attract more attention to those particular settings, at the expense of others not explained in the guidelines. This stands in contrast to the frameworks guidelines, which given the present state of learning, present a more exhaustive list of theories of harm. This major difference between the frameworks and applications guidelines could cause confusion in the courts, potentially working against the goal of stronger enforcement. The risk inherent in providing only a selected list of applications guidelines is a good reason as to why they were better positioned as a narrative to support explanation of the frameworks guidelines, not as discrete guidelines.

2. Questions Raised by the "Trends" and "Serial Acquisitions" Guidelines

311. The draft guidelines introduce scenarios that are the focus of applications guidelines, under which a merger is integral to a strategy of amassing market power *over time*. These include firms that engage in successive, or serial acquisitions that may further a trend toward consolidation from horizontal concentration, vertical integration, or incentives to bulk up to gain bargaining power. There are notable examples of settings involving both trends toward consolidation and serial acquisitions.

312. For example, a rapid spate of mergers in agricultural biotechnology markets occurred in the last decade, against the backdrop of rising concentration and consolidation. In 2015, six firms competed in the global market for the sale of genetic crop traits, transgenic seed, and agro-chemicals. In a two-year period, three major mergers reduced those six firms to three.[41] Two major mergers of pharmacy benefit managers (PBMs) and commercial health insurers also occurred in quick succession. The merger of CVS and Aetna (2017) and Express Scripts

39 Diana L. Moss et al., *Market Power and Digital Business Ecosystems: Assessing the Impact of Economic and Business Complexity on Competition Analysis and Remedies*, American Antitrust Institute (June 1, 2021), https://www.antitrustinstitute.org/work-product/aai-issues-report-market-power-and-digital-business-ecosystems-assessing-the-impact-of-economic-and-business-complexity-on-competition-analysis-and-remedies/.

40 *See, e.g.,* European Commission Press Release, Mergers: Commission Clears Acquisition of Fitbit by Google, Subject to Conditions, (Dec. 17, 2020), https://ec.europa.eu/commission/presscorner/detail/en/ip_20_2484.

41 James M. MacDonald, *Mergers in Seeds and Agricultural Chemicals: What Happened?* U.S. Dep't. of Ag. Econ. Research SVC. (Feb. 15, 2019), https://www.ers.usda.gov/amber-waves/2019/february/mergers-in-seeds-and-agricultural-chemicals-what-happened/.

and Cigna (2018) created two large, vertically integrated PBM-insurer systems. Together with UnitedHealth Group's homegrown PBM Optum, three major PBM-insurer systems came to dominate the industry in a short period of time.

313. The serial acquisition application guideline examines a merger that is part of a series of multiple acquisitions. Under this guideline, the Agencies may examine a single merger against the backdrop of the entire series, "...looking for a pattern or strategy of multiple acquisitions and challenge it even if no single acquisition would risk a substantial lessening of competition or tend to create a monopoly."[42] A leading example is the FTC's case against Anesthesia Partners mentioned earlier. Other private equity-backed roll-ups of markets in physician practices, nursing homes, and home healthcare raise similar issues and are generating significant scrutiny.[43] The digital business ecosystems are also home to significant growth by serial acquisition, especially in regard to small acquisitions that fly under the Hart-Scott-Rodino reporting thresholds.[44]

314. The "trends" and "serial acquisitions" applications guidelines flag patterns of consolidation that are a major reason for vigilant and vigorous merger enforcement. However, the final 2023 Guidelines provide only brief discussion of how the Agencies will evaluate mergers in these settings. For example, how will the Agencies determine what constitutes a "trend" or a "serial acquisition?" What period of time, number or size of previous acquisitions, and merger characteristics define a trend toward consolidation or a pattern of serial behavior? Moreover, both the "trends" and "serial acquisitions" guidelines refer repeatedly to the "industry," not the "relevant market." where concerns might arise. But the guidelines do not provide any framework for distinguishing these two very different concepts. Th questions remain largely unanswered by the 2023 Guidelines.

315. Moreover, mergers that are likely to be evaluated under both the "trends" and "serial acquisition" guidelines may well occur at lower levels of concentration. In strengthening the structural presumption, however, the 2023 Guidelines eliminated discussion of when moderately concentrative mergers can pose competitive concerns which was an important element of the 2010 and prior guidelines.[45] Retaining this discussion would have likely aided the agencies and courts in evaluating cases under these applications guidelines.

---

42 2023 Guidelines, *supra* note 1, at 24.

43 *See, e.g.,* Richard M. Scheffler et al., *Monetizing Medicine: Private Equity and Competition in Physician Practice Markets*, American Antitrust Inst, Petris Center, and Wash. Center for Equit. Growth (July 10, 2023), https://petris.org/monetizing-medicine-private-equity-and-competition-in-physician-and-practice-markets/.

44 Diana L. Moss & David Hummel, *Anticipating the Next Generation of Powerful Digital Players: Implications for Competition Policy*, American Antitrust Institute (Jan. 18, 2022), at 10, https://www.antitrustinstitute.org/work-product/new-aai-analysis-unpacks-acquisitive-growth-by-digital-firms-warns-of-next-wave-of-expansion-and-need-for-sector-wide-approach-to-competition-policy/.

45 2023 Merger Guidelines, *supra* note 1, at 6.

3. Overlooking Retrospective Analysis

316. A major feature of industrial organization and strategic management research over the last 15 years has been the development of merger retrospectives. Retrospectives assess whether completed mergers that were, and were not, the subject of *ex ante* merger reviews resulted in adverse effects or produced pro-competitive benefits claimed by merging parties. There is a valuable body of merger retrospectives that highlight merger outcomes that were contrary to *ex ante* predictions. Merger retrospectives analyze single mergers, but also multiple mergers, through the use of "meta-analysis."

317. Retrospective studies of post-merger effects have been performed for a wide variety of mergers, including for home appliances and food manufacturers, brewers, hospitals, and airlines.[46] There is also growing interest in retrospectives that evaluate whether the efficiencies claimed by parties to mergers actually materialized. Indeed, evidence from the strategic management literature indicates that mergers rarely produce benefits.[47] This evidence is particularly important in cases where the Agencies informally give credit to efficiencies claims in their investigations. But the probative value of such evidence is found in litigated merger proceedings. Namely, after the government has made the case for how a merger is likely to substantially lessen competition, the burden shifts to defendants to show pro-competitive efficiencies reduce their incentives to exercise their enhanced market power.

318. There are scant, if any, examples of litigated merger cases that were won on the basis of a defendant's successful rebuttal of the government's case. However, in reality, it is clear that the courts have given at least implicit deference to efficiencies claims. For example, in the vertical merger of AT&T and Time Warner, the court's decision formally relied on the failure of the government to make its case for why the merger was likely to substantially lessen competition. Nonetheless, the court noted that it was "…confident that defendants will achieve considerable efficiencies beyond those conceded by the Government,"[48] and that "…defendants have presented persuasive, probative evidence that the merger will produce even more efficiencies than those accounted for in this Opinion."[49]

319. In retrospect, rebuttal evidence offered by the defendants in AT&T–Time Warner was deeply flawed. For example, AT&T spun off Warner

---

46 *See, e.g.*, Manesh S. Patel, *Merger Breakups*, 2020 Wis. L. Rev. 975 (2020), https://papers.ssrn.com/sol3/papers.cfm?abstract_id=3469984.

47 *See, e.g.*, Scott A. Christofferson et al., *Where Mergers Go Wrong*, McKinsey Q. (May 1, 2004), https://www.mckinsey.com/capabilities/strategy-and-corporate-finance/our-insights/where-mergers-go-wrong. ["…most buyers routinely overvalue the synergies to be had from acquisitions," finding that almost 70% of the mergers in the database studied failed to achieve expected synergies related to obtaining access to a target's customers, channels, and geographies."]

48 U.S. v. AT&T Inc., et al., Opinion, Civil Case No. 17-2511 (RJL) (D.D.C. June 12, 2018), at 36–39.

49 *Id.* at 54–55. *See also*, n.17.

Media less than three years post-consummation. Retrospective analysis of efficiencies shows that few cost savings were realized in that short period of time, much less the promise to increase the subscriber base for HBO.[50] Indeed, the AT&T–Time Warner merger was never going to create significant benefits. Time Warner, which experienced declining operating margins, accounted for under 20% of total revenues and costs and contributed less than 6% to the company's overall performance in the time period after the merger.[51]

320. In sum, the 2023 Guidelines missed an important opportunity to marshal evidence from past mergers to provide transparency and context that could significantly strengthen enforcement. This omission of important economic and business analysis seems oddly out of sync with the guidelines' priority of introducing citation to legal precedent. On the whole, however, it is consistent with the theme of relegating non-legal analysis and precedent to a secondary role in the 2023 Guidelines. This is likely to work against promoting stronger enforcement in the future.

V. Conclusion

321. The 2023 Guidelines reflect the challenges of finding an ideological compromise for important antitrust agency guidance in a critical area of the law. Viewed from a 10,000-foot level, the final version of the 2023 Guidelines corrects, in many ways discussed herein, an ideological "over-correction" that was apparent in the draft version. The net result highlights the importance and appeal of center-left pro-enforcement thinking, versus ideological extremes. As the guidelines are applied and interpreted by the agencies and courts and further caselaw is developed, it remains to be seen what questions will arise over their transparency and administrability.

---

50 *See, e.g.*, Letter from the American Antitrust Institute and Public Knowledge to AAAG Richard Powers, Re: Strategic Consolidation, Market Power, and Efficiencies in the Media/Entertainment and Distribution Markets: Implications for Antitrust Reviews of Proposed Mergers, (Sept. 2, 2021), at § III, https://www.antitrustinstitute.org/wp-content/uploads/2021/09/AAI_PK-Ltr-on-Warner-Media-Disc_9.2.21.pdf.

51 *Id.*

The Missing Merger Guideline: On Efficiencies

Maureen K. Ohlhausen and Taylor M. Owings*
Wilson Sonsini Goodrich & Rosati

* Maureen K. Ohlhausen and Taylor M. Owings are Partners at Wilson Sonsini Goodrich & Rosati, where they are members of the Antitrust and Competition Practice Group. The views herein are the authors' own and do not necessarily represent that of any client. An earlier version of this piece was commissioned by the U.S. Chamber of Commerce and appears at https://www.uschamber.com/assets/documents/20230601-Merger-Efficiencies-White-Paper.pdf. This version has been updated to reflect the release of the FTC and DOJ 2023 Merger Guidelines in December 2023.

I. Merger Guidelines Grounded in Skepticism

322. The U.S. antitrust agencies have finalized their new Merger Guidelines ("2023 Guidelines").[1] Gone is the axiom that had appeared in every version of the merger guidelines since 1984, that "a primary benefit of mergers to the economy is their potential to generate significant efficiencies and thus enhance the merged firm's ability and incentive to compete, which may result in lower prices, improved quality, enhanced service, or new products."[2] Instead, the new 2023 Guidelines are structured as a list of anticompetitive reasons that a firm might seek to acquire new assets, giving the false impression that Agencies rarely see mergers undertaken to improve operations, create new capabilities, or otherwise expand a firm's output.[3] We think that the Guidelines' skeptical approach to the procompetitive potential of mergers weakens the force of the analytical framework and leaves businesses without clear guidance on what mergers they may pursue.

323. One of the most troubling weaknesses is the several suggestions that acquisitions leading to an improvement in the merged firm's performance would violate the antitrust laws.

324. For instance, Guideline 6 warns that various acquisitions can "entrench or extend a dominant position" but fails to articulate how acquisitions in this context differ from the analysis that the Agencies apply to vertical mergers where there is likelihood of consumer harm from the foreclosure of competitors (as outlined in Guideline 5). It explains that "if a dominant firm merges with a complementary product that interoperates with the dominant firm's competitors, it could reduce interoperability, harming competition for customers who value the complement."[4] But the acquisition of a complementary product also has the potential to improve the acquiring firm's product by creating more seamless interoperability.

---

1 Fed. Trade Comm'n and U.S. Dep't. of Justice, *Merger Guidelines* (2023) ("2023 Guidelines"), at 1, https://www.justice.gov/atr/2023-merger-guidelines.

2 Fed. Trade Comm'n and U.S. Dep't. of Justice, *Horizontal Merger Guidelines* (2010) ("2010 Guidelines"), at 1, https://www.justice.gov/atr/file/810276/download; *See also*, Fed. Trade Comm'n and U.S. Dep't. of Justice, *Merger Guidelines* (1997), https://www.justice.gov/sites/default/files/atr/legacy/2007/07/11/11251.pdf ("Mergers have the potential to generate significant efficiencies by permitting a better utilization of existing assets, enabling the combined firm to achieve lower costs in producing a given quantity and quality than either firm could have achieved without the proposed transaction. Indeed, the primary benefit of mergers to the economy is their potential to generate such efficiencies."); Fed. Trade Comm'n and U.S. Dep't. of Justice, *Merger Guidelines* (1992), https://www.justice.gov/sites/default/files/atr/legacy/2007/07/11/11250.pdf ("The primary benefit of mergers to the economy is their efficiency-enhancing potential, which can increase the competitiveness of firms and result in lower prices to consumers. Because the antitrust laws, and thus the standards of the Guidelines, are designed to proscribe only mergers that present a significant danger to competition, they do not present an obstacle to most mergers. As a consequence, in the majority of cases, the Guidelines will allow firms to achieve available efficiencies through mergers without interference from the Agency."); Fed. Trade Comm'n and U.S. Dep't. of Justice, *Merger Guidelines* (1984), https://www.justice.gov/sites/default/files/atr/legacy/2007/07/11/11249.pdf (substantially the same).

3 Approximately 98% of transactions subject to a Hart–Scott–Rodino filing never even receive an in-depth inquiry from the Agencies, suggesting that the vast majority of transactions accomplish goals that are not competitively concerning. *See* FED. TRADE COMM'N, HART–SCOTT–RODINO ANNUAL REPORT TO CONGRESS (2021), at 5, https://www.ftc.gov/system/files/ftc_gov/pdf/p110014fy2021hsrannualreport.pdf.

4 2023 Guidelines, *supra* note 1, at 19.

Of course, if complement foreclosure is likely and competitively significant, then the merger may be anticompetitive for the same reasons as it would be under Guideline 5. But the decision to make Guideline 6 separate from Guideline 5 tends to suggest that some mergers that improve products, without raising competitive concerns under typical foreclosure analysis, will nevertheless be treated skeptically under these Guidelines.

325. Guideline 9 has a similar problem. It discusses an analytical framework for mergers involving "multi-sided platforms," and suggests that the Agencies can challenge a merger merely because it "would create conflicts of interest" and would give a platform operator "an incentive to give its own products and services an advantage over other participants competing on the platform."[5] This conflicts with precedent indicating that vertical integration has competitive benefits, and that the government must establish a prima facie case with industry-specific evidence that foreclosing rivals (or raising their costs) is both likely and competitively harmful.[6]

326. Guideline 7 discusses the potential harm from mergers that are part of an industry trend toward consolidation. Conspicuously missing is any recognition that such trends are often caused by technological changes that improve economies of scale, reduce costs, expand output, and make a market more competitive.

327. The 2023 Guidelines' discussion of competition through innovation also ignores that acquisitions often play an important role in meeting consumer demands. Though it recognizes that: "The incentives to compete aggressively on innovation and product variety depend on the capabilities of the firms and on customer reactions to the new offerings," and "Development of new features depends on having the appropriate expertise and resources,"[7] it never seriously addresses the ways in which firms acquire the appropriate expertise and resources. It fails to grapple with the fact that acquisitions might be the best, fastest, or only way to enable this sort of innovative transformation that competition law seeks to protect.

328. Instead, the Guidelines explain all the reasons the Agencies will discredit claims that an acquisition would accomplish the benefits of innovative transformation to add new product features, reduce costs, or improve distribution of products. By discrediting the claims, the Agencies do not have to resolve a seeming conflict between the desire for horizontal competition (which incentivizes innovation) and a set of guidelines that may impede

---

5 *Id.* at 25.

6 In United States v. AT&T, Inc., 916 F.3d 1029, 1032 (D.C. Cir. 2019), the D.C. Circuit explained that the Agencies "must make a fact-specific showing that the proposed merger is likely to be anticompetitive." The district court in FTC v. Microsoft Corporation recently adopted this same language in describing the appropriate test in that vertical case, pointing out that vertical integration (or coordination between different levels of the supply chain) tends to reduce contracting inefficiencies and is therefore generally procompetitive. Preliminary Injunction Opinion, Case No. 23-cv-02880, slip op. at 21–22, 30 (N.D. Cal. July 11, 2023). *See also*, Phillip E. Areeda & Herbert Hovenkamp, Antitrust Law: An Analysis of Antitrust Principles and Their Application ¶ 755c (online ed. May 2023) ("Vertical integration is ubiquitous in our economy and virtually never poses a threat to competition when undertaken unilaterally and in competitive markets.")).

7 2023 Guidelines, *supra* note 1, at 39.

this competition by chilling vertical (or other non-horizontal) acquisition of expertise and resources.

329. In particular, the "Procompetitive Efficiencies" section of the 2023 Guidelines declares without support that "Competition usually spurs firms to achieve efficiencies internally."[8] And if the efficiencies can be achieved internally, then they can be discredited because the benefits are not merger specific. But instead of articulating administrable principles for when a merger is not necessary to achieve the efficiencies, the Guidelines merely list alternative ways that efficiencies (including the elimination of double marginalization) could be realized: through "organic growth," contracts, and other less concerning mergers.[9] It is unclear how a firm would prove that these alternatives were sufficiently unattractive, or even how unattractive is sufficiently unattractive, to allow a merger.

330. In some contexts, courts have been skeptical that alternatives to the merger were truly feasible. For instance, in *FTC v. Meta Platforms Inc.*, the court rejected that organic growth could have been a substitute for the merger. It found Meta's organic expansion into virtual reality fitness apps "impermissibly speculative" despite the Federal Trade Commission (FTC)'s claims that "the company considered organic entry" and had the "overall capability" to invest accordingly.[10] If other courts are also likely to discount the feasibility of paths not taken (i.e., alternatives to a merger), it may suggest that the Guidelines' preference for internal growth, and skepticism that a merger is necessary, may be out of step with the judiciary.

331. Elsewhere, too, the 2023 Guidelines express a policy of skepticism that mergers might accomplish benefits that result in enhanced competitiveness. There is a sense of hostility toward "claims" of such benefits (e.g. "A merger may substantially lessen competition or tend to create a monopoly regardless of the claimed intent of the merging companies or their executives")[11] and the presumption is always against merging parties (e.g. "To the extent efficiencies merely benefit the merging firms, they are not cognizable. The merging parties must demonstrate through credible evidence that, within a short period of time, the benefits will prevent the risk of a substantial lessening of competition in the relevant market").[12]

---

8 *Id.* at 32.

9 *Id.* at 32; *id.* at 16, n.31 (discussing that elimination of double marginalization could be achieved by contract).

10 Order Denying Plaintiff's Mot. For Prelim. Injunction, Case No. 5:22-cv-04325, slip op. at 53 (D.D.C. Jan. 31, 2023). The court rejected the FTC's merger challenge, finding that Meta was not likely to enter the market for virtual reality dedicated fitness apps because it did not have specific business-critical functionalities for such as "content development, instructors, studio production… , music rights & technology." Slip op. at 44. *See also*, FTC v. Steris Corp., 133 F. Supp. 3d 962 (N.D. Ohio 2015). *See also*, Alicia J. Batts et al., *The US District Court for the Northern District of Ohio denies the FTC bid for a preliminary injunction in a merger case (Steris/Synergy)*, E-COMPETITIONS Sept. 2015, art. No. 79584.

11 2023 Guidelines, *supra* note 1, at 17; see also *id.* at 34 ("Evidence that the merging parties intend or expect the merger to lessen competition … can be highly informative in evaluating the effects of a merger on competition. The Agencies give little weight, however, to the lack of such evidence or the expressed contrary intent of the merging parties.").

12 *Id.* at 33.

332. Perhaps this presumption against the benefits of mergers should come as no surprise. The agency heads wrote recently in a letter to a foreign enforcer that: "Our experience has been that efficiencies are often claimed but rarely proved."[13] Chair Khan hired an economic advisor, Professor John Kwoka, who is a prominent skeptic of merger efficiencies. In a 2018 piece suggesting reforms to merger control, he argued: "There is, in short, no good evidence that mergers generally result in substantial and verifiable cost savings, notwithstanding claims to the contrary."[14] One of Assistant Attorney General Kanter's advisors echoed a similar statement. Professor Eric Posner, who worked on the 2023 Guidelines as counsel in the Antitrust Division, recently wrote that they represent "new learning" since the "Obama-era 2010 Guidelines." According to Posner, "Economists have [] rethought many of their premises. It turns out that the efficiencies thought to be the birthright of every merger are often mythical."[15]

333. Both Agencies have also advanced litigation positions consistent with this skepticism. The FTC has argued that if a firm can build or borrow the resources it needs to achieve a strategic goal, then buying – that is, adding the resources through M&A – is prohibited by the antitrust laws.[16]

13 Letter from Fed. Trade Comm'n and U.S. Dep't. of Justice, re Ministry's Public Consultation Paper on the Future of Competition Policy in Canada (Mar. 31, 2023), https://www.ftc.gov/news-events/news/speeches/letter-chair-lina-khan-assistant-attorney-general-jonathan-kanter-canadian-ministry-innovation.

14 *See* John Kwoka, *Reviving Merger Control: A Comprehensive Plan for Reforming Policy and Practice* (Oct. 9, 2018), https://www.antitrustinstitute.org/wp-content/uploads/2018/10/Kwoka-Reviving-Merger-Control-October-2018.pdf (describing a McKinsey study showing that merger buyers overpay based on an overly optimistic view of synergies, a Blonigen & Pierce study using a dataset that we discuss at some length below, and two retrospective studies that showed efficiency gains of less than 1% and about 1.5%, respectively, across large samples). It is worth noting that the studies Professor Kwoka cites for his grim view of merger efficiencies all observe that the studied mergers did in fact result in efficiencies. *See e.g.,* Scott A. Christofferson et al., *Where Mergers Go Wrong*, McKinsey on Finance (2004), https://www.mckinsey.com/capabilities/strategy-and-corporate-finance/our-insights/where-mergers-go-wrong (finding 55 of 77 studied mergers achieved at least 50% of projected revenue synergies and 84 of 92 studied mergers achieved at least 50% of projected cost savings). The exception is the Blonigen & Pierce piece, which found no average, manufacturing industry-wide effect of mergers on plant-level productivity. *See* Bruce A. Blonigen & Justin R. Pierce, *Evidence for the Effects of Mergers on Market Power and Efficiency* (Nat. Bureau Econ. Rsch., Working Paper No. 22750, Oct. 2016). Other researchers using plant-level productivity gains on an industry-wide basis have reached the opposite conclusion. *See e.g.,* Mert Demirer & Omer Karaduman, *Do Mergers and Acquisitions Improve Efficiency: Evidence from Power Plants* (2022), https://www.ftc.gov/system/files/ftc_gov/pdf/demirerkaraduman.pdf.

15 Eric A. Posner, *The Revised Merger Guidelines Will Restore Principle of Competition to Merger Review*, ProMarket (July 19, 2023), https://www.promarket.org/2023/07/19/eric-posner-the-revised-merger-guidelines-will-restore-principle-of-competition-to-merger-review/.

16 The FTC made this affirmative argument in its failed challenge to Meta/Within. There, the FTC's theory of harm was that Meta would have been a new entrant in the virtual reality fitness app market if it had not purchased Within's capabilities, and under those circumstances was required to "build" rather than "buy." *See* FTC v. Meta Technologies, Inc., Plaintiff's Mem. of Points and Authorities ISO Mot. for a Prelim. Injunction, Case No. 5:22-CV-04325-EJD (N.D. Cal. Oct. 31, 2022), Dkt. 164 at 19. *See also*, Michael Moiseyev et al., *The US FTC abandons its challenge to the acquisition of a virtual reality fitness app by a social media giant following a District Court's denial of its request for a preliminary injunction (Meta/Within)*, e-Competitions Feb. 2023, art. No. 112748. In Illumina–Grail, the FTC raised a similar argument defensively. The Commission broke with the Administrative Law Judge's findings and opposed the parties' efficiencies arguments on several grounds, including that any benefits from the merger should not be legally cognizable because the parties did not foreclose the possibility of "building" or "borrowing" instead. *See* Opinion of the Commission (FTC Apr. 3, 2023), at 81, https://www.ftc.gov/system/files/ftc_gov/pdf/d09401commissionfinalopinion.pdf. Though the Commission ultimately prevailed on appeal, with the Fifth Circuit holding that the parties' claimed efficiencies were not cognizable for other reasons, the Court disagreed that there was sufficient evidence to support a claim that Illumina could have contracted with Grail to achieve the same effect as the merger. *See* Illumina, Inc. v. FTC, Case No. 23-60167, slip op. at 30 (5th Cir. Dec. 15, 2023) ("But the Commission did not fairly consider evidence that Grail – in coordination with its bankers at Morgan Stanley – had determined

The U.S. Department of Justice (DOJ) argued in its challenge to the U.S. Sugar–Imperial Sugar merger that courts "have expressed skepticism about efficiencies defenses" and asked the court in that case to reject the likelihood of a plant-level performance improvement, which turns out to be one of the most verified type of efficiencies in the empirical literature we collect below.[17]

334. In addition to specific remarks questioning efficiencies, we see an increasing amount of rhetoric equating consolidation with bad outcomes for consumers.[18] This oversimplification fails to acknowledge gains from consolidation like economies of scope or scale, the assets of poorly managed firms coming under direction of well managed ones, and the research and design benefits that come from the integration of complementary functions.

335. But how well-founded is this sort of generalized skepticism that mergers create efficiencies? Are Professors Kwoka and Posner right to label as "mythical" the idea that mergers can create sustained benefits of the type that enable firms to compete more aggressively? Even setting aside the legal precedent that would cast doubt on the authority (and wisdom) of enforcers substituting their judgment for that of a business,[19] we think the evidence shows reason to embrace M&A as a tool that improves the competitiveness of firms and markets.

---

that it lacked the leverage necessary to bring Illumina to the table on these alternative proposals, leaving merger as the only realistic option."). *See also*, Steven Cernak, *The US FTC unanimously votes to overturn its initial decision and orders a biotechnology company to divest the controlling stake in a rival that it had purchased (Illumina/Grail)*, E-COMPETITIONS Apr. 2023, art. No. 113586.

17 Plaintiff United States of America's Post-Trial Brief (redacted version), United States v. U.S. Sugar Corp., Case No. 21-cv-01644, Dkt. No. 218, 43-44 (D. Del. May 16, 2022). In its "findings of fact" the court ultimately credited that the acquiring firm would be able to "increase the capacity utilization of [the plant]," entered judgment against the government, and was *aff'd* on appeal. Redacted Memorandum Opinion, United States v. U.S. Sugar Corp., Case No. 21-cv-01644, Dkt. No. 256, 22 (D. Del. Sept. 23, 2022), *aff'd* by United States v. U.S. Sugar Corp., Case No. 22-2806 (3d Cir. July 13, 2023).

18 *See e.g., The Federal Trade Commission and the Department of Justice Should Abandon the Proposed Vertical Merger Guidelines and Embrace the Framework of the 1968 Guidelines* OPENMARKETS (Feb. 2020), https://www.ftc.gov/system/files/attachments/798-draft-vertical-merger-guidelines/comment_to_ftc-doj_re_vertical_merger_guidelines.pdf (arguing for a return to the 1968 approach using strict market-share-based thresholds for horizontal and vertical mergers to "reflect the Clayton Act's purpose to preserve and promote *market structures* conducive to competition"); Fed. Trade Comm'n FTC Chair, Prepared Statement of the Federal Trade Commission Before the United States Senate Committee on the Judiciary Subcommittee on Antitrust, Competition Policy and Consumer Rights, *Oversight of the Enforcement of the Antitrust Laws* (Sept. 20, 2022), https://www.ftc.gov/system/files/ftc_gov/pdf/P210100SenateAntitrustTestimony09202022.pdf (criticizing agency underenforcement for resulting in concentrated markets); Fed. Trade Comm'n FTC Chair, Lina Khan, Remarks Regarding the Request for Information on Merger Enforcement (Jan. 18, 2022), https://www.ftc.gov/system/files/documents/public_statements/1599783/statement_of_chair_lina_m_khan_regarding_the_request_for_information_on_merger_enforcement_final.pdf ("This inquiry comes against the backdrop of a broader reassessment of the effects of mergers across the U.S. economy. Evidence suggests that decades of mergers have been a key driver of consolidation across industries, with this latest merger wave threatening to concentrate our markets further yet. As President Biden noted in his Executive Order on Promoting Competition, industry consolidation and weakened competition have 'den[ied] Americans the benefits of an open economy,' with 'workers, farmers, small businesses, and consumers paying the price.'"). For a discussion of the history of the conduct–structure–performance paradigm and the research leading to reform of the 1968 approach, see Bruce H. Kobayashi & Timothy J. Muris, *Turning Back the Clock: Structural Presumptions in Merger Analyses and Revised Merger Guidelines,* COMPETITIVE ENTERPRISE INSTITUTE (Feb. 22, 2023), https://cei.org/wp-content/uploads/2023/02/KobayashiMuris-FINAL-Layout-RY-approved.pdf.

19 Under the U.S. antitrust laws, enforcement Agencies may block an M&A transaction only if they meet their burden to prove that the transaction's "effect [] may be substantially to lessen competition." 15 U.S.C. § 18. As courts have explained, this is a "totality-of-the-circumstances" inquiry, and they "weigh[] a variety of factors to determine the effects of particular transactions on competition" and "future competitiveness." United States v. Baker Hughes Inc., 908 F.2d 981, 984 (D.C. Cir. 1990).

336. If M&A can improve competitiveness, for instance by equipping a firm to reduce costs or offer new product features, then merger guidelines will be counterproductive in the effort to protect competition if they chill too much merger activity. The guidelines should instead help enforcers and the business community identify the types of mergers that tend to result in this sort of procompetitive transformation. For these mergers, enforcers may want to look for more evidence that their theory of harm will actually come to pass before they challenge the deal.

337. To be sure, classifying mergers based on observable pre-merger factors is not easy. There are empirical and data collection challenges in performing reliable retrospectives to determine whether a merger created a more competitive firm. But we have reviewed the literature and found that there are tractable ways to measure the beneficial effects from mergers, just like there are tractable ways to measure harms from a loss to competition.

338. We have published a compendium of the real-world evidence in previous articles.[20] Here, we summarize the findings, which we believe support what used to be common wisdom in the preamble to the guidelines: "a primary benefit of mergers to the economy is their potential to generate significant efficiencies." We think that the summary of methodologies and findings provides a guide for the work necessary to identify the types of mergers that are most likely to generate significant efficiencies. We hope this work can lead to more sensitive tools for reviewing mergers, and to a more procompetitive approach than is reflected in the new 2023 Guidelines.

II. Summary of Merger Efficiency Evidence

339. We have compiled papers measuring the real-world effects of mergers, corporate consolidation, or vertical integration, where at least one of the observed results was an increase in productivity or other improvement in performance (which we are, together, calling "efficiencies" throughout this paper).[21] For our purposes here, we were not focused on whether the efficiencies were passed through to consumers – that is, we were not just looking for mergers that were procompetitive overall. Instead, we aimed to compile and understand the evidence that mergers can accomplish benefits that policymakers might weigh positively in an overall cost-benefit analysis of an interventionist merger review policy.

340. One common theme of the literature is how difficult it is to measure accurately the effects of a merger.[22] As is often the case in antitrust,

20 *See* the authors' white paper, Evidence of Efficiencies in Consummated Mergers (Maureen K. Ohlhausen & Taylor M. Owings eds., (June 2023), https://www.uschamber.com/assets/documents/20230601-Merger-Efficiencies-White-Paper.pdf.

21 *See id.* (for additional details on methodology).

22 *See e.g.,* Demirer & Karaduman, *supra* note 14 ("A major challenge in analyzing the efficiency effects of mergers is distinguishing true efficiency gains from other factors, such as changes in market power, buyer power, and product quality."); David R. King et al., *Meta-Analyses of Post-Acquisition Performance: Indicators of Unidentified Moderators*, 25 Strat. Mgmt. J. 187 (2004) ("First, most post-acquisition performance

one difficulty is isolating the effect from the combination of assets and controlling for all the other changes that affect firm performance after the merger. Another difficulty is even more fundamental: What constitutes improved performance post-combination?[23] For instance, we are not interested in empirical evidence of outsized gains in stock price or revenue as such – those "improvements" in financial performance could come from the exercise of market power rather than the improvement of operations or the ability to better meet consumer demand.[24]

341. The studies that find improvements attributable to mergers answer these questions using different methodologies, which can be loosely categorized into seven buckets. We describe these seven categories below.

1. Difference-in-Differences Measures of Plant-Level Production after Acquisition

342. One group of studies finds efficiencies using rich datasets of plant-level manufacturing outputs and the changes in ownership of those plants. These studies look at a time series of data from entire industries where some of the plants were acquired across the period tracked. They measure the productivity of any given plant – that is, the amount of finished product produced from a given number of inputs.[25] They compare the productivity of acquired plants in a given moment to the productivity of plants that were not acquired. (A variation on this method is to measure productivity under different concentration levels, rather than after specific merger events.) This difference-in-differences methodology allows the researchers to draw conclusions about what gains in productivity were due to acquisition, rather than exogenous effects on the industry as a whole.

---

research has only employed stock market event studies, thus ignoring M&A effects on other potentially relevant dimensions of firm performance. The short-term nature of most event studies may not fully capture anticipated benefits from an acquisition due to information asymmetries."); Orly C. Ashenfelter et al., *Efficiencies Brewed: Pricing and consolidation in the U.S. Beer Industry*, 46 RAND J. Econ. 328, 328–29 (2015) ("[T]here is very little direct empirical evidence that efficiencies can offset the incentive to raise prices. This lack of direct evidence is likely due to the inherent difficulties in measuring if (and by how much) mergers lower firms' marginal costs.").

23 *See* Demirer & Karaduman, *supra* note 14, at 2 ("A major challenge when studying the efficiency effects of mergers is the lack of suitable data because most industries do not have reliable measures of cost and physical productivity.").

24 There is a large literature in the study of finance that attempts to measure "performance" improvements resulting from acquisitions, by which the researchers almost exclusively mean to forecast returns on investment. While there may be some results from this literature that shed light on the topic of efficiencies or other operational improvements, we do not attempt to catalogue this field of research. For a fairly comprehensive (if somewhat outdated) treatment of this sort of retrospective analysis of mergers and acquisitions, see Maruizio Zollo & Harbir Singh, *Deliberate Learning in Corporate Acquisitions: Post-Acquisition Strategies and Integration Capability in U.S. Bank Mergers*, 25 Strat. Mgmt. J. 1233 (2004); see also Paul M. Healy et al., *Does Corporate Performance Improve After Mergers?*, 31 J. Fin. Econ. 135 (1992).

25 Some studies we catalogue measure output by using revenue as a proxy. We recognize a debate in the literature about whether revenue is an inappropriate measure because it would reflect price effects from increases in market power. We do not attempt to resolve this debate here, but record in our table which type of measure was used.

2. Difference-in-Differences Measures of a Single Firm's Accounting Data

343. There is a wide variety of studies using a firm's accounting data to measure its improved performance after a merger by comparing it to an appropriate "but for" alternative, as measured by the performance of the rest of the industry, or a particular sample of the rest of the industry that has similar characteristics to the merged firm. Researchers measure this improved performance in many different ways. Some look at quality-adjusted prices – that is, they choose a measurable variable that serves as a proxy for the quality of a product or service (e.g. wait times) and measure changes in price, controlling for the variable. Price is only informative as a measure of reduced costs (i.e., efficiency) if the researcher is able to account for the price effects from any loss of competition (i.e., increases in market power or tacit coordination). Others look directly at measures of cost to produce goods or services. Still others compare output quantities to determine whether a combined firm is able to produce more from the same pre-merger assets.

3. Data Envelopment Analysis

344. Some researchers find performance improvements after mergers or during periods of industry concentration by using a measure of productivity called data envelopment analysis. Data envelopment analysis (DEA) is a statistical method that uses data measuring inputs and outputs in an industry to try to estimate the highest limits of possible production (i.e., "the production possibility frontier") and then measures a specific producer's performance against that potential performance to come up with a measure of efficiency. The method is only available where there is firm-level data available on the inputs used and outputs produced over time. When researchers also have a dataset tracking mergers in the industry, or concentration levels generally, they show how the DEA measure of efficiency improves with the M&A, or how the measure improves when the industry becomes more concentrated. Many of the DEA studies showing efficiency gains were focused on the banking industry, where the inputs and outputs seem to be more regularly measured by regulators.

4. Before-and-After Measures of a Single Firm's Performance

345. Some studies look only at operations of a firm before and after a merger, and directly measure improvements in the firm's costs of production (e.g. distances that goods must be shipped) after the combination. Unlike the difference-in-differences methodology, the before-and-after methodology cannot account for exogenous changes over time that would have lowered the cost of production, or other direct measures of performance, of the whole industry. As a result, many of these studies also show price decreases at the merged firm relative to the rest of the industry, and in doing so attempt to account for market-wide variables that also affect prices.

5. Industry-Wide Regression Analysis Using Accounting Data

346. Some studies measure the effects not of individual mergers, but of industry concentration or vertical integration generally on measures of price or performance. These studies include variables in the regressions that account for other explanations of movements in price or performance. These studies' findings of lower prices or higher-quality outputs in periods of greater consolidation or vertical integration may be explained by economies of scale and vertical efficiencies.

6. Before-and-After Measures of Market Share

347. One study is unlike the others; it makes a case for classifying mergers as "efficiency enhancing" if the post-merger market share (measured by quantity of a good produced) is greater than the sum of each firm's pre-merger market share.[26] Conversely, a merger is "market power enhancing" if the combined firm reduced output and their market share (after contracting aggregate output to internalize the infra-marginal losses that they impart to each other). The study uses a rich dataset from DRAM chip production to make the case that a group of "efficiency enhancing" mergers tended to cause less efficient firms to exit, and "market power enhancing" mergers tended to attract entry. The response of market participants, which is in line with theoretical expectation, tends to confirm the methodology for classifying a merger as "efficiency enhancing."

7. Case Studies

348. A final methodology does not purport to quantify efficiency effects in any way, rather it uses interviews, historical commentaries, or regulatory hearings to collect information on subjective understandings by managers or other informed observers to determine that mergers resulted in improved operations or created cost savings.

III. Takeaways from the Merger Efficiency Evidence

349. Our search for evidence of merger effects captured a wide and varied range of empirical work showing the realization of efficiencies from mergers. The most important takeaway is that there is no reason to doubt the once-settled wisdom underpinning the basic framework for merger review: mergers are considered a legitimate means to advance procompetitive business objectives unless there is evidence that the merger will cause quality-adjusted prices to increase or innovation to decrease.

---

26 Ralph B. Siebert, *Estimating Differential Dynamic Merger Effects on Market Structure and Entry in Related Markets*, 55 REV. OF INDUS. ORG. 431 (2019).

350. Many of the studies attempt to explain *when* or *why* mergers result in performance improvements. That result would be the panacea for antitrust enforcers, and it would also tell business managers when they should buy, rather than borrow or build, certain assets to advance their strategic growth plans. Unfortunately, the research as it exists today is largely inconclusive.[27] There is one helpful factor to observe, and it helps provide an indication of the type of finding that future work could uncover: several studies have results consistent with the explanation that better managed firms can acquire assets from underperforming firms and bring those assets up to the acquiring firm's level of performance. For a detailed discussion of this effect and the evidence corroborating it, we recommend Boyan Jovanovic & Peter L. Rousseau's paper from the *American Economic Review* in May 2002.[28] These results may give enforcers particular comfort when reviewing the acquisitions of firms with low levels of productivity.

351. We did not observe any robust evidence that certain types of mergers are especially *unlikely* to result in efficiencies.[29] Rather, we saw evidence of mergers leading to efficiencies in a wide range of industries, including for both goods and services, and for both highly commoditized products and differentiated products. For this reason, there is no empirically supported reason to alter our enforcers' case-by-case approach or for courts to change their assumption that business managers, who are closest to the industry in question, are best placed to judge which strategy – build, borrow, or buy – will best improve firm performance.[30] As the Supreme Court explained in *NCAA v. Alston*, "antitrust law does not require businesses to use anything like the least restrictive means of achieving legitimate business purposes. To the contrary, courts should not second-guess 'degrees of reasonable necessity' so that 'the lawfulness of conduct turn[s] upon judgments of degrees of efficiency.'"[31]

---

27 Equally inconclusive is the body of research trying to forecast the determinants of financial success for firms subject to M&A. See *supra* note 22.

28 *See* Boyan Jovanovic & Peter L. Rousseau, *The Q Theory of Mergers*, 92 Am. Econ. Rev. 198 (2002).

29 But see David J. Ravenscraft & F.M. Scherer, Mergers, Sell-Offs, & Economic Efficiency (1987). The authors conclude that the mergers they observed did not tend to lead to performance improvements, though they found performance improvements in some cases. Commentators have viewed this study, performed on a large dataset collected by the FTC and supplemented with interviews, as reaching conclusions that are idiosyncratic to the wave of conglomerate mergers completed in the 1960s. It nevertheless provides a model for the type of 6(b) study that could be useful for specific industries undergoing consolidation in the future.

30 For a strategy-focused discussion on factors that might support buying rather than building or buying, see Laurence Capron & Will Mitchell, Build, Borrow, or Buy: Solving the Growth Dilemma (2012) (explaining that buying may be the strategically optimal choice if existing internal resource have low relevance, the needed resource is difficult to trade or has principal-agent problems, and the resource must be closely integrated with other aspects of the business to achieve the growth strategy).

31 NCAA v. Alston, No. 20-512, slip op. at 26 (S. Ct. June 21, 2021) (quoting Rothery Storage & Van Co. v. Atlas Van Lines, Inc., 792 F.2d 210, 227 (D.C. Cir. 1986); Continental T.V., Inc. v. GTE Sylvania Inc., 433 U.S. 36, 58, n.29 (1977)). *See also*, Louis K. Fisher et al., *The US Supreme Court prohibits an association from restraining student-athlete education-related benefits while recognizing the association still retains considerable flexibility to regulate such benefits (NCAA/Alston)*, e-Competitions June 2021, art. No. 101244.

IV. Limitations of the Merger Efficiency Evidence

352. One obvious limitation in the literature is the relatively small number of industries where data are available to measure the costs and quantity of inputs and outputs. We think one critical learning from our effort to catalogue merger efficiency evidence is that the FTC has a unique power to collect data that would significantly improve the state of the research. For most industries, privately held data are necessary to test specific hypotheses about when mergers tend to lead to productive efficiencies, so the FTC's Section 6(b) power makes it uniquely qualified to clarify the empirical record in ways that private researchers have struggled to do.

353. If the FTC has a specific hypothesis about how theorized merger efficiencies are likely to play out in the real world, it can test that hypothesis by collecting a time series of data on inputs and outputs in an industry and doing a difference-in-differences analysis after firms, in the ordinary course, decide to merge. This would have benefits over the typical "merger retrospective," which usually works without relevant data from the industry before the merger of interest. Until such pre- and post-merger data is collected, policymakers will not be well-positioned to prove their skepticism of efficiencies, and their judgment will likely be considered less informed than business decisionmakers who turn to M&A to achieve operational efficiencies or other strategic goals that are broadly consistent with the imperative to compete.

V. Conclusion

354. The research we have summarized here tends to undermine the basis for generalized skepticism of merger efficiencies seen in the FTC and DOJ's 2023 Guidelines. Additionally, claims that more industries are more concentrated now than they were 40 years ago, even if accurate on their own terms, are not a sufficient basis to condemn the performance of antitrust enforcers.[32] Rather, as the research shows, increased concentration can mean better firm performance and better outcomes for consumers. Indeed, the destruction of inefficient firms (sometimes accompanied by the acquisition of their assets) is a fundamental part of the process of competition, which necessarily leads to consolidation as those who compete most strongly on the merits win out.

355. Though high-quality empirical evidence of mergers leading to improved performance is limited (relative to the huge number of mergers in the past 40 years), it exists for many industries where the necessary data were available to researchers. For industries or specific mergers with more limited data tracking, researchers have at least provided useful proxies

---

32 *See* Kobayashi & Muris, *supra* note 18.

for efficiency gains, again confirming the theoretical work modeling how consolidation can lead to welfare gains.

356. We should therefore reject the policy prescription that merger review be drastically altered to assume no gains from mergers, to doubt proffered strategic explanations, or to shift the burden to parties to prove why they could not achieve their goals through "organic growth." The Agencies should, as they have in the past, make enforcement decisions taking into account the likelihood of efficiencies in any particular case.[33] Moreover, as empirical evidence of explanatory factors for merger efficiencies improves, the Agencies will be able to name those factors and focus their enforcement efforts on mergers that are unlikely to result in the sorts of performance improvements that competition policy seeks to spur on.

33 *See* Malcolm B. Coate & Andrew J. Heimert, Merger Efficiencies at the Federal Trade Commission 1997–2007, (Feb. 2009), https://www.ftc.gov/reports/merger-efficiencies-federal-trade-commission-1997-2007. Staff considered efficiencies in 147 of the 186 "second request" cases during the period studied by Coate & Heimert. Bureau of Competition ("BC") staff discussed efficiencies in 115 of its recommendation memos, including 342 different efficiency claims. BC staff accepted 29 of the 342 claims (they rejected about a third of the claims, and did not come to a conclusion on the rest). The acceptances were correlated to a statistically significant degree with the outcomes of the investigations: BC accepted efficiency claims in 15.3% of the closed cases, compared to just 4.2% of cases where the Commission sought a settlement, and 6.9% of cases where the Commission challenged the merger.

Economics in the 2023 Merger Guidelines: Three Areas of Concern

JEREMY SANDFORD, LOREN SMITH AND NATHAN WILSON
Compass Lexecon*

* Jeremy Sandford (jsandford@compasslexecon.com), Loren Smith (lsmith@compasslexecon.com), and Nathan Wilson (nwilson@compasslexecon.com) are Executive Vice Presidents at Compass Lexecon. The views expressed in this article are the views of the authors only and do not necessarily represent the views of Compass Lexecon, its management, its subsidiaries, its affiliates, its employees, or its clients.

I. Introduction

357. In December 2023, the Department of Justice (DOJ) and the Federal Trade Commission (FTC) jointly released the 2023 Merger Guidelines ("2023 Guidelines").[1] The new Guidelines are improved relative to the July 2023 Draft Merger Guidelines ("2023 Draft Guidelines"), and we have found things to like in the 2023 Guidelines. However, many elements have not changed, and several of these worry us.[2] In particular, as economists, we are concerned that the 2023 Guidelines at times appear to substitute hardline rules and subjective priors for economic evidence.

358. In this chapter, we focus on the economics of three topics covered by the 2023 Guidelines: market definition, non-horizontal mergers, and efficiencies. For each topic, we discuss the Guideline's approach as compared with prior versions of the Merger Guidelines and discuss what the approach gets right – and wrong – from an economic perspective using examples drawn from recently litigated matters.

II. Market Definition

359. As others have observed, the role of market definition in antitrust matters is to identify the area of competition most likely to be affected by a merger (or other conduct).[3] Since, as the Supreme Court put it, "[e]very manufacturer is the sole producer of the particular commodity it makes but control [over price] depends upon the availability of alternative commodities for buyers,"[4] courts and agencies have found it useful to identify alternatives that are reasonably close substitutes for the products at issue, while excluding more distant substitutes. Market definition thus depends on demand-side substitution, with products that many consumers view as substitutes included in the market and those seen as more distant substitutes excluded.

360. To concretize this concept, courts and agencies have for decades relied upon the hypothetical monopolist test (HMT) to define markets, with the HMT first appearing in the 1982 Guidelines. A proposed market passes the HMT if a monopolist controlling all products in the market would be incentivized to increase price on at least one product and fails if competition from outside the market would disincentivize such a price increase. Application of the HMT often involves empirical measurement

---

1 *See* Fed. Trade Comm'n and U.S. Dep't. of Justice, *Merger Guidelines* (2023) ("2023 Guidelines"), https://www.ftc.gov/system/files/ftc_gov/pdf/2023_merger_guidelines_final_12.18.2023.pdf.

2 Since the Draft Merger Guidelines ("2023 Draft Guidelines") were published, 1,600 separate comments were posted to the docket, with another 3,300 comments received. *See* https://www.regulations.gov/docket/FTC-2023-0043.

3 *See, e.g.*, Gregory J. Werden, *Why (Ever) Define Markets? An Answer to Professor Kaplow*, 78 Antitrust L.J. 719, 729–46, 732 (2013) ("The relevant market is [...] the metaphoric arena in which in which the competition at issue occurs.")

4 United States v. E.I. du Pont de Nemours & Co., 351 U.S. 377, 404 (1956).

of demand substitution,[5] but it is fundamentally an algorithm that can be applied consistently across contexts in an effort to understand consumers' preferences.

361. Consistent with this view of the HMT, courts and practitioners sometimes additionally turn to qualitative evidence on demand substitution patterns in applying it. When qualitative evidence is incorporated into the HMT, it often is analyzed through the lens of several "practical indicia" enumerated by the Supreme Court in its *Brown Shoe* decision, such as industry recognition of a market.[6] In our experience, *Brown Shoe* factors are most productively considered in the service of the HMT, i.e., to provide additional evidence as to whether a monopolist would increase prices, as opposed to serving as some form of standalone test.

362. To their credit, the 2023 Guidelines largely keep the 2010 Guidelines' description of the HMT and its quantitative underpinnings. The draft also adds helpful additional explanation on applying the test to targeted customer markets, to cluster markets, and to markets involving bundles.

363. Beyond expanding the discussion of the HMT, the 2023 Guidelines also add a more explicit discussion of other potential sources of evidence on market definition, including "direct evidence of substantial competition between the merging parties", "direct evidence of the exercise of market power", and *Brown Shoe* indicia. This section discusses these additional sources of evidence and their relationship to the HMT.

364. First, "direct evidence of substantial competition between the merging parties" can be read as subordinating the market definition exercise to a competitive effects analysis. If analyses that do not depend on market definition indicate that consumers are likely to be harmed by lost competition between merging parties, we would agree that market definition may offer little incremental value over competitive effects analysis. Consequently, it may be appropriate to demote market definition in importance. Moreover, in our experience, the FTC and DOJ do (appropriately) give primacy to competitive effects analyses over market definition (particularly during their internal evaluations). Thus, this change may accurately and helpfully reflect their practice.[7]

365. Second, it is less clear what "direct evidence of the exercise of market power" adds, or under which circumstances such evidence could alleviate the need

---

5 The HMT is described in greater detail in Section 4.3 of the 2023 Guidelines.

6 Brown Shoe Co. v. United States, 370 U.S. 294, 324 (1962).

7 For instance, the FTC argued to the DC Circuit in FTC v. Whole Foods Market, Inc., 548 F.3d 1028 (D.C. Cir. 2008) that market definition is unnecessary in merger cases, stating that market definition is but one way of measuring market power, and thus a means to an end, and not an end in itself. While the DC Circuit rejected this reasoning by saying that "the FTC itself made market definition key" in its complaint and briefs to the district court, it agreed that "market definition will [not] always be crucial" to merger cases. *See* DC Circuit opinion at 10–12, https://www.cadc.uscourts.gov/internet/opinions.nsf/D7E40F1331EE35CF85257 80000523CE4/$file/07-5276-1130155.pdf. *See also*, James W. Lowe et al., *The US Court of Appeals for the District of Columbia Circuit overturns a district court's denial of FTC's request for a preliminary injunction against an acquisition in the organic food sector (Whole Foods/Wild Oats)*, e-Competitions July 2008, art. No. 37167.

for market definition. In our experience, the term "market power" lacks a consistent definition, and – in large part because the term is ill-defined – it can be challenging to credibly establish market power by methods other than defining a market and demonstrating large shares in that market (and this too may be subject to legitimate critiques). Nonetheless, given the well-known "cellophane fallacy," commonly applied market definition techniques may break down when a firm faces few close competitors and has already increased its price to reflect the lack of competition.[8] In such circumstances, it may indeed be appropriate to deemphasize market definition in favor of competitive effects analyses. If the "exercise of market power" language is applied to address such situations, then it could prove a useful addition. However, it remains to be seen just what the Agencies intended with this new language.

366. Third, language referencing the *Brown Shoe* indicia as relevant for market definition last appeared in the 1982 and the 1984 Guidelines. In those documents, the context was in regards to their use as "circumstantial evidence" of product substitutability, including "buyers' perceptions that the products are or are not substitutes" and "similarities or differences between the products in customary usage, design, physical composition, and other technical characteristics."[9] The 1982 and 1984 Guidelines explained that qualitative indicia of substitutability were to be applied in support of the HMT, which those guidelines established as the "general" benchmark for market definition.[10] In other words, the *Brown Shoe* factors could be relevant because they could help answer the HMT, not because they offered clear guidance as to the appropriate contours of the relevant market outside of the HMT framework.

367. Consistent with this view, the 1992, 1997, and 2010 Guidelines do not emphasize *Brown Shoe* criteria. Indeed, the 1992 Guidelines dropped references to qualitative indicia of substitutability, specifically linking the relevant market to the HMT.[11] For instance, the 1992 Guidelines deleted prior guidelines' appeals to "buyers' perceptions" in favor of evidence on actual or considered substitution; they also dropped references to

---

8 While the cellophane fallacy more commonly arises in matters involving single-firm conduct, it can also implicate market definition in merger matters. By way of example, suppose that a dominant seller of a product proposed to acquire a fringe supplier or an importer of the product. It may be that a hypothetical monopolist seller of the product would not increase price by very much above the price charged by the dominant seller, who may be constrained mainly by alternative product types. It is unclear why the legality of such a merger should depend on the ability of a hypothetical monopolist to increase prices by some fixed amount, and thus market definition may not meaningfully add to analyses of the merger.

9 Fed. Trade Comm'n and U.S. Dep't. of Justice, *Merger Guidelines* (1982) ("1982 Guidelines"), https://www.justice.gov/archives/atr/1982-merger-guidelines; Fed. Trade Comm'n and U.S. Dep't. of Justice, *Merger Guidelines* (1984) ("1984 Guidelines"), https://www.justice.gov/archives/atr/1984-merger-guidelines.

10 *Id.*

11 Fed. Trade Comm'n and U.S. Dep't. of Justice, *Merger Guidelines* (1992) ("1992 Guidelines"), https://www.justice.gov/archives/atr/1992-merger-guidelines (Section 1.11, "Absent price discrimination, the Agency will delineate the product market to be a product or group of products such that a hypothetical profit-maximizing firm that was the only present and future seller of those products ("monopolist") likely would impose at least a small but significant and nontransitory increase in price"). This language was repeated verbatim in the 1997 Guidelines.

"similarities or differences" between products in favor of criteria that were likely to be more objectively measurable. The 2010 Guidelines downgraded the importance of market definition relative to that of competitive effects analyses,[12] while maintaining the primacy of the HMT as a market definition tool.[13]

368. In contrast to the 1982–2010 Guidelines, the 2023 Guidelines characterize the HMT as but one of several tools used to define markets, with the Agencies able to "rely on any one or more" of the tools to "demonstrate the validity of a candidate relevant antitrust market," including *Brown Shoe* qualitative indicia. The 2023 Guidelines do not provide guidance as to the circumstances under which the Agencies may place relatively greater or lesser weight on either *Brown Shoe* indicia or on the HMT. Nor do they indicate that *Brown Shoe* indicia will be used in support of the HMT, as did the 1982 and 1984 Guidelines.

369. While the *Brown Shoe* indicia have been excised from the last several iterations of the Guidelines, in our experience they can be important inputs into market definition, both in practice at the Agencies and as a matter of legal necessity in litigation. In particular, in matters in which quantitative evidence of actual or likely substitution patterns is unavailable, *Brown Shoe* factors may comprise the best available evidence on demand substitution, and thus market definition. Thus, their return to the 2023 Guidelines may reflect agency thinking, and therefore be useful guidance.

370. In our experience, however, qualitative indicia are generally less reliable indicators of demand substitution than are the quantitative measurements that an HMT using data on customer substitution patterns provides. This is particularly true in the common scenario in which *Brown Shoe* indicia may produce ambiguous results or rely on subjective characterizations of evidence that may point in different directions. Qualitative factors are even less likely to be persuasive if untethered from the motivating question that underlies the HMT. How can an analyst know the importance of some similarities unless explicitly linked to tangible outcomes.

371. In short, we believe *Brown Shoe* indicia are most likely to be useful as inputs into, or complements for, the HMT, and not – as seemingly posited for the first time in over 40 years by U.S. Merger Guidelines – as alternatives to the HMT.

372. In the remainder of this section, we consider the relationship between *Brown Shoe* indicia and the HMT, with examples drawn from recent Agency enforcement. In our view, these examples illustrate the value of quantitative implementations of the HMT as both a complement to and

12 Fed. Trade Comm'n and U.S. Dep't. of Justice, *Horizontal Merger Guidelines* (2010) ("2010 Guidelines"), https://www.justice.gov/atr/horizontal-merger-guidelines-08192010. (See Section 4, stating "The Agencies' analysis need not start with market definition. Some of the analytical tools used by the Agencies to assess competitive effects do not rely on market definition.")

13 *Id.* (See Section 4.1.1, "The Agencies employe the hypothetical monopolist test to evaluate whether groups of products in candidate markets are sufficiently broad to constitute relevant antitrust markets.")

substitute for *Brown Shoe* indicia. While *Brown Shoe* indicia may in some cases strengthen the conclusions of a quantitative HMT, or stand in for quantitative evidence when such evidence is unavailable, the indicia would be poor replacements for the HMT itself as a general matter.

373. **Illumina/–PacBio (2019) and Illumina/–Grail (2021):** In seeking to block this merger, the FTC alleged a "Next Generation Sequencing" or "NGS" product market including both the "short-read" technology used by Illumina systems and the "long-read" technology used by PacBio systems. While the FTC's complaint cited "some instances" in which switching between the parties occurred, it did not allege significant substitution between the parties.[14] Indeed, the complaint alleged that long-read NGS systems like PacBio's had only recently become a closer substitute for Illumina's short-read technology, and then only "for some customers in some projects" (with more substitution alleged to come in the future).[15]

374. In support of an NGS product market, the FTC relied entirely on *Brown Shoe* factors as evidence of demand substitution, by referencing "internal documents [in which] both Illumina and PacBio routinely recognize the existence of an NGS market" and the recognition of "other market participants" of an NGS market.[16] The FTC also stated that "PacBio's long-read systems have characteristics and uses similar to those of Illumina's short-read systems."[17]

375. The FTC's case would doubtlessly have been stronger had there been robust quantitative evidence on actual customer substitution between the merging parties. However, the absence of such information may be expected for newer products, or for evolving products for which past substitution patterns may not be good indicators of future substitution. In our view, the absence of quantitative evidence need not be gating, and in such matters *Brown Shoe* indicia can be helpful in assessing demand substitution and thus in establishing an antitrust market, especially if supported by testimony or other qualitative evidence on likely demand substitution.

376. In a similar vein, the Fifth Circuit recently found that the FTC "was not required to use the hypothetical monopolist test to define the relevant product market" when assessing the proposed merger between Illumina and Grail, one of several companies developing cancer detection products using Illumina's platform.[18] In reaching this conclusion, the court noted that "requiring such hard metrics to prove the bounds of a market where

---

14 *See* Fed. Trade Comm'n. v. Illumina Inc., Complaint, Case No. 09-387https://www.ftc.gov/system/files/documents/cases/d9387_illumina_pacbio_administrative_part_3_complaint_public.pdf, at 5.

15 *Id.*

16 *Id.*

17 *Id.*

18 *See* Illumina, Inc. v. FTC, Case No. 23-60167, slip op. at 13 (5th Cir. Dec. 15, 2023), https://www.ca5.uscourts.gov/opinions/pub/23/23-60167-CV0.pdf.

only one product has been commercialized but there is indisputably ongoing competition to bring additional products to market would, in effect, prevent research-and-development markets from ever being realized for antitrust purposes."[19] We agree with the court that a quantitative implementation of the HMT would have been effectively impossible in this matter. In lieu of such quantitative analyses, the court not unreasonably turned to *Brown Shoe* indicia to define a product market around cancer detection products like Grail's.

377. **Whole Foods–Wild Oats (2007):** In seeking to block this merger, the FTC alleged a product market consisting of "premium natural organic supermarkets" (PNOS). The FTC defined PNOS as distinct from other retailers in that PNOS offer "more amenities", "promote a lifestyle of health and ecological sustainability", and set higher prices reflecting "a lifestyle to which their customers aspire."[20] To support its definition, the FTC relied in part on party documents describing Whole Food's focus on "high quality perishables" and its "superior store experience" and indicating that conventional supermarkets had not taken share from Whole Foods even as they added organic food items.[21] In arguing for a market encompassing a broader array of retailers, Whole Foods produced documents indicating that it tracks a broad array of retailers for the purposes of setting prices and choosing locations, that conventional supermarkets had shifted towards offering more organic items, and that most products that Whole Foods sells are not organic.[22]

378. The district court found that the sum of the qualitative evidence indicated that "other supermarkets, including Safeway, Wegmans and Delhaize, compete today for the food purchases of customers who shop at Whole Foods and Wild Oats," and that Whole Foods did not uniquely compete with Wild Oats.[23] In part based on this qualitative evidence, the district court concluded that "the relevant product market in this case is [...] at least all supermarkets."[24]

379. In our view, this matter nicely illustrates the limitations of qualitative *Brown Shoe* evidence. Such evidence in this matter was contradictory and ambiguous, with the litigants able to find support in the qualitative evidence for both a narrow market and a broader market. In our experience, this is often the case in matters involving differentiated products that compete to varying extents with a wide range of other products. In such markets, *Brown Shoe* criteria may be of limited value, with courts

---

19 *Id.*

20 *See* FTC v. Whole Foods Market, Inc., et al, Complaint, Case No. 07-1021 (D.D.C. 2007), https://www.ftc.gov/sites/default/files/documents/cases/2007/06/070605complaint.pdf.

21 *Id.*

22 *Id.* (The Kavanaugh dissent summarizes evidence produced by the defendants, e.g., at 7).

23 *Id.*, at 28–29.

24 *Id.*, at 31.

and agencies appropriately placing greater emphasis on quantitative implementations of the HMT backed by data on customer substitution patterns. In fact, both the district court and the DC Circuit on appeal extensively discussed quantitative arguments put forward by both the FTC and Whole Foods, with the district court finding that Whole Foods' critical loss analysis indicated that a price increase to PNOS customers would be unprofitable,[25] and the DC Circuit finding that the district court erred in interpreting the econometric evidence by giving too much weight to marginal as opposed to core customers.[26]

380. While the litigants' quantitative analyses ostensibly produced contradictory quantitative evidence, such evidence can be traced back to assumptions and basic measurements, which often can be tested and either accepted or rejected. In contrast, qualitative evidence produced by party documents does not easily lend itself to such testing. Thus, while *Brown Shoe* factors can be helpful in matters involving differentiated products, we think there is considerable value in looking beyond such factors to quantitative evidence on customer substitution. When, as here, the qualitative indicia appear to be inconclusive, a quantitative implementation of the HMT should receive greater weight than qualitative factors.

381. **Peabody–Arch (2020):** Peabody and Arch own the two largest coal mines in the South Powder River Basin ("SPRB"). The FTC sued to block their proposed joint venture, arguing that SPRB coal was a market unto itself, despite some competition with coal derived from other basins and alternative sources of energy like natural gas. The FTC's complaint highlighted qualitative factors distinguishing SPRB coal from other types of coal (e.g., as compared to other coals, SPRB coal contains more heat and less sulfur and sodium) and stated that "industry and public recognition" confirmed the distinction.[27] The complaint also made quantitative claims, namely that shipping costs made coal from other basins uneconomical for many power plants, and that the cost of converting a plant to use alternative fuels was prohibitive.[28]

382. In finding for the FTC, the district court devoted 35 pages to product market definition, considering both quantitative and qualitative evidence. The court concluded that "[b]oth sides have argued persuasively that certain *Brown Shoe* factors support the Court's use of their preferred market."[29] In particular, the court found persuasive both defendants' evidence of there being "robust industry and public recognition of interfuel competition and that the prices for SPRB coal are affected by the prices of other

25 *Id.*, at 16.

26 *See* D.C. Circuit opinion, *supra* note 7.

27 *See* Fed. Trade Comm'n v. Peabody Energy Corp. Complaint, Case No. 4:20-cv-00317-SEP (E.D. Mo. Apr. 1, 2020), https://www.ftc.gov/system/files/documents/cases/d09391_peabody_energy-arch_coal_administrative_complaint_0.pdf.

28 *Id.*

29 *Id.*, at 36.

fuels" and the FTC's evidence of there being both public recognition of an SPRB coal market and SPRB coal having distinct customers, characteristics, and production facilities as compared to other fuel sources.

383. While the court found that the FTC established "that the SPRB coal market has the 'practical indicia' of a relevant product market," the opinion led with an extensive review of quantitative evidence and the litigants' application of the HMT.[30] The FTC used various data sets to estimate the elasticity of demand for SPRB coal, and argued that under any estimate a price increase would be jointly profitable for SPRB coal producers.[31] Defendants argued that a coal price increase would trigger the conversion of power plants to alternative fuel sources, and that econometric estimates indicated that this dynamic effect (which it said the FTC did not fully account for) would render unprofitable an increase in the price of SPRB coal.[32] Both sides put forward econometric estimates of switching from SPRB coal, with the FTC examining variation in the price of coal caused by a 2020 tax increase,[33] and defendants examining variation in the price of coal relative to that of natural gas.[34] The court found the FTC's quantitative assessments more credible, and noted the "HMT's usefulness as an analytical tool for determining how to define the relevant product market."[35]

384. In our view, this example illustrates two principles. First, the court attempted to trace differing interpretations of quantitative evidence back to differences in modelling or assumptions, and to understand which approaches were more credible. The opinion appears to pinpoint modelling differences and to explain why the court found the FTC's modelling more persuasive. Second, market definition is most probative when qualitative and quantitative factors point in the same direction. In this matter, *Brown Shoe* indicia appeared to complement HMT analyses, strengthening the court's conclusions.

385. Ultimately, we believe that both *Brown Shoe* indicia and quantitative evidence can be useful tools for defining markets and explaining competitive dynamics within those markets. However, as the case studies we have provided illustrate, an HMT based on quantitative evidence of customer switching provides more objective evidence that is appropriately preferred to *Brown Shoe* indicia when available. When data on switching are unavailable, as may be the case with mergers involving new or rapidly evolving products, it is appropriate to increase the weight placed on *Brown Shoe* factors. However, we believe they are more impactful if testimony or

30 *Id.* at 36.

31 *Id.* at 26.

32 *Id.* at 27–28.

33 *Id.* at 34.

34 *Id.* at 31.

35 *Id.* at 35.

other qualitative evidence clearly supports their connection to the HMT. While the draft guidelines do not indicate when the Agencies will give greater emphasis to one or the other source of evidence for market definition, we view courts as likely to consider *Brown Shoe* factors but to continue to prefer rigorous implementations of the HMT when available.

III. Non-Horizontal Mergers

386. Most merger-related litigation concerns horizontal transactions, which combine firms that provide (or are at least alleged to provide) the same type(s) of product to the same type(s) of customer. However, mergers can also be non-horizontal in nature when they involve products that are not directly substitutable.

387. One type of non-horizontal transaction is known as a "vertical" merger. Vertical mergers integrate a buyer and seller of a given product. For example, a manufacturer acquiring a retailer of its products would represent a vertical merger. Clearly, the manufacturer and the retailer are not directly competing. But they interact with each other as the retailer purchases products from the manufacturer to sell to final consumers.

388. Another form of non-horizontal transaction that may give rise to competition effects is a "conglomerate" merger, whereby the merging parties sell complementary products that are sometimes consumed with each other or are otherwise "related."[36] An example of a transaction combining complements would be the merger of a computer hardware maker and a software publisher. The hardware and software firms do not directly compete with each other. However, demand for software and hardware is related since computer hardware is more valuable when paired with high quality software and vice versa.[37]

389. Although vertical and conglomerate transactions often are discussed separately, their underlying economics are quite similar. That is because a vertical relationship is simply a specific form of complementarity.[38] Whether the different products are part of the same production chain,

36 *See, e.g.*, discussion in United States, "Conglomerate effects of mergers – Note by the United States" (2020), https://www.ftc.gov/system/files/attachments/us-submissions-oecd-2010-present-other-international-competition-fora/oecd-conglomerate_mergers_us_submission.pdf. *See also*, European Union, "Conglomerate effects of mergers – Note by the European Union" (2020), https://one.oecd.org/document/DAF/COMP/WD(2020)8/en/pdf. We are using the term "conglomerate merger" to refer to mergers of complements. We agree with the Agencies' submission to the OECD that "Conglomerate mergers that raise neither vertical nor horizontal concerns are unlikely to be problematic under U.S. merger Law."

37 Other examples of products that have been lumped into discussions of "conglomerate" mergers include products that only sometimes (or even rarely) are consumed together by end consumers but are purchased together by intermediaries, such as grocery products that are not strong complements or substitutes but would be purchased together by grocery retailers after their merger, or pharmaceuticals that are rarely purchased together by end consumers but potentially share positions on health plan formularies. Theories of harm related to such products still are developing but most likely would stem from relationships between the products for intermediaries as opposed to end consumers.

38 When final consumers' demand for merging parties' products is uncorrelated, there will generally not be any reason to anticipate competitive effects. *See, e.g.*, Michael D. Whinston, *Tying, Foreclosure, and Exclusion*, 80 Am. Econ. Rev. 837–59 (1990).

and thus vertically related, as opposed to being sold separately but often consumed in combination, and thus categorized as conglomerate, is not important for the economic assessment of incentives.[39]

390. Guideline 5 in the 2023 Guidelines describes how the Agencies assess both vertical and conglomerate transactions "non-horizontal" transactions. Guideline 5 is focused on complementary transactions of all kinds and mandates that "mergers can violate the law when they create a firm that may limit access to products or service that its rivals use to compete." For Guideline 5, the underlying concern is that when complementary products are combined inside the same firm there may be an incentive for the merged firm to change how it treats unaffiliated rivals that ultimately harms consumers.

391. The economic basis for Guideline 5 is mixed, at best. On the one hand, in some cases, the ultimate impact on consumers from the internalization by the merging parties of the impact of their respective products' prices (or characteristics) on the profits of those of the merger partner may be harmful. Thus, there is a basis for scrutinizing whether a given non-horizontal transaction will result from some form of raising rivals' costs. However, the 2023 Guidelines ignore that this same process of internalization also creates procompetitive incentives. Below, we briefly discuss how non-horizontal transactions give rise to these contrasting impulses.

392. The intuition for how and why non-horizontal transactions may be anticompetitive is straightforward. For example, a vertical merger may cause an upstream firm to realize that its downstream merger party would benefit if the upstream firm charged a higher wholesale price to the downstream firm's rivals (or cut them off entirely).[40] Such price increases would be expected to cause the downstream rivals to raise their prices to cover their higher costs, which in turn could lead some final customers to decide to switch to the downstream merger partner's product. In either circumstance, affected final consumers would be worse off relative to the pre-merger world.

393. Analogously, a conglomerate transaction could lead the combined firm to increase the price of one of its products when it would be used in conjunction with those of rival firms (or render its products entirely incompatible with those of rivals). Once more, the antitrust concern would be that the combined firm's action would weaken competition as rivals' products would be at a disadvantage relative to the pre-merger world. That is because consumers would have to pay extra for the merged firm's products when used with rivals (if the option remained available at all).

394. The basic logic for why integrating complements can have important procompetitive effects is similar. When demand for two products is correlated

39 However, there may be important differences between vertical and conglomerate transactions insofar as there may be variation in the combined firm's practical ability to accomplish certain strategies depending on whether one party's product is a direct input into others' or is simply a complement.

40 *See, e.g.*, Michael A. Salinger, *Vertical Mergers and Market Foreclosure*, 103 Q.J. Econ. 345–56 (1988). *See also*, Jay P. Choi, *Mergers with Bundling in Complementary Markets*, 56 J. Indus. Econ. 553–77 (2008).

and both products face downward sloping demand curves, meaning that the seller earns a margin on each sale, the end price to consumers will be lower if the same firm controls both products. This is because lowering the price of one of the goods encourages consumption of both products, a benefit that financial integration encourages that separate ownership does not.[41] The incentive to lower the final price is often characterized in the economic literature as a stemming from the "elimination of double marginalization" (EDM). In addition to benefits stemming from EDM, economic theory and evidence shows that non-horizontal transactions may also be associated with other benefits, such as reductions in transactions costs and/or increased investment in quality improvements.[42]

395. In general, non-horizontal transactions will simultaneously give rise to both types of incentive, the procompetitive and the anticompetitive. In other words, there will be some incentive for the merged firm to use their control of products used by or in conjunction with the products of rivals to reduce the competitiveness of those rivals' products. Simultaneously, there will be downward pressure on the price of the bundle of the combined firm's products or (in the case of a vertical merger) on the price of the final good (in addition to possibly other beneficial effects). These contrasting impulses, in turn, will interact with each other, leading to an overall impact on competition and consumers that is theoretically ambiguous and deeply dependent on the specific nature of competition in a given market.[43]

396. Further compounding the complexity is the fact that standard economics shows that the types of situations that can give rise to raising rivals' costs concerns are often also associated with the greatest scope for price reductions. For example, when an upstream firm earns a very sizable margin, it may have the ability to increase prices to downstream rivals of its merger partner. However, the same circumstances would be expected to give rise to a large EDM effect, so the merger may benefit consumers on balance because any raising rivals cost effects are outweighed by EDM (or other benefits).[44]

---

41 The essence of this insight dates back to Antoine-Augustin Cournot, Researches into the Mathematical Principles of the Theory of Wealth (1838).

42 *See generally* Oliver E. Williamson, *The Vertical Integration of Production: Market Failure Considerations*, 61 Am. Econ. Rev. (1971) (discussing efficiency motivations for integration). *See also*, Mark A. Israel & Daniel P. O'Brien, *Vertical Mergers with Bilateral Contracting and Upstream and Downstream Investment*, (July 13, 2021), https://papers.ssrn.com/sol3/papers.cfm?abstract_id=3886048.

43 Steven C. Salop, *Invigorating Vertical Merger Enforcement*, 127 Yale L. J. 1962–94, 1974 (2018) ("In short, in the real world of imperfectly competitive markets, the direction of the net competitive effect is a question of fact, not theory. While vertical mergers in oligopoly markets should not be subject to near-per se illegality, they also are not entitled to near-per se legality. Both of these per se rules would lead to unacceptable errors. Instead, competitive-effects analysis, enforcement, and law should be balanced and fact-based"). However, at least with linear demand, the result is generally to the benefit of final consumers. *See, e.g.*, Michael A. Salinger, *The Complicated Simple Economics of Vertical Mergers* (May 1, 2021), https://papers.ssrn.com/sol3/papers.cfm?abstract_id=3799273.

44 Daniel P. O'Brien, *Tethering Vertical Merger Analysis*, CPI Antitrust Chron. (Mar. 18, 2022), https://papers.ssrn.com/sol3/papers.cfm?abstract_id=4061410. That fact patterns seemingly consistent with an ability to foreclose may also imply strong incentives to act in pro-competitive ways makes the 2023 Guideline's assertion that vertical mergers involving an upstream firm with a 50% or larger market share are presumptively anticompetitive especially concerning from an economic point of view (2023 Guidelines, n.30).

397. Consistent with this theoretical ambiguity, an expanding empirical literature underscores that there is no clear argument that non-horizontal transactions are *typically* on net harmful to consumers.[45] The 2023 Guidelines de-emphasize this nuance by consigning EDM to a footnote, describing EDM as "a common rebuttal argument" subject to the processes described in Section 3.3. of the 2023 Guidelines for the analysis of efficiencies.[46]

398. To understand how both anticompetitive and procompetitive effects may arise in the context of a non-horizontal transaction, as well as the importance of a detailed, fact-specific interrogation of which effect dominates, it is useful to think about these issues in the context of a specific case. Consider the 2017 challenge by the DOJ of AT&T's proposed acquisition of Time Warner (TW). At the time, AT&T–TW was notable as the first litigation of a non-horizontal transaction in decades. Since that time, however, non-horizontal merger challenges have become more common, including United Healthcare–Change, Meta–Within, Microsoft–Activision, Amgen–Horizon, and IQVIA–Propel Media.

399. AT&T–TW was a vertical transaction in the sense that TW content is an input into TV packages offered by providers such as AT&T's DirecTV, Comcast, and Cox. The DOJ's central theory of harm was that the merger would lead to cable providers paying higher prices for TW content, which ultimately would result in consumers paying higher quality-adjusted prices for their cable packages. The prices paid by cable companies like DirecTV or Comcast to content providers like TW generally are set via bargaining wherein all aspects of the transaction are subject to negotiation. This stands in contrast with how business is conducted in many consumer-facing industries where firms "post" their prices and then consumers buy – or don't buy – as much as they want at that price.

400. The economics of bargaining can be thorny. While there may be broad agreement on some core tenets – e.g., neither party accepts terms that leave it worse off than not transacting and parties do not leave available surplus unclaimed – the ways that mergers affect outcomes when prices are negotiated can be particularly dependent on factors that are difficult to measure. For example, a key element may be what each party earns should they fail to reach agreement. These "disagreement" payoffs – and how they impact prices – were at the core of AT&T–TW.

401. The government specifically attributed predicted price increases to a change in the leverage that TW would possess in its negotiations with

---

45 *See, e.g.*, Marissa Beck & Fiona M. Scott Morton, *Evaluating the Evidence on Vertical Mergers*, 59 Rev. Indus. Org. 273–302 (2021). *See also*, Francine Lafontaine &Margaret E. Slade, *Presumptions in Vertical Mergers: The Role of Evidence*, 59 Rev. Indus. Org. 255–72 (2021).

46 Defenders of the 2023 Guidelines may claim that EDM is indeed like any other potential cost-saving efficiency, and should be scrutinized as such under Section 3.3. We disagree. As discussed in the body of this chapter, the procompetitive incentives that arise from non-horizontal mergers stem from the same internalization of effects on product demand as potentially give rise to anti-competitive effects. In other words, they involve no alterations to the nature of the combined firm or other aspects of the market. As such, we do not see how it makes sense to impose a seemingly different evidentiary standard – as suggested by Section 3.3 – for EDM and other procompetitive impulses than the 2023 Guidelines appear to require for anticompetitive ones.

cable providers. The DOJ alleged that when TW became integrated with AT&T, which owned DirecTV, it would have less to lose from a breakdown in negotiations over the price of TW content. A breakdown that led to TW content not being on a cable provider at all could cause some customers of Comcast (or other cable providers) to switch to DirecTV so they could continue consuming TW content, and this switching would allow AT&T to recoup some of the profits lost by TW when negotiations broke down. It should be noted that the DOJ did not dispute that the combined firm would suffer from the loss of revenue from Comcast (or other cable providers) if agreement could not be reached, but argued that the shift in relative outcomes would lead to an increase in negotiated rates. In other words, because disagreement would not be quite so bad for TW as previously, they would be able to extract a higher fee.

402. Meanwhile, the merging parties emphasized the scope for lower prices through the internalization of the complementarity between TW and DirecTV leading to procompetitive effects through via EDM. Pre-merger, when TW negotiated with DirecTV, the two entities did not recognize that a lower cost of TW content as part of a package would lead to greater utilization of DirecTV.[47] However, post-merger, this relationship would be recognized. Thus, while DirecTV would continue to pay a "transfer" fee to TW for its content, the merger would incentivize TW and DirecTV to set the transfer price to maximize corporate-wide profits, rather than the profits of TW in isolation, as TW did before the merger. Because any transfer price from DirecTV to TW does not directly affect corporate-wide profits (just where those profits are booked), while a lower transfer price makes DirecTV more competitive with its rivals, economic theory predicts that the combined company should optimally lower the transfer price all the way down to TW's cost, "selling" the content at zero margin to DirecTV. This lower cost would increase DirecTV's margin, incentivizing it to increase sales, by lowering price. Ultimately, the elimination of the TW margin benefits not only DirecTV, but its consumers.

403. In some ways, AT&T–TW provided the framework for subsequent non-horizontal transactions. The antitrust authorities focused on the scope for raising rivals' costs, and the merging parties emphasized benefits from the internalization of multiple margins. However, in other ways, the case stands apart. That is because in contrast to subsequent challenges, there was broad agreement between the litigants over the underlying economics. For example, the government's expert, Dr. Carl Shapiro, acknowledged that the transaction would lead to an incentive to lower DirecTV's costs, which would benefit consumers.[48] However, he opined that this effect

47 Analogously, lower DirecTV prices could lead to more subscribers that would result in higher payments to TW.

48 *See, e.g.*, Expert Report of Carl Shapiro § 10 (Feb. 2, 2018), https://www.justice.gov/atr/case-document/file/1081336/download. ("The proposed merger may also create an incentive for DTV to lower its price to subscribers if that lower price would benefit Turner by expanding the number of viewers with access to Turner Content. Prior to the merger, DTV does not account for this potentially positive effect on Turner's profits

would not dominate the price increasing effects that the transaction also would give rise to. Meanwhile, the defendants disputed the materiality of the marginal change in disagreement payoffs identified by Dr. Shapiro and the DOJ. In short, they focused on whether the evidence supported the government's argument that if failing to reach agreement with Comcast shifted from being awful to slightly less awful for TW then TW would be able to extract meaningfully higher payments.

404. In other words, both the DOJ and the parties recognized that non-horizontal transactions are complex, involving incentives to boost, as well as hinder, competition. They just disagreed with how best to think about the net effect of these contrasting impulses.

405. Ultimately, the parties prevailed in convincing Judge Leon of the DC District Court that the transaction would not violate the antitrust laws. It is difficult to pin down precisely why, but a number of factors appear in Judge Leon's opinion as influential. First, the fact that there had never been a breakdown in negotiations between TW and a cable provider meant that there was no data for the DOJ to leverage as to just how important TW content was to subscribers, which would affect their propensity to switch to DirecTV. This necessitated the use of survey data, which ultimately proved unsatisfying.[49]

406. Second, the defense was able to point to a number of instances of vertical integration which had not led to price increases. Although the DOJ noted that these past instances also involved antitrust or regulatory interventions that may have been instrumental in forestalling effects, the defense was able to point to the fact that they had committed themselves to "baseball-style arbitration" in the event of disagreements. This voluntary resolution resembled the regulatory interventions to the past transactions. Thus, the defense was able to argue that past experience showed that the instant transaction would not result in harm to consumers or competition.[50]

407. Third, TW had long-term contracts with several cable companies. The fact that these contracts would continue to be in force for some time implied that any consumer harms would not occur for some time. In contrast, the potential benefits from internalizing the presence of two margins would be immediate. The parties argued that Dr. Shapiro did not account for this temporal aspect.[51]

---

when setting its price. After the merger, if the resulting expansion of DTV subscribers benefits Turner, then the combined DTV and Turner would find it profitable to decrease price to some degree.")

49 U.S. v. AT&T Inc., 310 F. Supp. 3d 161, 123–29 (D.D.C. 2018). *See also*, Jonathan M. Barnett, *A major telecommunications company resolves to unwind a failed acquisition of a mass media and entertainment conglomerate, notwithstanding rulings greenlighting the merger at both District Court and Appeals Court level (AT&T/Time Warner)*, E-COMPETITIONS May 2021, art. No. 108426.

50 *AT&T Inc.*, 310 F. Supp. 3d 161, 99–108. *See also*, Nathaniel L. Asker et al., *The US District Court for the District of Columbia rejects the DOJ's challenge to a vertical merger in the entertainment sector (AT&T/Time Warner)*, E-COMPETITIONS June 2018, art. No. 90032.

51 *Id.*, at 146–48.

408. Fourth, Judge Leon appears not to have been convinced by the DOJ's arguments about how modest variation in disagreement payoffs as a result of the merger would lead to material differences in negotiated outcomes. In particular, in footnote 36, he notes as "particularly persuasive" the TW CEO's comment that the threat of a 950lb weight falling on one's head may be perceived as quite similar to the threat of a 1000lb weight.[52] In other words, a blackout wherein TW's content was not available on a cable provider would remain catastrophic for both sides after the merger. Therefore, in Judge Leon's view, the integration with DirecTV provided no incremental leverage that could be used in actual negotiations.[53]

409. Reasonable minds may disagree with the outcome of AT&T–TW – as they may on many litigations.[54] But it seems hard to dispute that Judge Leon's 172-page opinion engaged seriously with the record evidence and addressed a general view of competition that was agreed to by all sides. That seems like a procedural outcome that all participants in the antitrust ecosystem should cheer. Given their predominantly one-sided portrayal of non-horizontal transactions, we fear that non-horizontal cases brought as guided by the 2023 Guidelines will involve less substantive debate than was observed in AT&T–TW, as well as possibly cause the Agencies to focus investigations on factors other than those that are likely to be at issue in litigation.

410. As has been described elsewhere, the myopic view of non-horizontal mergers articulated in the 2023 Guidelines seems predicated on the belief that nuance unduly favors the merging parties.[55] Based on the Agencies' track record in their vertical challenges since AT&T–TW, wherein the Agencies have generally dismissed the procompetitive rationales for and implications of non-horizontal transactions, we think that acknowledging only a fraction of the effects that economics predicts is not the route to more successful enforcement. In our experience, courts do not lack common sense. This matters as common sense as well as basic economic principles point to the potential for material benefits from integrating complements. Consequently, we anticipate that courts will be loath to dismiss these without firmer showing that they are outweighed by anticompetitive effects, which will generally involve a forthright grappling with the fact that non-horizontal transactions may benefit as well as harm competition.

52 *Id.*, at n.36.

53 *Id.*, at 111–17.

54 For the pro-enforcement perspective, see Carl Shapiro, *Vertical Mergers and Input Foreclosure Lessons from the AT&T/Time Warner Case*, 59 Rev. Indus. Org. 303–41 (2021). For the defense's side, see Dennis W. Carlton et al., *A Retrospective Analysis of the AT&T/Time Warner Merger*, 65 J.L. Econ. S461-S498 (2022).

55 *See, e.g.*, Mark A. Israel et al., *Guidelines Lacking Guidance: Improving the FTC/DOJ Draft Merger Guidelines*, (Oct. 16, 2023), https://papers.ssrn.com/sol3/papers.cfm?abstract_id=4575390. *See also*, Daniel Francis, *Comments on the 2023 Draft Merger Guidelines*, (Sept. 12, 2023), https://papers.ssrn.com/sol3/papers.cfm?abstract_id=4569469. For broadly similar views, see Jonathan B. Baker et al., *Comments of Economists and Lawyers on the Draft Merger Guidelines*, (Sept. 18, 2023), https://papers.ssrn.com/sol3/papers.cfm?abstract_id=4574947.

IV. Efficiencies

411. Economists have long recognized that improvements in economic efficiency often can be a natural outcome of mergers. Most basically, merging firms can take advantage of each other's strengths in ways they cannot when operating as independent entities. Consistent with this, the different Merger Guidelines have historically recognized merger efficiencies, both implicitly and explicitly. The 2023 Guidelines move the line on both implicit and explicit recognition of merger efficiencies in a direction that would give efficiencies less credit in merger investigations. In our view, the new standard lacks a clear empirical foundation.

412. Implicit recognition of merger efficiencies is evident from the fact that neither antitrust authorities nor courts advocate that *every* merger be blocked.[56] That is, in the case of horizontal mergers, absent efficiencies, as a matter of basic economics every merger reduces competition and causes upward price pressure. And, in the case of vertical mergers, absent EDM and other procompetitive benefits, nearly every merger raises foreclosure concerns. Hence, Merger Guidelines' establishment of market concentration thresholds above which a merger raises competitive concerns could be interpreted as an implicit recognition of merger efficiencies.[57]

413. Merger efficiency benefits have also explicitly been recognized in Merger Guidelines. That is, although guidelines have expressed varying degrees of skepticism about merging parties' efficiency claims, recognition that merger benefits are possible has explicitly been written in Merger Guidelines, including the 2023 Guidelines. However, the 2023 Guidelines show greater reluctance to recognize merger efficiencies than previous versions in at least two ways.

414. First, the 2023 Guidelines have reduced the measures of market concentration and changes in market concentration that create a "presumption" that a merger may substantially reduce competition. Specifically, the 2023 Guidelines move the thresholds for post-merger Herfindahl–Hirschman Index (HHI) and change in HHI for such significant concern down from 2500/200 in the 2010 Guidelines to 1800/100.[58] The 2023 Guidelines also add a new threshold for the merging parties' combined market share following a horizontal merger of 30%, that "presents an undue threat of undue concentration," regardless of whether post-merger market

---

56 *See also*, Frederick R. Warren-Boulton, *Merger Policy and Enforcement at the Antitrust Division: The Economist's View*, 54 Antitrust L.J. 109–16, 112 (1985) ("I should preface this discussion by saying that the very existence of 'safe harbor' Herfindahls in the Guidelines already implies a 'standard deduction' for efficiencies. Such a standard deduction is implicit in a policy that allows mergers that increase concentration to some extent, even without a showing of any efficiency gains").

57 In a November 2010 speech as Deputy Assistant Attorney General, Carl Shapiro made this recognition more explicit, suggesting a 5% "safe harbor" for gross upward pricing pressure, noting "[t]he 'safe harbor' outlined here does not indicate any tolerance for anti-competitive price increases[; r]ather, it reflects the fact that a small amount of upward pricing pressure is unlikely, at the end of the day, to correspond to any actual post-merger price increase." (*See* https://www.justice.gov/atr/file/518246/download, at 24–25.)

58 2010 Guidelines, at § V; 2023 Guidelines, at § II.1.

concentration is less than 1800.[59] Hence, a merger between two of six equally sized firms that would not have triggered a structural presumption in the 2010 Guidelines is condemned by the 2023 Guidelines. As described above, this movement of the structural thresholds implicitly gives less credit to merger efficiencies.

415. Second, the 2023 Guidelines set burdens of proof for explicit merger efficiency claims that generally are more challenging to meet than in previous Guidelines.

416. Agency doubts about merging parties' efficiency claims are not new. Merging parties have incentives to make self-serving efficiency claims, and thus it is reasonable for the Agencies to be wary of such claims. Moreover, it is often more difficult for the Agencies to gain information on likely merger efficiencies than it is to gain information on likely competitive effects. Hence, the 2023 Guidelines are not the first iteration of the Guidelines to treat merger efficiencies with a healthy dose of skepticism.

417. That said, the 2023 Guidelines have added some new challenges to merger efficiency claims. First, although previous Guidelines have required efficiencies to be merger-specific, which in our experience meant that the efficiencies are a direct outcome of the merger, the 2023 Guidelines have added language that shift the merger-specific requirement more toward "merger-required." For example, the 2023 Guidelines characterize merger-specificity as achieving procompetitive benefits that "could not be achieved" without the merger, as compared to the 2010 Guidelines characterization of efficiencies that are "unlikely to be accomplished" in the absence of the merger.[60] The 2023 Guidelines list out potential alternative means to achieving merger efficiencies as including: "organic growth of one of the merging firms, contracts between them, mergers with others, or a partial merger involving only those assets that give rise to the procompetitive efficiencies."[61] The 2023 Guidelines also remove a sentence from the 1997 and 2010 Guidelines that stated that the Agencies do not "insist upon a less restrictive alternative that is merely theoretical."[62]

418. Second, while previous Guidelines required merging parties to substantiate efficiency claims so that "the Agencies can verify by reasonable means the likelihood and magnitude of each asserted efficiency,"[63] the 2023 Guidelines introduce language that appears to shift the burden and requires greater certainty in the evaluation of efficiency claims, i.e., that efficiency claims "have been verified, using reliable methodology not

59 2023 Guidelines, at § II.1. *Id.* n.30 also appears to create a structural threshold for vertical mergers of a "50 percent" "foreclosure share." It is unclear to us what exactly this means and thus we do not consider its importance in the assessment of merger efficiencies.

60 *Id.* at § 3.3; 2010 Guidelines, at § 10.

61 2023 Guidelines, at § 3.3.

62 1997 Guidelines, at § 4; 2010 Guidelines, at § 10.

63 *See, e.g.*, 2010 Guidelines, at § 10.

dependent on the subjective predictions of the merging parties."[64] The 2023 Guidelines further introduce a novel claim that "[p]rocompetitive efficiencies are often speculative" and remove a sentence from previous Guidelines stating that "efficiency claims substantiated by analogous past experience are those most likely to be credible."[65]

419. Third, the 2023 Guidelines impose new dimensions on which merger efficiencies must be demonstrated to be "not anticompetitive."[66] These requirements are written:

> Any benefits claimed by the merging parties are cognizable only if they do not result from the anticompetitive worsening of terms for the merged firm's trading partners.[67]

420. There is a footnote to this requirement noting that "[t]he Agencies will not credit efficiencies if they reflect or require a decrease in competition in a separate market. For example, if input costs are expected to decrease, the cost savings will not be treated as an efficiency if they reflect an increase in monopsony power."[68]

421. These new requirements present a stark set of conditions that would not necessarily result in competitive outcomes or even allow for the acknowledgment of efficiencies. The following examples illustrate how efficiencies analyses have affected past matters.

422. **Anthem–Cigna (2017):** In the proposed Anthem–Cigna merger, the merging parties claimed that the merger would create benefits because the combined firm would have increased bargaining leverage in negotiations with healthcare providers through which it would negotiate better terms of service that it could pass on to customers. The DOJ argued that any better terms negotiated by the combined firm should not count as a merger efficiency because they would derive from increased monopsony power. An economic expert for the parties, Dr. Mark Israel, proposed a three-part test to distinguish procompetitive price reductions from monopsony power. These parts were: (i) decreases in the negotiated price of healthcare services will be passed through to consumers in the form of lower insurance prices, (ii) output, i.e., the quantity of insurance plans purchased, will not decrease, and (iii) healthcare services prices will remain above the applicable competitive level.[69]

---

64 2023 Guidelines, at § 3.3.

65 *Id.*

66 *Id.*

67 *Id.*

68 *Id.*

69 Mark A. Israel, *Are You Pushing Too Hard? Lower Negotiated Input Prices as a Merger Efficiency*, 82 Antitrust L. J. 623–42 (2019) describes this level of costs as follows: "As a matter of economics, the competitive level is the price that yields zero economic profits. In practice, this means that the price is high enough to cover marginal accounting costs and to cover a firm's weighted average cost of capital (WACC). Put differently, it is the price that enables a firm to cover its costs and earn a competitive return on investments." (*Id.* at n.3).

423. Dr. Israel presented evidence that procurement savings that would occur through the Anthem–Cigna merger would satisfy the three parts of his proposed test and thus would be a merger benefit. Although the court ruled that efficiencies failed for other reasons (merger-specificity and verifiability), it also expressed skepticism that the claimed lower procurement savings should count as an efficiency because it saw them as deriving from an increase in monopsony power.[70]

424. The new requirements in the 2023 Guidelines are consistent with Dr. Israel's proposed tests but may be significantly and unduly more burdensome. For instance, part (i) of Dr. Israel's test resembles the pass-through requirement in the 2023 Guidelines and previous Guidelines.[71] Parts (ii) and (iii) coincide with the "not anticompetitive" requirement in the 2023 Guidelines and the attached footnote. That is, parts (ii) and (iii) of Dr. Israel's proposed test would be failed when insurance prices would be pushed below the competitive level or the quantity/quality of insurance plans is reduced. The 2023 Guidelines language quoted above may align exactly with Dr. Israel's test if the "*anticompetitive* worsening of terms" can be understood to mean prices below the competitive level and/or a reduction in quantity or quality of output.[72] However, the footnote attached to the quoted text goes a step further, suggesting that the Agencies will not credit any price decreases that derive from increased bargaining leverage gained through merger.[73] That is, the 2023 Guidelines appear to propose that input price reductions that are passed through to consumers and increase output will not be considered if they derive from an increase in the merging parties' share of purchases in input markets. This is not necessarily a new agency position, but it represents a strengthening of the language in the 2010 Guidelines, which expressed skepticism toward but allowed for the possibility of efficiencies from lower input prices.[74]

425. **Rite Aid–Eckerd (2007):** In its post-transaction press release, Rite Aid noted that with increased scale it would better be able to compete with its major drug store rivals, as "[w]ith a much larger Rite Aid, we're confident we will have substantial opportunities to reduce costs…."[75] Under the 2023 Guidelines, such economies of scale, even if resulting in a more competitive combined firm, could be viewed with skepticism given Guideline 7, which expresses concerns about mergers that continue a trend

70 *See, e.g.*, United States v. Anthem, Inc., 236 F. Supp. 3d 253 (D.D.C. 2017). *See also*, Clifford H. Aronson et al., *The US District Court for the District of Columbia blocks two proposed mergers in the insurance sector brought and litigated under the Obama administration (Aetna/Humana and Anthem / Cigna)*, E-COMPETITIONS Feb. 2017, art. N° 83761.

71 2023 Guidelines, at § 3.3; 2010 Guidelines, at § 10.

72 2023 Guidelines, at § 3.3.

73 *Id.*

74 2010 Guidelines, at § 10 ("Yet other [cost savings], such as those relating to *procurement*, management, or capital cost, are less likely to be merger-specific or substantial, or may not be cognizable for other reasons.")

75 Rite Aid Press Release, Rite Aid Completes Acquisition of 1,854 Brooks and Eckerd Stores, (June 4, 2007), https://www.sec.gov/Archives/edgar/data/84129/000134100407001770/exhibit99_1.htm

of increased concentration wholly distinct from changes in competition or outcomes for consumers.

426. Taking Rite Aid's statements at face value, it was struggling to compete with larger, growing chains, suggesting those chains were able to achieve lower costs through scale economies. However, if it is true that larger retail pharmacy firms are in general more efficient, a merger that is driven by a procompetitive incentive to lower costs and compete more effectively may result in both increased scale and concentration.

427. It is unclear how the Agencies would evaluate the Rite Aid–Eckerd situation under the 2023 Guidelines. But we worry that the 2023 Draft Guideline's statement that efficiencies are not cognizable if they "accelerate a trend toward concentration," would mean that a primary claimed efficiency of the Rite Aid–Eckerd transaction would not be credited, since such efficiencies by definition result in increased concentration.[76]

V. Conclusion

428. We see some helpful changes in the 2023 Guidelines, both relative to the 2023 Draft Guidelines and relative to past Guidelines. However, in other cases, we worry that they echo the Draft Guidelines in giving greater weight to qualitative, noneconomic evidence and presumptions than did past Guidelines. In places, this change in emphasis may have the effect of suggesting the reasonableness of substituting qualitative for quantitative evidence, or of downgrading the importance of basic economic principles. We hope the discussion and examples in this paper begin to illustrate the value of quantitative, economic evidence, and its role in the analysis of mergers. For decades, such economic evidence has helped the Agencies bring and win cases, including matters in which the qualitative evidence was ambiguous. While a shift to bright-line rules would seem to lower the Agencies' burden in bringing merger challenges, it may also result in the Agencies and parties focusing on issues unlikely to be pivotal in litigation, and thus ultimately serve to undermine enforcement.

76 2023 Draft Guidelines, at 34.

The Evolution (and Devolution) of Market Structure Reasoning

SEAN P. SULLIVAN*
University of Iowa College of Law

* Professor of Law & Bauma Faculty Fellow in Law, University of Iowa College of Law.

I. Introduction

429. "The language of a nation," wrote F.L. Lucas, "like the land it lives by, needs constant cultivation and weeding."[1] Untended evolution was as likely to degrade language, in Lucas's experience, as it was to improve it. Lucas was specifically concerned with linguistic style, here, but his warning about the frailty of accomplishment was more general. "Such indeed is the common law of life," he groaned, "It is only too easy to go downhill. Oysters and barnacles once had heads."[2]

430. We may quibble whether crustacea really need our pity, but Lucas's broader point finds powerful application in decisional law, where clarity and grace are always as fleeting as a fact pattern, and where the downhill slide of one clumsily reasoned decision or policy statement can corrupt in an instant what took years of labor to develop. Untended evolution is particularly fraught for merger law, complex and fact specific as it is, and even more so for this law's reliance on market structure reasoning. Little in merger law can boast the tenure or pedigree of structural reasoning. And nothing is in greater need of weeding.

431. Since the late 1960s, U.S. federal antitrust agencies have enjoyed the opportunity, and tacit approval, to gently guide merger law along its evolutionary path in the form of published merger guidelines, statements, and revisions. The Agencies have contributed much to merger law in this way but have often trembled to prune it. As market structure reasoning has been allowed to grow more of less untended since 1968, decades of growth, overgrowth, and decay are now on display in the variety of structural inferences in the 2023 Merger Guidelines.[3] This chapter surveys the evolution and devolution of market structure reasoning in the Merger Guidelines, starting in 1968 and ending with the insights and errors of the 2023 update.

II. Four Evaluative Criteria

432. Because market structure reasoning spans seven decades and nearly as many schools of thought in the Merger Guidelines, we might start with some criteria that can be used to evaluate the quality of this reasoning over time. The following four propositions are dryly descriptive accounts of antitrust law, economics, and logical reasoning. They should not be contentious. They are, however, for various reasons, frequently forgotten and ignored.

---

1 Frank L. Lucas, The Art of Writing Well 24 (3rd ed. 2012).

2 *Id.*; *see also* Frank L. Lucas, *Party of One*, Holiday, Mar. 1960, at 11 ("Languages evolve like species. They can degenerate; just as oysters and barnacles have lost their heads.").

3 Fed. Trade Comm'n and U.S. Dep't. of Justice, *Merger Guidelines* (2023) ("2023 Guidelines").

433. First, aside from the structural consequence of a merger itself – reallocating ownership of competitive assets from one firm to another – market structure and concentration information should not be treated as having direct significance in U.S. merger law. This follows from the plain language of the statutory standard. Section 7 of the Clayton Act proscribes mergers for their effects on competition, not their effects on concentration.[4] Changes in numbers of competitors, in market shares, and in concentration can all be relevant and important considerations – but only to the extent that they help us understand the competitive effects of mergers – not as ultimate objectives themselves.

434. The legal record on this point is not interestingly varied. True, some Warren Court opinions included strong language about market concentration. *Brown Shoe* embellished the text of Section 7 with the gloss that Congress hoped the statute would help maintain "fragmented industries and markets."[5] In *Von's Grocery*, the Court extended this embellishment to the Sherman Act,[6] and in *Philadelphia National Bank* it invoked "Congress' design in § 7 to prevent undue concentration"[7] as justifying heavy reliance on market structure evidence.[8] But these statements are outliers against decades of prior and subsequent statements, in both merger law and broader antitrust law, that show how market structure informs competitive effects, rather than constitutes it. Examples include the statement that markets should be defined in ways that help evaluate effects on competition,[9] that market shares should be assigned in ways that help predict effects on competition,[10] that market shares should be used to predict competitive dynamics and market power,[11] and that effects

4 Clayton Act, ch. 323, § 7, 38 Stat. 730, 731–32 (1914) (current version at 15 U.S.C. § 18 (2022)) (prohibiting mergers, "the effect [of which] may be substantially to lessen competition, or to tend to create a monopoly").

5 Brown Shoe Co. v. United States, 370 U.S. 294, 344 (1962).

6 United States v. Von's Grocery Co., 384 U.S. 270, 275 (1966) ("Like the Sherman Act in 1890 … the basic purpose of the 1950 Celler-Kefauver Act was to prevent economic concentration in the American economy by keeping a large number of small competitors in business.").

7 United States v. Phila. Nat'l Bank, 374 U.S. 321, 363 (1963).

8 Conflation of concentration and competition was also a frequent occurrence. *E.g.*, United States v. Pabst Brewing Co., 384 U.S. 546, 552 (1966) ("Congress, in passing s 7 and in amending it … was concerned with arresting concentration in the American economy, whatever its cause."); United States v. Cont'l Can Co., 378 U.S. 441, 458 (1964) ("Where a merger is of such a size as to be inherently suspect, elaborate proof of market structure, market behavior and probable anticompetitive effects may be dispensed with in view of § 7's design to prevent undue concentration.").

9 FTC v. Indiana Fed'n of Dentists, 476 U.S. 447, 460 (1986) ("[T]he purpose of … inquiries into market definition and market power is to determine whether an arrangement has the potential for genuine adverse effects on competition.")

10 United States v. Gen. Dynamics Corp., 415 U.S. 486, 503 (1974) (instructing that market shares should be computed to reflect firms' "probable future ability to compete"); *id.* at 510 (affirming the lower court's discretion to reject competitive effects inferences drawn from market share that were not "proper indicators of future ability to compete").

11 United States v. Grinnell Corp., 384 U.S. 563, 571 (1966) ("The existence of [power to control prices or exclude competition] ordinarily *may be inferred* from the predominant share of the market." (emphasis added)); United States v. Baker Hughes Inc., 908 F.2d 981, 982–83 (D.C. Cir. 1990) (treating market structure evidence as the basis of a burden shifting presumption that could be rebutted in many ways).

on competition, not formalistic line drawing, are the measure of illegality.[12] Even the Warren Court cases that exalted market structure considerations were quick to tether this reliance to economic consensus that increased concentration meant decreased competition.[13] In short, treating market structure as a predictor of competitive effects – not an end concern itself – reconciles merger practice with both the statutory standard and the broader corpus of antitrust law.

435. Second, market structure should not be treated as having economic or legal significance outside the context of a particular method of defining markets. This follows from the inescapable logic that the competitive effects of a merger are a consequence *of the merger*, not of the markets that happen to be used to evaluate the merger. A problematic merger is not rendered innocuous by an over-broad market; an innocuous merger is not made problematic by an excessively narrow market. Because the legal significance of market structure derives from its ability to predict the economic consequences of a merger, and because the predictive value of market structure evidence derives from the way that markets are defined,[14] market structure evidence cannot be interpreted independently of the way that markets are defined.

436. The logic of this proposition may be inescapable, but the lesson escapes many during times of strong and stable market definition practices. For the past forty years, relevant markets in merger cases have been defined using the Hypothetical Monopolist Test (HMT).[15] By construction, a HMT market identifies a scope of trade in which anticompetitive harm could occur as a result of extreme market concentration; this is the very definition of a valid HMT market.[16] Market shares in HMT markets thus have reliable economic and legal significance. But nothing prevents relevant markets from being defined by other tests, like *Brown Shoe*'s practical indicia test.[17] And when markets are defined by methods as vacuous as

---

12 Am. Needle, Inc. v. Nat'l Football League, 560 U.S. 183, 191 (2010) ("[W]e have long … eschewed … formalistic distinctions in favor of a functional consideration of how the parties involved in the alleged anticompetitive conduct actually operate."); Cont'l T.V., Inc. v. GTE Sylvania Inc., 433 U.S. 36, 58–59 (1977) ("[D]eparture from the rule-of-reason standard must be based upon demonstrable economic effect rather than … upon formalistic line drawing."); *see also* Lynn Diamond, *The US Supreme Court applies a functional test to determine whether joint venture activity triggers antitrust liability (American Needle/National Football League)*, e-Competitions May 2010, art. No. 32779.

13 *E.g.*, Brown Shoe Co. v. United States, 370 U.S. 294, 333 (1962) ("The market share which companies may control by merging is one of the most important factors to be considered *when determining the probable effects of the combination* on effective competition in the relevant market." (emphasis added)); United States v. Phila. Nat'l Bank, 374 U.S. 321, 363 (1963) (defending reliance on market structure evidence as "fully consonant with economic theory" and asserting that the underlying structural inference was both "common ground among most economists" and "undoubtedly a premise of congressional reasoning about the antimerger statute").

14 *See* Sean P. Sullivan, *Modular Market Definition*, 55 UC Davis L. Rev. 1091, 1117–29 (2021) (describing the different purposes served by different ways of defining markets).

15 *See generally* David Glasner & Sean P. Sullivan, *The Logic of Market Definition*, 83 Antitrust L.J. 293 (2020); Gregory J. Werden, *The History of Antitrust Market Delineation*, 76 Marq. L. Rev. 123 (1992).

16 *See infra* note 50 and accompanying text.

17 *Brown Shoe*, 370 U.S. at 325.

lists of practical indicia, nothing guarantees that market shares will have economic significance as predictors of market power or competitive effects.

437. Third, market structure evidence should be treated as having different significance for evaluating different competitive concerns – what David Glasner and I have referred to as the theory-dependence of market-based inferences.[18] It is convenient shorthand to say that merger law tries to prevent acquisitions from enhancing market power.[19] But market power takes different forms and arises from different sources. The relevance of market structure evidence is not that it tells us how a merger influences some platonic account called "market power." The relevance of market structure evidence is that it tells us specific things about each of several specific ways that a merger might allow firms to exercise certain types of market power.

438. As an example, take a merger of clothing stores in a city center. If competing clothing stores had previously been on the cusp of tacitly colluding on changes in price or terms of service, then the merger could be the thing that tips this market into collusion. Market structure can help to gauge the severity of this risk, since it is easier for a few independent competitors to tacitly collude than it is for many. But the same merger could raise other concerns. If the merging firms were two of three high-end clothing stores, then the merged firm might unilaterally raise its prices to exploit captive customers of the merging firms. Market shares in a high-end clothing market might give some guidance on how closely the merging firms compete, and thus how great this unilateral incentive might be. The important point is that the unilateral effects inference is different than the coordination inference – these are different types of market power in different relevant markets and are informed in different ways by different aspects of market structure.

439. Fourth, market structure evidence should not be treated as a reliable proxy, presumption, or safe harbor for evaluating competitive effects without theoretical or empirical justification for believing that it is probative of the effects in question. This requirement follows directly from the effects-based mandate of the statutory standard.[20] It is not excused by aspirations to reduce the costs or increase the predictability of merger review.[21] Ease and predictability are nothing to treasure if the easy and predictable results are also consistently wrong.

---

18 Glasner & Sullivan, *supra* note 15, at 324–26.

19 *E.g.*, Fed. Trade Comm'n and U.S. Dep't. of Justice, *Horizontal Merger Guidelines* § 1 para. 5 (2010) ("2010 Guidelines") ("The unifying theme of these Guidelines is that mergers should not be permitted to create, enhance, or entrench market power or to facilitate its exercise.").

20 *See supra* note 4 and accompanying text.

21 *E.g.*, 2023 Guidelines, *supra* note 3, at § 2.1 para. 2 ("In the Agencies' experience, [presuming harm from market structure] provides a highly administrable and useful tool for identifying mergers that may substantially lessen competition."); Fed. Trade Comm'n and U.S. Dep't. of Justice, *Merger Guidelines* § 2 para. 1 (1968) ("1968 Guidelines") (stating that restricting enforcement policy to "a limited number of structural factors … facilitates both enforcement decision-making and business planning").

440. This is not a demand for certainty in proof of effects or for precise quantification of predicted harm to competition. Merger law is still law and reasonable inferences can and should be drawn on less than sterling demonstrations of cause and effect. But even in the rough and tumble of litigation, *something* must be available to provide foundation for suggested structural inferences. Euphemistic retreat to unpublished agency "experience" is not enough.[22]

III. Evolution and Devolution

441. With these four evaluative criteria in mind, we can move efficiently through the development of market structure reasoning in the Merger Guidelines. There is no point in trying to tackle the difficult subject of structural reasoning in vertical merger analysis in this review. Even in the comparatively simple area of horizontal merger analysis, it soon becomes apparent that market structure reasoning is still wobbling about on unsure legs.

1. 1968 Merger Guidelines

442. The first Merger Guidelines staked a strong but not unfair position on the use of market structure in merger review. True, the weight these guidelines placed on market structure and changes in concentration is unmatched in any of the subsequent revisions. An opening statement aptly captures this focus: "the primary role of Section 7 enforcement is to preserve and promote market structures conducive to competition."[23] But the 1968 Guidelines were less interventionist and perhaps even less structural than they might have been. Then-prevalent economic thinking and recent merger decisions would have justified extreme deference to market structure and hostility to even small increases in market concentration. Measured by this context, the 1968 Guidelines roamed safely within the boundaries of what surrounding circumstances allowed.[24]

443. Starting with the economic context, the structuralism of the 1968 Merger Guidelines was supported by widespread acceptance of the (now maligned) Structure–Conduct–Performance (SCP) paradigm. In the typical modern recounting, the SCP paradigm drew a strong and simplistic inverse relationship between market concentration and economic performance.[25]

---

22 *E.g.*, 2023 Guidelines, *supra* note 3, at § 2.1 para. 2; *id.* at para. 4 n.14; 2010 Guidelines, *supra* note 19, at § 5.3 para. 6.

23 1968 Guidelines, *supra* note 21, at § 2 para. 1; *see also id.* at § 4 para. 1 ("[E]nforcement activity … has the following interrelated purposes: … (iii) preventing significant increases in concentration in a market; and (iv) preserving significant possibilities for eventual deconcentration in a concentrated market.").

24 *See* Frank H. Easterbrook, *Is There a Ratchet in Antitrust Law*, 60 Tex. L. Rev. 705, 711–12 and n.30 (1982) (observing that tighter concentration thresholds would have been justified by caselaw); *see also* William E. Kovacic, *The Modern Evolution of U.S. Competition Policy Enforcement Norms*, 71 Antitrust L.J. 377, 434 (2003) (discussing how the 1968 Guidelines declined to take some economically unsupported enforcement opportunities).

25 *E.g.*, Douglas H. Ginsburg & Joshua D. Wright, *Philadelphia National Bank: Bad Economics, Bad Law, Good Riddance*, 80 Antitrust L.J. 377, 382–84 (2015).

Markets consisting of a few large competitors performed poorly; markets comprised of thousands of atomic competitors performed well.[26] The modern recounting is perhaps unfair to the SCP program, whose members included respected economists with ideas more nuanced than this lifeless summary suggests.[27]

444. But, in broad strokes, the modern recounting is accurate. The SCP thesis of a strong, causal link between market structure and performance was widely accepted, with a combined share of as little as 20% taken to be evidence of a merger's likely anticompetitive effect.[28] And the thesis *was* simplistic in the sense that it offered no theory to explain the connection between market structure and performance. Models existed to lend tentative support, like Stigler's use of market concentration to predict collusion,[29] or applications of Cournot's models of oligopoly to reason from concentration to market power.[30] But the broadly accepted thesis was defended more on intuition and a perceived empirical link between concentration and price or profits than on any specific, logical explanation of the causal link between market concentration and market power.[31]

445. On the legal front, things were much the same. Warren Court opinions of the 1960s embraced structural reasoning as previously noted. In *Philadelphia National Bank*, the Court held that a merger resulting in a combined share of at least 30% of the relevant market was presumptively illegal,[32] and endorsed reliance on concentration statistics as a general shortcut to establishing the illegality of horizontal mergers,[33] again, on the support

---

26 Donald I. Baker & William Blumenthal, *The 1982 Guidelines and Preexisting Law*, 71 Calif. L. Rev. 311, 315 (1983) ("[M]erger policy during the 1960's tended to flow from a simple equation: increases in concentration lead to less efficient performance.").

27 *See* Joe S. Bain, *Structure versus Conduct as Indicators of Market Performance: The Chicago-School Attempts Revisited*, 18 Antitrust L. & Econ. Rev. 17, 21 (1986) (describing a step-function relationship between concentration and performance, possibly tied to a critical point at which competitors become aware of their interdependence); Leonard W. Weiss, *The Structure-Conduct-Performance Paradigm and Antitrust*, 127 U. Pa. L. Rev. 1104, 1105 (1979) (identifying specific SCP predictions: "(1) that concentration will facilitate collusion, whether tacit or explicit, and (2) that as barriers to entry rise, the optimal price-cost margin of the leading firm or firms likewise will increase"); *see generally* Matthew T. Panhans, *The Rise, Fall, and Legacy of the Structure-Conduct-Performance Paradigm*, J. Hist. Econ. Thought 1 (2023), https://www.cambridge.org/core/journals/journal-of-the-history-of-economic-thought/article/abs/rise-fall-and-legacy-of-the-structureconductperformance-paradigm/3BA4E9F9FE29BAED06E9F1860BD37052 (providing a history of the SCP paradigm and its proponents).

28 *E.g.*, George J. Stigler, *Mergers and Preventive Antitrust Policy*, 104 U. Pa. L. Rev. 176, 182 (1955) ("Every merger by a firm which possesses one-fifth or more of an industry's output after the merger shall be presumed to violate the statute."); Carl Kaysen & Donald F. Turner, Antitrust Policy: An Economic and Legal Analysis 133 (1959) (similar for a combined share exceeding 20%); *see also* Jesse W. Markham, *Merger Policy under the New Section 7: A Six-Year Appraisal*, 43 Va. L. Rev. 489, 522 (1957) (estimating that the Agencies were using a threshold of 25%).

29 George J. Stigler, *A Theory of Oligopoly*, 72 J. Pol. Econ. 44 (1964).

30 *But cf.* Stephen W. Salant et al., *Losses from Horizontal Merger: The Effects of an Exogenous Change in Industry Structure on Cournot-Nash Equilibrium*, 98 Q.J. Econ. 185 (1983) (questioning whether Cournot competitors would have the profit incentive to undertake output-suppressing mergers).

31 *See* Panhans, *supra* note 27, at 4 (noting that the SCP paradigm was less concerned with theory than with empirical demonstration of its claimed causal link).

32 United States v. Phila. Nat'l Bank, 374 U.S. 321, 364 (1963).

33 *Id.* at 363.

of general economic acceptance of the SCP thesis.[34] In *Von's Grocery*, the Court demonstrated how strong this shortcut could be, finding a merger illegal when it would have yielded a combined share of less than 8% of a relatively unconcentrated market.[35]

446. Against this backdrop, the structuralism of the 1968 Guidelines was unremarkable. In markets with a C_4 greater than 75%, the guidelines predicted challenges to mergers with a combined share of more than 8%.[36] In less concentrated markets, a combined share between 10 and 26% spelled potential doom.[37] Without any apparent economic foundation,[38] the guidelines also followed the Supreme Court in making evidence of a "trend toward concentration" an exacerbating feature that would justify intervention against a merger causing a share increase of as little as 2%.[39]

447. Looking back today, this approach to market structure reasoning was simplistic and clumsy. Its conflation of market structure with competition was later shown to be unjustified as the early empirical foundations of the SCP thesis crumbled under scrutiny.[40] This is not to say that market structure cannot provide useful information for evaluating mergers; merely that the link between concentration and performance is not as simple or as universal as it was thought to be in 1968.[41] With the demise of the SCP thesis fell the only economic justification for the market share thresholds and structuralism of the 1968 Guidelines. Strong reliance on the SCP thesis proved to be a weakness of the document, but the independent errors of the 1968 Guidelines are found elsewhere: in how the guidelines handled market definition and how they attempted to infer unspecific injury from market structure evidence.

448. On market definition, the 1968 Guidelines presented about as loose a standard as one could imagine. Apparently satisfied to follow vapid Supreme Court platitudes, the guidelines adopted a blend of language from *Brown Shoe* and *General Motors* to delineate markets by an observational process similar to the way lawyers might try to distinguish adverse legal precedent: "any product or service which is distinguishable as a matter of commercial practice from other products or services will ordinarily

---

34 *See supra* note 13 and accompanying text (indicating judicial and perhaps Congressional reliance on SCP economics as the justification for structural reasoning).

35 United States v. Von's Grocery Co., 384 U.S. 270, 272 (1966).

36 1968 Guidelines, *supra* note 21, at § 5.

37 *Id.* at § 6.

38 *See* Donald F. Turner, *Observations on the New Merger Guidelines and the 1968 Merger Guidelines*, 51 Antitrust L.J. 307, 307 (1982) ("[T]he horizontal merger guidelines for prospective illegality were in some respects too severe, particularly where there was a so-called trend … .").

39 1968 Guidelines, *supra* note 21, at § 7.

40 *See generally* Richard Schmalensee, *Inter-industry Studies of Structure and Performance*, *in* 2 Handbook Of Industrial Organization 951 (Richard Schmalensee & Robert D. Willig eds., 1989).

41 *See generally* Sherrill Shaffer, *Structure, Conduct, Performance, and Welfare*, 9 Rev. Indus. Org. 435 (1994) (identifying conditions in which commonly supposed associations with market structure are provably violated).

constitute a relevant product market."[42] In fairness, the guidelines did elsewhere connect market boundaries to the assumption of some competitive insulation of in-market competitors from out-of-market competitors,[43] but the capacity of the 1968 Guidelines to arrive at excessively narrow markets is beyond dispute.

449. The immediate consequence of this undisciplined approach to market definition was that market shares under the 1968 Guidelines lacked reliable content as indicators of market power or as predictors of the competitive consequences of mergers. More than a decade after their release, Donald Turner conceded this error in a critical review of his own guidelines:

> [S]ome language in the discussion of market definition may have suggested the adoption of unduly narrow markets, which of course undermine, if not destroy, the significance of the resulting market share figures and the reasonableness of any presumptive tests based upon them.[44]

450. The severity of unprincipled market definition for market structure reasoning cannot be overstated. Even in a parallel universe in which the SCP thesis had proved entirely accurate, market definition under the 1968 Guidelines would still have precluded sensible outcomes in many cases.

451. On the absence of specific inferences of injury, the 1968 Guidelines embraced the SCP paradigm's general refusal to commit to a specific explanation of how or why an increase in concentration would cause a negative effect on competition. Demand for specificity in merger challenges can be taken too far,[45] to be sure, but here the absence of a coherent logical narrative undermined the 1968 Guidelines in two ways. First, it left nothing to support the guidelines' market concentration thresholds when the SCP paradigm fell. Second, it prevented dialogue between market structure evidence and the many other factual considerations that were supposed to be important in merger law.[46] It is impossible to say whether a particular fact about a market or the history of interaction between competitors increases or decreases concern about a merger when the basis for concern has never been identified in the first place.

---

42 1968 Guidelines, *supra* note 21, at § 3(i) para. 1.

43 *Id.* at § 3 para. 1.

44 Turner, *supra* note 38, at 307.

45 *See* D. Daniel Sokol & Sean P. Sullivan, *The Decline of Coordinated Effects Enforcement and How to Reverse It*, 76 Fl. L. Rev. § IV.C (forthcoming 2024) (identifying excessive demand for specificity and quantification as causes of underenforcement for coordinated effects theories).

46 *Compare* Brown Shoe Co. v. United States, 370 U.S. 294, 322 n.38 (1962) ("Statistics reflecting the shares of the market controlled by the industry leaders and the parties to the merger are, of course, the primary index of market power; but only a further examination of the particular market – its structure, history and probable future – can provide the appropriate setting for judging the probable anticompetitive effect of the merger."), *with* 1968 Guidelines, *supra* note 21, at § 2 para. 2 ("In certain exceptional circumstances … the structural factors used in these guidelines will not alone be conclusive … .").

2. 1982 and 1984 Merger Guidelines

452. In 1982, the Merger Guidelines were revised about as wrenchingly as they have been again in 2023. A snapshot of the shock, elation, and gloom surrounding these changes is captured in a symposium sponsored by the *California Law Review* in 1983.[47] Enough has been written about the philosophical underpinnings of the 1982 Guidelines to dispense with detailed rehashing, here. Suffice it to say, Reagan's appointed agency leaders cleaved small-business protectionism, strong structuralism, and most social and political considerations out of the guidelines, leaving behind only a few specific theories of harm – chiefly the risk that a merger would facilitate tacit collusion among a remaining group of competitors.[48]

453. There is room to disagree whether these changes were good or bad from social, economic, and policy perspectives. Regardless, they deserve credit as one of the few instances in which the drafters of U.S. Merger Guidelines attempted to prune any of the overgrowth from merger law. The 1982 Merger Guidelines did more than just cut, though. They also contributed new ideas and approaches to merger law. In terms of market structure reasoning, their greatest contributions were the introduction of the Hypothetical Monopolist Test and the exposition of coordinated effects as a specific theory of harm.

454. While something like the HMT was probably an inevitable invention,[49] the 1982 Guidelines were the entry point for this type of effect-oriented market definition in conventional merger practice. As articulated in a slight revision of the 1982 Guidelines in 1984, the HMT scoped relevant markets around the identification of potential exercises of market power through coordinated conduct:

> [F]or each product of each merging firm, the Department seeks to define a market in which firms could effectively exercise market power if they were able to coordinate their actions. Formally, a market is defined as a product or group of products and a geographic area in which it is sold such that a hypothetical, profit-maximizing firm, not subject to price regulation, that was the only present and future seller of those products in that area would impose a "small but significant and nontransitory" increase in price above prevailing or likely future levels.[50]

455. The emergence of the HMT was an evolutionary leap in the guidelines' approach to market structure reasoning.[51] For the first time, market

47 Symposium, *1982 Merger Guidelines*, 71 Calif. L. Rev. 280 (1983).

48 *See* Donald I. Baker & William Blumenthal, *The 1982 Guidelines and Preexisting Law*, 71 Calif. L. Rev. 311, 317 (1983) ("Where economic, social, and political considerations once received more or less equal billing as the basis for merger policy, economic considerations have now achieved primacy." (footnote omitted)).

49 *See* Sullivan, *supra* note 14, at 1109 n.87 (collecting similar expressions of this approach to defining markets).

50 Fed. Trade Comm'n and U.S. Dep't. of Justice, *Merger Guidelines*, § 2.0 para. 1 (1984) ("1984 Guidelines").

51 *See* Sullivan, *supra* note 14, at 110 (collecting praise for the HMT by antitrust commentators).

shares held at least theoretically reliable evidentiary value for predicting the competitive effects of mergers. Collusion in a market not satisfying the HMT would be ineffective by definition. But within a market validated by the HMT, collusion could in principle lead to higher prices and other anticompetitive effects. The risk that a merger would facilitate this type of collusion turned on factors including the number and relative size of competitors in the potential collusive set. This structure was precisely what the HMT revealed.

456. The connection between market structure and coordinated effects also restored economic content to the type of market concentration thresholds put forth in the 1968 Guidelines. The 1982 revision replaced the C_4 index with the Herfindahl–Hirschman Index (HHI), in view of its perceived better fit with anticompetitive coordination;[52] a new definition of highly concentrated markets – a HHI of at least 1800 – roughly equated to the previous C_4 of greater than 75%.[53] Mergers resulting in unconcentrated markets – a HHI below 1000 – were set aside as unlikely to be challenged "[b]ecause implicit coordination among firms is likely to be difficult [in this region]."[54] But mergers increasing the HHI by more than 100 points in highly concentrated markets were designated likely to be challenged.[55] And those increasing the HHI by 50 to 100 points in the highly concentrated markets, or by over 100 points in less concentrated markets, were to be evaluated on market structure and other evidence.

457. The identification of "other evidence" was another area of improvement. In contrast to the incommensurability of structural and non-structural evidence in 1968, adoption of a coordinated effects focus allowed the 1982 and 1984 Guidelines to transition from market structure evidence – primary evidence for the prediction of coordinated effects – to other relevant factors for evaluating coordination. Relevant factors included perceived determinants of the ease and stability of tacit price coordination, such as ease of entry,[56] similarity of economic interests,[57] market transparency,[58] and other now familiar considerations.[59]

458. But while the pivot to coordinated effects unlocked significant improvements in market structure reasoning in the 1982 and 1984 Guidelines, some aspects of the approach continued to hold market structure reasoning back.

---

52 Fed. Trade Comm'n and U.S. Dep't. of Justice, *Merger Guidelines* § III.A para. 2 (1982) ("1982 Guidelines").

53 *See id.* para 3 ("An empirical study by the Department of the size dispersion of firms within markets indicated that the critical HHI thresholds at 1000 and 1800 correspond roughly to four-firm concentration ratios of 50% and 70%, respectively.").

54 *Id.* at § III.A.1 para. 2.a.

55 *Id.* at para. 2.c.

56 *Id.* at § III.B.

57 *Id.* at § III.C.1.

58 *Id.* at § III.C.2.

59 *Id.* at § III.C; *see also* 1984 Guidelines, *supra* note 50, at § 3.2.

One problem was that the strong focus on coordinated effects crowded out similarly thoughtful treatment of how market structure could inform other concerns. The 1982 Guidelines devoted a single paragraph to a type of unilateral effect under the title of the "Leading Firm Proviso:"

> [T]he Department is likely to challenge the merger of any firm with a market share of at least 1 percent with the leading firm in the market, provided that the leading firm has a market share that is at least 35 percent and is approximately twice as large as that of the second largest firm in the market.[60]

459. While conceding that non-structural coordination factors were "of little relevance to the ability of a single dominant firm to exercise market power,"[61] the guidelines where quiet about what factors did matter, or why markets scoped around possible collusion were the appropriate context for evaluating this concern.

460. Another problem of the 1982 and 1984 Guidelines was that they commanded little outside authority for their retooled market concentration thresholds. Where the 1968 Guidelines were at least arguably supported by then-relevant scholarship and caselaw, the 1982 Guidelines could point to no similar external authority for the thresholds they propounded. To his credit, William Baxter candidly admitted this weakness:

> The present state of the theoretical and empirical literature on collusion precludes a rigorous basis for any particular thresholds. Those used in the Guidelines were adopted because they were consistent with the experience of those in the Division and also with empirical literature.[62]

461. On the 35% threshold for the leading firm proviso, Baxter similarly retreated: "As with the selection of HHI thresholds in those cases involving the danger of collusion, the selection of a threshold for the leading-firm proviso was somewhat arbitrary."[63]

462. Any bright line rule is bound to be somewhat arbitrary. But arbitrary selection between well-supported options is different than arbitrary selection between well-intended guesses. And the thresholds of the 1982 and 1984 Guidelines were of the latter sort. Future decades would see improvements in the understanding of structural predictors of coordination in the form of experimental economics research and retrospective studies.[64] At the time of drafting, the empirical literature was unimpressive and not

---

60 1982 Guidelines, *supra* note 52, at § III.A.2.

61 *Id.*

62 William F. Baxter, *Responding to the Reaction: The Draftsman's View*, 71 Calif. L. Rev. 618, 626–27 (1983).

63 *Id.* at 627–28.

64 Sokol & Sullivan, *supra* note 45, at § IV.A (surveying experimental and retrospective evidence on the connection between market structure and coordination).

addressed to the type of narrow relevant markets scoped by the newly minted HMT. Thus, the "experience of those in the Division" seems to have been the only serious authority for these concentration thresholds. One need not question the experience or intentions of the staff of the Division to feel some modest skepticism toward concentration thresholds emerging from the *ipse dixit* of interested parties.

3. 1992 and 1997 Horizontal Merger Guidelines

463. In the 1990s, market structure reasoning took another evolutionary leap. A more sophisticated understanding of market structure and antitrust injuries was emerging to replace the vacuum left by the collapse of the SCP thesis. But devolution was happening, too, as the growing sophistication of some market structure reasoning began to grate against the coarser reasoning of other parts of the same document. The locus of these evolutionary dynamics was the intersection of two areas of significant revision: (1) the expansion and separation of specific theories of coordinated and unilateral effects; and (2) the retreat from structural reasoning under market concentration thresholds.

464. The expanded treatment of specific theories of harm was the more notable change. The drafters of the 1992 Horizontal Merger Guidelines set aside non-horizontal mergers and used the space to introduce a new section on "Potential Adverse Competitive Effects of Mergers."[65] This section was further subdivided into anticompetitive harms arising from coordinated interactions and anticompetitive harms arising from unilateral effects of mergers. The treatment of unilateral effects embraced two broad theories of how a post-acquisition firm could exercise market power without competitor cooperation. First, in differentiated-product markets, mergers of particularly close rivals could produce unilateral incentives for the merged firm to raise its prices.[66] Second, in undifferentiated markets, mergers of firms with substantial market shares could produce unilateral incentives for the merged firm to suppress its output, thereby elevating the market price.[67]

465. Another change was a revised interpretation of market structure thresholds. The 1992 Guidelines continued a retreat from giving dispositive weight to market concentration evidence that had begun in 1984.[68] They added an affirmative commitment to evaluate structural evidence while also considering theory-relevant non-structural evidence:

> "[M]arket share and concentration data provide only the starting point for analyzing the competitive impact of a merger. Before determining whether to challenge a merger, the Agency also will

65 Fed. Trade Comm'n and U.S. Dep't. of Justice, *Merger Guidelines* § 2 (1992) ("1992 Guidelines").

66 *Id.* at § 2.21.

67 *Id.* at § 2.22.

68 1984 Guidelines, *supra* note 50, at § 3.11 ("[M]arket share and concentration data provide only the starting point for analyzing the competitive impact of a merger").

assess the other market factors that pertain to competitive effects, as well as entry, efficiencies and failure."[69]

466. This addressed, for theories other than coordinated effects, the market structure puzzle left open in 1968: how does structural reasoning interact with non-structural evidence? The answer was that market structure constituted one form of evidence about risk that a merger would have specific effects on competition. Non-structural considerations suggested by the relevant theory constituted other evidence. In arriving at a prediction about the competitive effect of a merger, both sources of evidence would be considered simultaneously.

467. Another subtle but important change to the market structure thresholds in 1992 was the introduction of several broad assertions about the likely absence of competitive effects. Mergers resulting in post-merger HHIs of less than 1000 were described as "unlikely to have adverse competitive effects."[70] Below a post-merger HHI of 1800, mergers creating an HHI delta of less than 100 points were similarly said to be "unlikely to have adverse competitive consequences,"[71] and so, too, mergers with an HHI delta of less than 50 points when the post-merger HHI was greater than 1800.[72] Though these assertions might be labeled "safe harbors," they went further than that in not just promising safety from challenge but in affirmatively asserting the likely absence of competitive effects.

468. At the intersection of these changes, evolutionary dynamics were mixed. The 1982 Guidelines had already drawn the connection between market structure and coordinated effects, but the 1992 revision expanded upon it.[73] The 1992 Guidelines also contributed a new and conceptually distinct link between market structure and unilateral output suppression.[74] The economic theory of differentiated-product unilateral effects outpaced the associated market structure reasoning in these guidelines, but the initial step was in a positive direction.[75]

469. That final quibble about structural reasoning was, unfortunately, one facet of a larger problem. The 1992 Guidelines, and the minor 1997 revision,[76] introduced new theories of competitive harm without making corresponding revisions to market definition or market concentration thresholds to

---

69 1992 Guidelines, *supra* note 65, at § 2.0.

70 *Id.* at § 1.51 para. 1.a.

71 *Id.* at para. 1.b.

72 *Id.* at para. 1.c.

73 *Id.* at § 2.1

74 *Id.* at § 2.22.

75 The asserted connection between market shares and price effects rested on questionable assumptions. *See* Robert D. Willig, *Merger Analysis, Industrial Organization Theory, and Merger Guidelines*, 22 Brookings Papers on Econ. Activity: Microeconomics 281, 299–304 (1991) (providing formal exposition of the model and its sensitivity).

76 Fed. Trade Comm'n and U.S. Dep't. of Justice, *Merger Guidelines*, § 0.1 (1997) ("1997 Guidelines").

adjust structural reasoning to the distinct competitive mechanics underlying each type of harm. The HMT, designed to identify potential collusive groups, was put to off-label use scoping markets for differentiated-product unilateral effects theories.[77] Market concentration thresholds – asserted in the 1980s to be probative of likely coordinated effects – were suddenly promoted to plenary predictors of three distinct forms of anticompetitive effect. What were inadequately supported economic assertions in 1982 had become nearly incoherent economic assertions in 1992.

470. This confusion came to a head in the safe harbor provisions. In 1984, the presence of many competitors in a market defined around a potential collusive group was seen as evidence against the need for intervention "[b]ecause implicit coordination among firms is likely to be difficult" in this setting.[78] Now, the same feature of the same method of defining markets was also being interpreted as evidence that unilateral price increases could not result from mergers of close competitors in a differentiated product space.[79] In fairness, careful enforcers could wiggle their way to sensible results by targeting the HMT at extremely narrow markets when pursuing unilateral effect cases.[80] But this was proceeding to a sensible result despite the framework, not because of it.

4. 2010 Horizontal Merger Guidelines

471. The 2010 Horizontal Merger Guidelines improved upon previous iterations with a clearer explanation of unilateral effects theories and a better separation of analysis according to different theories of harm. The first of these contributions was transparent in an extended treatment of unilateral effects.[81] The treatment of unilateral effects in a differentiated product space was particularly improved, with redirected emphasis from market shares to diversion ratios fixing some questionable structural assertions in the prior guidelines.[82]

472. The 2010 Guidelines also made the evolutionary leap of rejecting any uniform process for the evaluation of mergers and surrounding evidence. As the guidelines put it:

> [M]erger analysis does not consist of uniform application of a single methodology. Rather, it is a fact-specific process through which the Agencies… apply a range of analytical tools to the reasonably available and reliable evidence to evaluate competitive concerns … .[83]

77 As a quirk of the different mechanism of predicted harm, the HMT did generalize quite well to defining market in homogenous-good unilateral effects cases. *See* Sullivan, *supra* note 14, at 1136–37.

78 1984 Guidelines, *supra* note 50, at § 3.11 para. 2.

79 1992 Guidelines, *supra* note 65, at § 1.51 para. 1.

80 *See* Sullivan, *supra* note 14, at 1116 (explaining how predicted price effects justify narrow HMT markets).

81 2010 Guidelines, *supra* note 19, at § 6.

82 *See supra* note 75 and accompanying text.

83 2010 Guidelines, *supra* note 19, at § 1 para. 4.

473. This laid the foundation for evaluating different theories of harm according to different evidence and techniques. It supported, for example, the use of hypothesized injuries to guide market definition,[84] a major improvement on the previous suggestion that market definition preceded competitive effects analysis.

474. But, despite these and other advances, a series of missteps prevented the 2010 Guidelines from realizing their potential to improve market structure reasoning. On net, the 2010 revision probably did more harm than good.

475. One error was the missed opportunity to reconcile diversion ratios with market structure reasoning. Market shares had long ago lost legal significance except to the extent that evidence of past trades predicted a firm's future competitive significance.[85] Diversion ratios similarly use evidence of current or past purchasing patterns to draw inferences about the relative future competitive significance of firms in a differentiated product space. It would have been helpful and clarifying to introduce diversion ratios as a species of market structure evidence – something like a generalized market share better suited to the multidimensional competitive significance of firms in a differentiated product space.[86]

476. Instead, diversion ratios and market structure evidence were presented as categorically distinct types of evidence. The 2010 Guidelines drove that interpretive wedge in the presentation of unilateral effects theories:

> Diagnosing unilateral price effects based on the value of diverted sales need not rely on market definition or the calculation of market shares and concentration. The Agencies rely much more on the value of diverted sales than on the level of the HHI for diagnosing unilateral price effects in markets with differentiated products.[87]

477. The guidelines did the same for market definition. Where unilateral effects predictions could have been presented as a form of market definition useful to the evaluation of specific types of competitive effect,[88] the guidelines instead opted to distance these concepts, asserting that "[s]ome of the analytical tools used by the Agencies … do not rely on market definition,"[89] and specifically that "merger simulation methods need not rely on market definition."[90]

---

84 *See* Glasner & Sullivan, *supra* note 15, at 316–24 (explaining that the HMT base price and price increase should fit the anticipated anticompetitive harm if the resulting market is to be helpful in evaluating potential competitive effects).

85 United States v. Gen. Dynamics Corp., 415 U.S. 486, 503, 510 (1974).

86 *Cf.* Christopher Conlon & Julie Holland Mortimer, *Empirical properties of diversion ratios*, 52 RAND J. ECON. 693 (2021) (describing other interpretations of diversion ratios, some specific to particular empirical specifications).

87 2010 Guidelines, *supra* note 19, at § 6.1 para. 6.

88 Sullivan, *supra* note 14, at 1115–17 (arguing that there is no conceptual difference between the HMT and the predicted price effects of a merger simulation model).

89 2010 Guidelines, *supra* note 19, at § 4 para. 2.

90 *Id.* at § 6 para. 7.

478. Semantically isolating market definition and market concentration evidence from other sources of information about the structure of competition allowed the 2010 Guidelines to clean up selected unilateral effects theories without addressing the broader structural confusion of the 1992 Guidelines. Thus, the 2010 Guidelines continued to interpret concentration thresholds as somehow simultaneously predictive of a range of potential competitive injuries.[91] Worse, without support from external authority,[92] the guidelines raised the concentration thresholds, redefining "highly concentrated" markets as those with HHI above 2500 and "unconcentrated" markets as those with HHI below 1500.[93] If the objective of these changes was merely to fit the thresholds to agency enforcement patterns,[94] it would have made sense to speak in terms of agency actions: mergers falling in a certain range would be labeled "likely" or "unlikely" to be challenged.[95]

479. Instead, the 2010 Guidelines spoke in terms of likely adverse competitive effects.[96] The implication, under the raised thresholds, was that some mergers that would have "raise[d] significant competitive concerns" in 1997 were suddenly declared "unlikely to have adverse competitive effects" in 2010.[97] Since, logically, at least one of these claims about likely competitive effects must have been wrong, it would have been nice to know how the 2010 Guidelines arrived at the thresholds and likely competitive effect predictions that they did. As in previous guidelines, however, vague reference to agency "experience" was the only answer.[98]

480. The confused safe harbor provision of the 1992 and 1997 Guidelines was also preserved and even expanded in these guidelines. Carl Shapiro directed attention to the illogic of the safe harbor in commentary on the 2010 Guidelines. After noting that HHI figures played a limited role in differentiated-product unilateral effects analysis,[99] he continued:

> The express acknowledgement that HHI levels typically are not very helpful diagnostics in these [unilateral effects] cases has led to concerns that the valuable screening role played by the HHI thresholds since 1982

91 *Id.* at § 5.3.

92 Dennis W. Carlton & Mark A. Israel, *Will the New Guidelines Clarify or Obscure Antitrust Policy?*, Antitrust Source, Oct. 2010, 1 ("[W]e know of no body of economic research that provides either an econometric or a theoretical basis for the HHI thresholds in the 2010 Guidelines (or for that matter in previous versions of the Guidelines).").

93 2010 Guidelines, *supra* note 19, at § 5.3 para. 6.

94 Christine E. Varney, *The 2010 Horizontal Merger Guidelines: Evolution, not Revolution*, 77 Antitrust L.J. 651, 659 (2011) (stating that "the increased HHI thresholds more accurately describe actual practice").

95 *Cf.* 1982 Guidelines, *supra* note 52, at § III.A para. 2 (using concentration thresholds to describe when the Division was "likely" or "unlikely" to challenge a merger).

96 2010 Guidelines, *supra* note 19, at § 5.3 para. 6.

97 *Compare* 1997 Guidelines, *supra* note 76, at § 1.51, *with* 2010 Guidelines, *supra* note 19, at § 5.3.

98 2010 Guidelines, *supra* note 19, at § 5.3 para. 6.

99 Carl Shapiro, *The 2010 Horizontal Merger Guidelines: From Hedgehog To Fox In Forty Years*, 77 Antitrust L.J. 701, 720 (2010).

has been reduced or lost. In fact, the 2010 Guidelines recognize the importance of these HHI thresholds to help identify mergers that are "unlikely to have adverse competitive effects and ordinarily require no further analysis." Indeed, the 2010 Guidelines not only retain HHI thresholds but raise them. DOJ continues to apply the HHI thresholds to all horizontal mergers.[100]

481. The statement speaks for itself.

5. 2023 Merger Guidelines

482. Today, the 2023 Guidelines stand as another wrenching revision to the document. In contrast to other recent guidelines, they present a dazzling display of potential theories of harm. They also diverge from previous guidelines in asserting now dated Supreme Court opinions as primary authority for statements about competitive effects and what evidence can be used to prove them. Whatever the overall merits of this approach, it motivates the 2023 Guidelines to adopt an eclectic mix of market structure inferences – some thoughtful, some careless.

483. In one important point of consistency with all Merger Guidelines since 1982, the 2023 Guidelines use market structure as evidence of likely competitive effects – not as an end objective of merger law itself.[101] This would be unremarkable if an earlier draft had not appeared to conflate changes in market concentration with changes in competition.[102] Edits to the final document mostly foreclose that interpretation.

484. The 2023 Guidelines also keep with prior iterations in largely preserving the haphazard separation of market structure reasoning by competitive effects that held back the 1992, 1997, and 2010 Guidelines. Like the 2010 Guidelines, the 2023 Guidelines are of two minds about the relevance of market concentration evidence in the evaluation of unilateral effects theories: they embrace the presumption of harm from evidence of high and increasing concentration,[103] while insisting that harm can also be proved without the support of concentration evidence,[104] and while apparently denying that structural reasoning can disprove unilateral effects.[105] Market

100 *Id.* at 720–21.

101 2023 Guidelines, *supra* note 3, at § 1 para. 8 ("Market concentration is often a useful indicator of a merger's likely effects on competition.").

102 Fed. Trade Comm'n and U.S. Dep't. of Justice, *Draft Merger Guidelines* § 1 para. 9 (2023) ("2023 Draft Guidelines") ("Mergers Should Not Significantly Increase Concentration in Highly Concentrated Markets… . [In some cases,] the Agencies presume that a merger may substantially lessen competition based on market structure alone.").

103 2023 Guidelines, *supra* note 3, at § 2.2 para. 1 ("Although a change in market structure can also indicate risk of competitive harm (see Guideline 1), an analysis of the existing competition between the merging firms can demonstrate that a merger threatens competitive harm independent from an analysis of market shares.").

104 *Id.*

105 *See infra* note 111 and accompanying text (discussing the absence of a safe harbor provision in these guidelines).

shares are given appropriate weight in an elaborated discussion of output suppression theories,[106] but this follows the almost complete neglect of market shares and market concentration information in an enumeration of evidence generally considered in unilateral effects analysis.[107]

485. One area of evolutionary improvement is the clarified use of structural reasoning in coordinated effects analysis. Consistent with the suggestions of recent scholarship,[108] the 2023 Guidelines emphasize the importance of market structure for evaluating coordination theories.[109] Evidenced that a merger would significantly increase concentration, leading to a highly concentrated market, is treated as evidence "that post-merger market conditions are susceptible to coordinated interaction and that the merger materially increases the risk of coordination."[110]

486. Another evolutionary improvement in the 2023 Guidelines is the quiet elimination of the plenary safe harbor provision of the 1992, 1997 and 2010 Merger Guidelines.[111] With this omission, the 2023 Guidelines escape the disastrous logic of interpreting evidence against the plausibility of coordinated effects in one relevant market as evidence against all potential competitive effects in all potential relevant markets. The inclusion of theory-specific or market-specific safe harbors might have been a better approach, but the existing document provides the foundation for future changes in this direction.

487. Elsewhere, the 2023 Guidelines make some baffling decisions. In another chapter of this volume, Gregory Werden critiques the relaxed approach that the 2023 Guidelines take to market definition. The new guidelines preserve the HMT as one method of defining markets,[112] but also embrace *Brown Shoe*'s practical indicia test as another method of defining markets,[113] as well as other vague language about inferring market boundaries from "direct evidence" of observed competition or exercises of market power.[114]

488. The problem with this approach is the same problem that hobbled the 1968 Guidelines. Unless relevant markets are defined in ways that ensure market shares have economic significance, market structure provides no reliable basis for drawing inferences about the competitive effects of

106 2023 Guidelines, *supra* note 3, at § 4.2.D para. 2.

107 *Id.* at § 4.2.A.

108 *E.g.*, Sokol & Sullivan, *supra* note 45, at § IV.A (advocating for greater emphasis of structural evidence); *id.* at 48 (collecting similar advocacy).

109 2023 Guidelines, *supra* note 3, at § 2.3.

110 *Id.* at § 2.3.A.

111 *Id.* at § 2.1.

112 *Id.* at § 4.3.

113 *Id.*

114 *Id.*

mergers.[115] To their credit, the 2023 Guidelines do recognize this problem, noting that "[a]lthough any market that is properly identified using the methods [in these guidelines] is valid, the extent to which structural measures calculated in that market are probative in any given context depends on a number of considerations."[116] The suggestion that a relevant market could still be "valid," even when no aspect of its structure would be probative of any competitive effect, is curious to say the least.

489. Even more curious is a subsequent statement that, in clarifying the previous proposition, limits the scope of structural reasoning to markets defined by the HMT:

> [T]he market used to estimate shares should be broad enough that it contains sufficient additional products so that a loss of competition among all the suppliers of the products in the market would lead to significantly worse terms for at least some customers of at least one product. Markets identified using the various tools in [these guidelines] can satisfy this condition – for example, all markets that satisfy the HMT do so.[117]

490. The question is what markets *except* those that satisfy the HMT would meet this requirement. The condition "that a loss of competition among all the suppliers ... would lead to significantly worse terms for at least some customers" simply restates the HMT inquiry.

491. The puzzling result is that the 2023 Guidelines embrace multiple methods of defining markets, but only stand behind market structure evidence when markets are defined by the HMT. Relying on the HMT when engaging in market structure reasoning is sensible and aligns these guidelines with many of the advances of prior iterations. What role this leaves for the other three tests is a mystery perhaps best left unsolved.

492. Finally, the 2023 Guidelines make some simple missteps. The new guidelines reverse the 2010 Guidelines in returning the definitions of "highly concentrated" markets and of "significant increase[s]" in concentration to the levels initially set in 1982.[118] In a footnote, the 2023 Guidelines defend this change:

> The first merger guidelines to reference an HHI threshold were the merger guidelines issued in 1982. These guidelines referred to mergers with HHI above 1,000 as concentrated markets, with HHI between 1,000 and 1,800 as "moderately concentrated" and above 1,800 as "highly concentrated," while they referred to an increase in HHI of 100 as a "significant increase." Each subsequent iteration until 2010 maintained those thresholds... . Although the Agencies

115 *See supra* note 44 and accompanying text.

116 2023 Guidelines, *supra* note 3, at § 4.4 para. 2.

117 *Id.* at para 4.

118 *Id.* at § 2.1.

raised the thresholds for the 2010 guidelines, based on experience and evidence developed since, the Agencies consider the original HHI thresholds to better reflect both the law and the risks of competitive harm suggested by market structure and have therefore returned to those thresholds.[119]

493. The now predictable justification of agency "experience" is here augmented by "evidence developed since [2010],"[120] but the result is little different and no less opaque.

494. The optics of this wobble are the concerning part. The 2010 Guidelines offered no persuasive justification for raising the "highly concentrated" threshold;[121] the 2023 Guidelines offer no persuasive justification for lowering it. Both guidelines treat evidence of concentration above this threshold, initially suggested to identify opportunities for tacit collusion, as somehow plenary evidence of various different competitive effects. But while the substance of the revised threshold is no more lacking than before, the act of self-aggrandizement might have demanded better justification in 2023 than the act of self-restraint did in 2010. Claims made in knowing concession of agency enforcement power are different than claims made in arrogation of it.[122]

495. There is less room for equanimity when considering other structural assertions introduced in the 2023 Guidelines. The claim that a "trend toward concentration in an industry" raises a merger's threat to competition is a triumph of rhetoric over reason.[123] The claim that unspecific competitive effects can be presumed when a merger produces a firm with a combined share of 30%, at a change in HHI of at least 100 points, is similarly specious.[124] Though this proposition looks a bit like the leading firm proviso of 1982,[125] it actually appears to be inspired by the Supreme Court's reasoning in *Philadelphia National Bank*,[126] the sole authority the guidelines cite for the claim.[127]

496. As already discussed, *Philadelphia National Bank* was decided at a time when broad acceptance of the SCP thesis meant that many economists

---

119 *Id.* at n.15.

120 *Id.*

121 *See supra* note 92 and accompanying text.

122 *Cf.* Fed. R. Evid. 804(b)(3) (reflecting the common-sense assumption that people are less likely to mislead when the result would be damaging to their own self-interest).

123 2023 Guidelines, *supra* note 3, at § 2.7. This assertion also raises the new question of what defines an "industry." This is evidently something different than a "relevant market," yet it is also evidently a scope of trade in which concentration statistics have economic significance.

124 *Id.* at § 2.1.

125 1982 Guidelines, *supra* note 52, at § III.2 (discussing a situation in which "the leading firm has a market share that is at least 35% and is approximately twice as large as that of the second largest firm in the market").

126 United States v. Phila. Nat'l Bank, 374 U.S. 321 (1963).

127 2023 Guidelines, *supra* note 3, at § 2.1 n.16.

agreed with the Court's reasoning. The *Philadelphia National Bank* majority specifically defended its approach as "fully consonant with economic theory," since concern about significant market shares was "common ground among most economists."[128] This is no longer the case. Market structure and market concentration can still be probative of market power and competitive effects, but the strong form of SCP reasoning that the Court invoked to defend its market share reasoning in *Philadelphia National Bank* was discredited decades ago. If there is a defensible basis, today, for believing that this 30% share threshold is an empirically accurate predictor of competitive effects, it will not be found in the pages of *Philadelphia National Bank*. The guidelines are only a hair less vulnerable on the claim that this 30% threshold still reflects antitrust law.[129]

IV. Discussion

497. Merger Guidelines evolve over time. We might hope that this evolution would be in the direction of clearer thinking and better predictions. But change is never that certain. Market structure reasoning has both evolved and devolved over the history of the Merger Guidelines, and both trends are evident in the latest revision. Market structure reasoning is better and more informed in the 2023 Guidelines than it was in 1968 or even 1982. But there is still vast room for improvement. Like all Merger Guidelines, the current revision began to age the instant it was published. It will fall to the drafters of future revisions to decide what branches of structural reasoning will be kept, what branches will be cut, and whether it makes sense to start again from seed.

---

128 *Phila. Nat'l Bank*, 374 U.S. at 363.

129 *See* Kimble v. Marvel Entm't, 576 U.S. 446, 461 (2015) ("We have … felt relatively free to revise our legal analysis as economic understanding evolves and … to reverse antitrust precedents that misperceived a practice's competitive consequences."); *id.* at 461–62 (reasoning that in cases where effects on trade need to be predicted "the Court's rulings necessarily turn[] on its understanding of economics" and thus that "to overturn [earlier] decisions in light of sounder economic reasoning [is] to take them on [their] own terms" (internal quotation marks removed)); *see also* Seth D. Greenstein, *The US Supreme Court hears arguments before the decision on whether post-expiration license royalty obligations are caught in the web of patent policies or antitrust analysis (Kimble/Marvel)*, e-Competitions Mar. 2015, art. No. 72308.

Market Delineation under the New Merger Guidelines: Gerrymandering Redux

Gregory J. Werden*

Mercatus Center at George Mason University

* Gregory J. Werden is a visiting scholar at the Mercatus Center at George Mason University. After earning a Ph.D. in economics at the University of Wisconsin in 1977, he worked in the Antitrust Division of the U.S. Department of Justice until 2019. He is the only Antitrust Division employee to be recognized with the Department's Mary C. Lawton Lifetime Service Award. Werden has 200 published works, and more than two dozen of them concern the delineation of the relevant market. He was deeply involved in preparing the 1982 Merger Guidelines, and involved in varying capacities in all subsequent merger guidelines through 2019.

498. The new Merger Guidelines ("2023 Guidelines") abandon some critical principles that governed market delineation since 1982. The Department of Justice (DOJ) and the Federal Trade Commission (FTC) evidently contemplate gerrymandering markets as in the 1960s, when the relevant market in merger cases was whatever collection of products and places made the best case against the merger. This chapter provides context then details problematic policy choices embodied in the 2023 Guidelines.

I. The Centrality of the Relevant Market

499. For decades, antitrust law operated without a statutory provision specifically directed at mergers and without a well-articulated relevant market concept.[1] The concept was first clearly articulated in the 1948 *Columbia Steel* decision,[2] in which the Supreme Court rebuffed a DOJ merger challenge under the Sherman Act.[3]

500. The *Columbia Steel* decision used the word "market" many times. And the Court explained that, before assessing the likely competitive effects of a proposed merger, it is "first necessary to delimit the market in which the concerns compete and then determine the extent to which the concerns are in competition in that market."[4]

501. DOJ's failure to block the merger in *Columbia Steel* helped break an impasse in Congress over pending anti-merger legislation. The 1950 Celler-Kefauver Act,[5] amended Section 7 of the Clayton Act to prohibit a merger or acquisition, "where in any line of commerce in any section of the country, the effect of such acquisition may be substantially to lessen competition, or to tend to create a monopoly."[6]

502. From the outset, courts read the amended Section 7 to require market delineation. An early district court decision interpreting the statute observed that:

> The ultimate question of whether a merger comes within the ban of Section 7 requires a consideration of the relevant market. Like other sections of our antitrust laws, Section 7 does not contain the word "market." It is clear, however, that "line of commerce" signifies a product market and "section of the country" refers to a geographic market.[7]

---

1 *See* Gregory J. Werden, *The History of Antitrust Market Delineation*, 76 Marquette L. Rev. 123, 125–40 (1992).

2 United States v. Columbia Steel Co., 334 U.S. 495, 520, 527 (1948).

3 Ch. 647, 26 Stat. 209 (1890) (current version codified at 15 U.S.C. §§ 1–7).

4 *Columbia Steel*, 334 U.S. at 520, 527.

5 Pub. L. 81-899, ch. 1184, 64 Stat. 1125 (1950).

6 15 U.S.C. § 18.

7 United States v. Bethlehem Steel Corp., 168 F. Supp. 576, 587–88 (S.D.N.Y. 1958).

503. A half-century later, a judge scoffed at the FTC's contention that "market definition is not necessary in a § 7 case," describing the contention as "in contravention of the statute itself."[8]

504. Before interpreting the amended Section 7, the Supreme Court gave meaning to the concept of the relevant market in other cases.[9] In a 1953 tying case, the Court declared that: "For every product, substitutes exist. But a relevant market cannot meaningfully encompass that infinite range. The circle must be drawn narrowly to exclude any other product to which, within reasonable variations in price, only a limited number of buyers will turn … ."[10]

505. In 1956, the Court was called upon to decide whether cellophane traded in a distinct relevant market from other flexible wrapping materials.[11] The Court observed that the relevant "market is composed of products that have reasonable interchangeability for the purposes for which they are produced – price, use and qualities considered."[12]

506. The first Supreme Court merits decision under the amended Section 7 declared that: "The market share which companies may control by merging is one of the most important factors to be considered when determining the probable effects of the combination on effective competition in the relevant market."[13] The centrality of the relevant market was cemented a year later when the Court held that

> a merger which produces a firm controlling an undue percentage share of the relevant market, and results in a significant increase in the concentration of firms in that market, is so inherently likely to lessen competition substantially that it must be enjoined in the absence of evidence clearly showing that the merger is not likely to have such anticompetitive effects.[14]

507. The relevant market would be central to Section 7 analysis even if market shares had no special significance. The relevant market is "the area of

---

8 FTC v. Whole Foods Market, Inc., 548 F.3d 1028, 1036 (D.C. Cir. 2008) (opinion of Brown, J.) (The case yielded no majority opinion.). *See* FTC v. H.J. Heinz Co., 246 F.3d 708, 719 n.17 (D.C. Cir. 2001) ("Courts interpret 'line of commerce' as synonymous with the relevant product market.").

9 For a full discussion of the cases and commentary of this period, see Werden, *supra* note 1, at 130–56.

10 Times-Picayune Publ'g Co. v. United States, 345 U.S. 594, 612 n.31 (1953). The decision was authored by Justice Tom C. Clark who had worked in the DOJ's Antitrust Division from 1937 to 1943. He spent his last five months in the Division as the Assistant Attorney General in charge, succeeding Thurman W. Arnold.

11 United States v. E.I. du Pont de Nemours & Co., 351 U.S. 377 (1956).

12 *Id.* at 404. The Court's focus on interchangeability in use was proper but standardless. The Court held that cellophane was part of a much broader "flexible packaging material market." *Id.* at 400. Scholarly opinion has consistently held that the Court erred. *See, e.g.*, George W. Stocking & Willard F. Mueller, *The Cellophane Case and the New Competition*, 45 Am. Econ. Rev. 29 (1955); George W. Stocking, *Economic Tests of Monopoly and the Concept of the Relevant Market*, 2 Antitrust Bull. 479 (1957).

13 Brown Shoe Co. v. United States, 370 U.S. 294, 343 (1962).

14 United States v. Phila. Nat'l Bank, 374 U.S. 321, 363 (1963).

effective competition"[15] that must be examined in evaluating the likely competitive effects of a merger. Delineating the relevant market separates the active and primary competitive forces from passive and secondary forces, and this separation is fundamental to the economic analysis of competition.[16]

508. The legal concept of "the relevant market" is closely related to the economic concept of "the market," which is the focus of most work in microeconomics. Market-level economics, termed "partial equilibrium analysis," places a spotlight on one narrow sector of the economy, while holding all else constant. The most familiar application is supply and demand, in which the spotlighted sector is termed the "market" and outside prices are held constant.

509. Partial equilibrium analysis of competition posits strategic interaction within a narrow scope. Outside prices are held constant, treating competition from the outside as passive. The best choice generally is to model strategic interaction as congruent with the relevant market. Positing a broader interaction injects complexity without offering insight; positing narrower interaction misspecifies the competitive process and risks materially distorting the analytic conclusions.[17]

II. The Dark Ages of Market Delineation

510. For market delineation, the 1960s were like the early 16th Century was for anatomy (before Vesalius) or astronomy (before Copernicus). *Brown Shoe*[18] was the first case under the amended Section 7 decided on the merits by the Supreme Court. To avoid tension with the cellophane case, the Court asserted that a relevant market defined on the basis of reasonable interchangeability could contain "submarkets," which also "constitute product markets for antitrust purposes."[19]

---

15 Tampa Elec. Co. v. Nashville Co., 365 U.S. 320, 327–28 (1966) (Clark, J.).

16 *See* Gregory J. Werden, *Why (Ever) Define Markets? An Answer to Professor Kaplow*, 78 Antitrust L.J. 719, 735–40 (2013).

17 *See* Gregory J. Werden, *The Relevant Market Concept in Antitrust Law* in Global Antitrust Economics: Current Issues in Antitrust Law & Economics 117, 118–20 (Douglas H. Ginsburg & Joshua D. Wright eds. 2016); Gregory J. Werden, *Antitrust Needs the Relevant Market, in* 2012 Fordham Competition Law Institute 235, 252–53 (Barry Hawk ed. 2013).

18 Brown Shoe Co. v. United States, 370 U.S. 294 (1962).

19 *Id.* at 325. The submarket concept was disparaged by commentators. *See, e.g.*, G.E. Hale & Rosemary D. Hale, *A Line of Commerce: Market Definition in Anti-Merger Cases*, 52 Iowa L. Rev. 406, 426 (1966) ("[T]he notion of a submarket is an odd one: … If the line of commerce is men's shoes, it should not also be men's golf shoes: if one boundary is right, the other must be wrong."); George R. Hall & Charles F. Phillips, *Antimerger Criteria: Power, Concentration, Foreclosure and Size*, 9 Vill. L. Rev. 211, 219 (1964) (the submarket concept is an "intellectual monstrosity … providing almost unlimited authority to the courts in choosing a market"); Bryce J. Jones, *The Brown Shoe Case and the New Antimerger Policy: Comment*, 54 Am. Econ. Rev. 407, 408 (1964) ("It is within the broad market, not the submarket, that the stuff of price determination and competitive rivalry is found."); Lawrence C. Maisel, *Submarkets in Merger and Monopolization Cases*, 72 Geo. L.J. 39 (1983) ("[T]he holding in *Brown Shoe* that smaller relevant markets can exist within broader relevant markets should be overruled and the word 'submarket' banished from the antitrust lexicon.")

511. The court went on to declare that: "The boundaries of such a submarket may be determined by examining such practical indicia as industry or public recognition of the submarket as a separate economic entity, the product's peculiar characteristics and uses, unique production facilities, distinct customers, distinct prices, sensitivity to price changes, and specialized vendors."[20]

512. During the 1960s, the Supreme Court accepted any market definition the government contrived.[21] In *Philadelphia National Bank*, the merger combined two banks, and the relevant market was the "cluster of products ... and services denoted by the term 'commercial banking.'"[22] Non-bank financial institutions provided most of same products and services, but they were excluded from the relevant market, which consisted of non-substitutable products and services.

513. In *Rome Cable*, the merger combined two manufacturers of electrical conductor, and the relevant market was bare and insulated aluminum conductor.[23] Those products did not significantly compete, and a close substitute for insulated aluminum conductor was excluded from the market. Dissenting Justice Potter Stewart lamented that the majority had overruled an "impeccable ... [trial court] decision with little more than a wave of the hand."[24]

514. In *Continental Can*, the merger combined manufacturers of metal cans and glass jars, and the relevant market was glass and metal containers.[25] The Supreme Court majority combined bottles and jars together with cans to "conform to competitive reality,"[26] but dissenting Justice John Marshall Harlan found the Court's market "unrelated to any reality whatsoever."[27] The reality was that the merging firms did not compete significantly. In beer containers, the Herfindahl–Hirschman Index increase was less than 100; in soft drink containers, it was less than 5.[28]

515. In his 1964 annual lecture before the Association of the Bar of the City of New York, Professor Milton Handler lampooned the state of merger law with a parody Supreme Court decision condemning the merger of Joe's

---

20 *Brown Shoe*, 370 U.S. at 325. The practical indicia determined only the product dimensions of the relevant market, but the Court also asserted that, "just as a product submarket may have § 7 significance as the proper 'line of commerce,' so may a geographic submarket be considered the appropriate 'section of the country.'" *Id.* at 336.

21 During the 1960s, government prevailed in all 14 merger cases decided by the Supreme Court.

22 United States v. Phila. Nat'l Bank, 374 U.S. 321, 356 (1963).

23 United States v. Aluminum Co. of Am., 377 U.S. 271, 267–77 (1964). The appellation *Rome Cable* is the name of the acquired firm.

24 *Id.* at 284 (Stewart, J., dissenting).

25 United States v. Cont'l Can Co., 378 U.S. 441, 457 (1964).

26 *Id.*

27 *Id.* at 472 (Harlan, J., dissenting).

28 *See* United States v. Cont'l Can Co., 217 F. Supp. 761, 795, 798 (S.D.N.Y. 1964).

Delicatessen and Victor's Meat Market.[29] The decision limited the geographic market to the intersection at which both merging firms operated, along with Gordon's Vegetable Store and an A&P supermarket.[30] All four of shops competed in an "all food products" market, but the decision focused on the "meat-delicatessen submarket."

516. In a leading business magazine, Professor Handler later criticized the Court's market definitions in *Rome Cable* and *Continental Can*.[31] The section of the article on the former case was headed "Gerrymandering the Market," and it bemoaned "the sorry state of affairs in which markets are gerrymandered to magnify the [market share] percentages, the tolerated percentages dwindle over time, and nothing else seems to matter."[32]

517. The Supreme Court's disdain of market delineation principles was on display in two decisions released June 13, 1966. *Grinnell* involved monopolization allegations relating to burglar, fire, and other alarm services.[33] The Court placed all in the same relevant market, although they were not substitutes, and the Court limited the relevant market to "central station" services, which transmitted signals to manned monitoring stations.[34] Dissenting Justice Harlan lambasted the "gerrymandered market definition."[35]

518. In *Pabst*, the Supreme Court could have accepted the government's arguments for a three-state beer market. Instead, the Court declared that the relevant market need not be defined "by metes and bounds" and that "the failure of the Government to prove by an army of expert witnesses what constitutes a relevant 'economic' or 'geographic' market is not an adequate ground on which to dismiss" the case.[36] Dissenting Justice Harlan observed that "the possibilities for 'gerrymandering' are limitless" in the majority's approach.[37]

---

29 Milton Handler, *Recent Antitrust Developments – 1964*, 63 Mich. L. Rev. 59, 70–78 (1964). The lecture was delivered four days before the *Continental Can* decision, and the parody decision coincidentally carried the date of the *Continental Can* decision.

30 The intersection was 21st & K Streets, N.W., Washington, D.C. George Washington University is nearby, and the White House is six blocks away.

31 Milton Handler & Stanley D. Robinson, *The Supreme Court vs. Corporate Mergers*, Fortune, Jan. 1965, at 164.

32 *Id.* at 165.

33 United States v. Grinnell Corp., 384 U.S. 563 (1966).

34 *Id.* at 571–72.

35 *Id.* at 591 (Harlan, J., dissenting).

36 United States v. Pabst Brewing Co., 384 U.S. 546, 549 (1966).

37 *Id.* at 555–56 (Harlan, J., dissenting). Commentators jumped on bandwagon, asserting that the agencies and the courts routinely gerrymandered relevant markets. *See, e.g.*, Gordon F. Hampton, *The Merger Movement in Historic Perspective – A Lawyer's View*, 39 Antitrust L.J. 107, 111 (1969) (In the "flood of decisions following *Brown Shoe*, … a 'gerrymandering' process has occurred, giving the appearance of markets with high percentage shares."); Richard A. Solomon, *Why Uncle Same Can't Lose a Case under Section 7 of the Clayton Act*, 53 A.B.A. J. 137, 138 (1967) (accusing the FTC of "gerrymandering the relevant market" and of asserting the "prerogative to carve out relevant markets on the basis of any approach that may be convenient.").

519. *Grinnell* and *Pabst* were DOJ cases, and DOJ Antitrust Division AAG Donald F. Turner signed the government's briefs. While the cases were pending, he began work on the first Merger Guidelines,[38] which were not released until May 30, 1968.[39] This was the opening paragraph of the market delineation section of the 1968 Guidelines:

> A rational appraisal of the probable competitive effects of a merger normally requires definition of one or more relevant markets. A market is any grouping of sales (or other commercial transactions) in which each of the firms whose sales are included enjoys some advantage in competing with those firms whose sales are not included. The advantage need not be great, for so long as it is significant it defines an area of effective competition among the included sellers in which the competition of the excluded sellers is, *ex hypothesi*, less effective. The process of market definition may result in identification of several appropriate markets in which to test the probable competitive effects of a particular merger.

520. The 1968 Guidelines were a praiseworthy attempt to place clear and reasonable limits on which mergers would be challenged,[40] but the treatment of market delineation fell short. A prominent group of experts made this comment:

> The delineation of a relevant market within which to appraise the lawfulness of a merger is crucial, for if the market is drawn narrowly enough, virtually any merger can be made to seem monopolistic in its effects. Unfortunately, as they are presently drafted the Guidelines seem to invite a substantial degree of market gerrymandering, especially in delineating regional or local markets.[41]

III. Rationalizing Market Delineation

521. With the 1980 election of Ronald Reagan, William F. Baxter became the AAG in charge of the Antitrust Division, and issuing new merger guidelines was one of his priorities. While work on new merger guidelines was underway, economist George J. Stigler[42] delivered a high-profile lecture on

---

38 By one account, a first draft of the Merger Guidelines was prepared about the time *Grinnell* and *Pabst* were decided, but it was not circulated even inside the Antitrust Division. *See* Donald I. Baker, *Donald Turner's Merger Guidelines as an Antitrust Watershed*, 53 Rev. Indus. Org. 435, 439 (2018).

39 *Merger Guidelines* (1968) ("1968 Guidelines"), https://www.justice.gov/sites/default/files/atr/legacy/2007/07/11/11247.pdf.

40 *See* Gregory J. Werden, *The 1968 Merger Guidelines: In Praise of Committing to Restraint*, 53 Rev. Indus. Org. 445 (2018).

41 *Report of the Task Force on Productivity and Competition*, 1 J. Reprints Antitrust L. & Econ. 827, 847 (1969). This confidential report (the *Stigler Report*) was made public in June 1969.

42 Stigler was awarded the 1982 Nobel Prize in economics for work in and related to industrial organization. He occasionally worked as an expert witness in antitrust cases, and he chaired the task force cited in the previous paragraph.

the contributions of economics to antitrust policy in which he caricatured the practice of market delineation:

> The typical antitrust case is an almost impudent exercise in economic gerrymandering. The plaintiff sets the market, at a maximum, as one state in area and including only aperture-priority SLR cameras selling between $200 and $250. This might be called J-Shermanizing the market, after Senator John Sherman. The defendant will in turn insist that the market is worldwide, and includes not only all cameras, but also portrait artists and possibly transportation media because a visit is a substitute for a picture. This might also be called T-Shermanizing the market, this time after the Senator's brother, General William Tecumseh Sherman. Depending on who convinces the judge, the concentration ratios will be awesome or trivial, with a large influence on his verdict.[43]

522. AAG Baxter was determined to put an end to market gerrymandering and made great strides with Merger Guidelines released on June 14, 1982.[44] The 1982 Guidelines set out market delineation principles, all of which were reasserted by successor policy statements until now. With these principles, the 1982 Guidelines sought to assure that *Brown Shoe*'s "practical indicia" could no longer be used as a checklist to confirm whatever market maximized a merger's apparent competitive significance.[45]

523. One foundational principle was the hypothetical monopolist test (HMT), which holds that a candidate market is a market only if a hypothetical monopolist over it would raise price significantly. The HMT had been developed by the DOJ in 1978 to analyze competition in the coal industry.[46] The HMT was then used to explain why it made sense to define relatively narrow coal markets around points of production even though coal was shipped great distances.[47]

524. As the Supreme Court observed in the cellophane case: "Every manufacturer is the sole producer of the particular commodity it makes but its control … over the relevant market depends upon the availability of alternative commodities for buyers … ."[48] To delineate the relevant market is to evaluate the alternatives that can constrain the exercise of market power. The insight behind the HMT was that the economic theory of monopoly provided a useful framework in which to do it.

---

43 George J. Stigler, *Economists and the Problem of Monopoly*, 72 Am. Econ. Rev. (Papers & Proc.) 1, 8–9 (1982).

44 *Merger Guidelines* (1982) ("1982 Merger Guidelines"), https://www.justice.gov/archives/atr/1982-merger-guidelines.

45 *See* Maisel, *supra* note 19, at 59–69; Werden, *supra* note 1, at 173–79.

46 *See* U.S. Dep't of Justice, Antitrust Division, Competition in The Coal Industry 26–27 (May 1978).

47 *See* Gregory J. Werden, *On the Use and Misuse of Shipments Data in Defining Geographic Markets*, 26 Antitrust Bull. 719 (1981).

48 United States v. E.I. du Pont de Nemours & Co., 351 U.S. 380 (1956).

525. The conventional wisdom had been that substitutability in both demand and supply should be accounted for in the delineation of the relevant market.[49] But a second foundational principle set out in the 1982 Guidelines was that the relevant market is delineated solely in the basis of substitutability on the demand side of the market. The 1982 Guidelines accounted for supply substitutability in identifying a market's competitors. Any supplier that reasonably could be expected to compete, over the near term, in providing the relevant product in the relevant place, was treated as a competitor and assigned an appropriate share.

526. The 1982 Guidelines also provided for the possibility of aggregation as "a matter of convenience" when a case involved many relevant markets with very similar competitive conditions, as when the products were good substitutes in supply. The 1982 Guidelines did not permit clustering, as in *Philadelphia National Bank*, when competitive conditions differed.[50]

527. When initially formulated in 1978, the HMT only defined markets around suppliers. The 1982 Guidelines, however, articulated the concept of price discrimination markets, which were defined around consumers. The third foundational principle articulated by the 1982 Guidelines was that relevant markets are always delineated around suppliers, but when price discrimination is possible, additional relevant markets – "price discrimination markets" – can be delineated around consumers.

528. In a market delineated around suppliers, the competitors are the producers in the defined area, and their market shares are determined by the capacities or outputs in the area. In a relevant market delineated around customers, more is involved in identifying the competitors in the relevant market and assigning them shares. A competitor making no sales in a market might be a significant competitor because it could divert product there if prices rose.[51]

529. The 1982 Guidelines prevented gerrymandering by combining the foundational principles with size and shape principles to assure a unique relevant market for every starting point.[52] The size of the relevant market was governed by the Smallest Market Principle stated by footnote 11: "The Department normally will not expand the market beyond the point at which this standard is satisfied unless it is convinced that independent competitive concerns exist in a larger market."

---

49 *See, e.g.*, Steven M. Edwards et al., *Proposed Revision of the Justice Department's Merger Guidelines*, 81 Colum. L. Rev. 1543, 1557, 1559–60 (1981); Note, *The Role of Supply Substitutability in Defining the Relevant Product Market*, 65 Va. L. Rev. 129 (1979). Of the six *Brown Shoe* practical indicia, two related to supply-side substitutability (unique production facilities and specialized vendors). And the Court appended a footnote to the list of practical indicia beginning with: "The cross-elasticity of production facilities may also be an important factor in defining a product market within which a vertical merger is to be viewed." Brown Shoe Co. v. United States, 370 U.S. 294, 325 n.42 (1962).

50 The DOJ, thereafter, argued that the relevant market in bank merger cases was not the cluster of products and services provided by commercial banks. *See, e.g.*, United States v. Cent. State Bank, 817 F.2d 22, 23–24 (1987).

51 In the early 1980s, a hot topic in antitrust policy was the proper treatment of imports, and a prominent commentary argued that shares of foreign competitors should be based on their world-wide sales. William M. Landes & Richard A. Posner, *Market Power in Antitrust Cases*, 94 Harv. L. Rev. 937, 963–64 (1981).

52 *See* Gregory J. Werden, *Market Delineation under the Merger Guidelines: A Tenth Anniversary Retrospective*, 38 Antitrust Bull. 517 (1993).

530. The shape of the relevant market was governed by the Circle Principle, which was stated in separate footnotes relating to the product and geographic dimensions of the market. Footnote 12 stated: "In constructing and expanding the provisional market, the Department will not exclude any product that is at least as good a substitute as any product included." Footnote 24 stated: "In constructing and expanding the provisional market, the Department will not exclude any area if production there is at least as good a substitute as production that is included."[53]

531. A common initial reaction to the 1982 Guidelines was that the HMT would lead to excessively broad relevant markets.[54] This reaction had no rational basis, and experience proved it wrong. The HMT became universally embraced by the courts,[55] which have cited the HMT and the Smallest Market Principle in rejecting defense arguments for broad markets.[56]

IV. A Formal Statement of the HMT Procedure

532. The 1982 Guidelines stated the procedure for implementing the HMT this way:

> Taking the product of the merging firm as a beginning point, the Department will establish a provisional product market. The Department will include in the provisional market those products that the merging firm's customers view as good substitutes at prevailing prices… . The Department will add additional products to the market if a significant percentage of the buyers of products already included would be likely to shift to those other products in response to a small but significant and non-transitory increase in price. As a first approximation, the Department will hypothesize a price increase of five percent and ask how many buyers would be likely to shift to the other products within one year. The Department will continue expanding the provisional market until it satisfies the general profitability standard stated above.[57]

53 1982 Merger Guidelines, *supra* note 44.

54 *See, e.g.*, Robert G. Harris & Thomas M. Jorde, *Market Definition in the Merger Guidelines: Implications for Antitrust Enforcement*, 71 Calif. L. Rev. 464, 486 (1983) ("the Guidelines use procedures which have the effect of increasing the size of the market").

55 *See* Gregory J. Werden, *The 1982 Merger Guidelines and the Ascent of the Hypothetical Monopolist Paradigm*, 71 Antitrust L.J. 253 (2003).

56 *See* Vasquez v. Ind. Univ. Health, Inc., 40 F.4th 582, 587 (7th Cir. 2022), *see also* Brittany Nieves, *The US Court of Appeals for the Seventh Circuit rules that the hypothetical monopolist test remains the "best approach" for geographic market analysis in the healthcare context (Vasquez / Indiana University Health)*, e-Competitions July 2022, art. No. 108431; FTC v. Sysco Corp., 113 F. Supp. 3d 1, 26–27 (D.D.C. 2015), *see also* Allison F. Sheedy, *The US District Court for the District of Columbia grants the FTC a preliminary injunction to halt the proposed merger between the largest US food distributors, leading them to abandon the merger plans (Sysco / US Foods)*, e-Competitions June 2015, art. No. 74459; United States v. H & R Block, Inc., 833 F. Supp. 2d 36, 59 (D.D.C. 2011), *see also* James A. Keyte et al., *The US District Court for the District of Columbia grants DoJ request to enjoin a merger between two digital do-it-yourself tax preparation software providers (H&R Block / TaxAct)*, e-Competitions Nov. 2011, art. No. 45126.

57 For a contemporaneous explication of market delineation under the 1982 Merger Guidelines, see Gregory J. Werden, *Market Delineation and the Justice Department's Merger Guidelines*, 1983 Duke L.J. 514.

533. The 1984 Guidelines[58] changed little in the 1982 Guidelines, but did improve the articulation of the procedure:

> [T]he Department will begin with each product (narrowly defined) produced or sold by each merging firm and ask what would happen if a hypothetical monopolist of that product imposed a "small but significant and nontransitory" increase in price. If the price increase would cause so many buyers to shift to other products that a hypothetical monopolist would not find it profitable to impose such an increase in price, then the Department will add to the product group the product that is the next-best substitute for the merging firm's product and ask the same question again. This process will continue until a group of products is identified for which a hypothetical monopolist could profitably impose a "small but significant and nontransitory" increase in price. The Department generally will consider the relevant product market to be the smallest group of products that satisfies this test.[59]

534. A more precise, and more complete, statement of the procedure requires terminology and notation not found in the 1982–84 Guidelines.[60]

535. A relevant market is delineated around a *focal good*, g_0, sold by one of the merging firms. Substitutes for g_0 are denoted g_i.[61] The g_i are ordered on the basis of their closeness to g_0, as a matter of consumer preference. Closeness is reflected in a *closeness metric*,[62] $c(g_i|g_0)$, derived from the demand curve for g_0. For example, the metric could be the diversion ratio from g_0 to g_i when the price of g_0 is increased.[63]

536. This ordering yields the *next-best substitute sequence*: $(g_0, g_1, g_2, g_3, \ldots)$, where g_1 is the best substitute for g_0, g_2 is the second-best substitute, and so forth. The *candidate market sequence* is then formed such that $\mathbf{C}_0 = \{g_0\}$, $\mathbf{C}_1 = \{g_0, g_1\}$, and so forth.[64] The HMT is applied only to the candidate market sequence.[65]

---

58 *Merger Guidelines* (1984) ("1984 Merger Guidelines"), https://www.justice.gov/archives/atr/1984-merger-guidelines.

59 This passage was quoted by Olin Corp. v. FTC, 986 F.2d 1295, 1299–300 (9th Cir. 1993).

60 The following is based on Gregory J. Werden, *Market Delineation Algorithms Based on the Hypothetical Monopolist Paradigm* (U.S. Dep't of Justice, EAG Discussion Paper No. 02-8, Aug. 2002).

61 If consumers view two goods as completely interchangeable, they are a treated as a single good.

62 The closeness metric differs from a metric in mathematics in one respect: A metric in mathematics is a sort of distance, and the distance from point x to point y must be the same as the distance between point y and point x. But consumers can find good x to be a close substitute for good y and yet find good y to be a distant substitute for good x.

63 The choice of the closeness metric sometimes matters. Case experience indicates that the best closeness metric is the relative diversion ratio, i.e., the diversion ratio from g_i to g_0, divided by what the diversion ratio would be if diversion were proportionate to share. *See* Gregory J. Werden, *Demand Elasticities in Antitrust Analysis*, 66 Antitrust L.J. 363, 402–06 (1998).

64 If equally close substitutes exist, they are added in together. Thus, if $c(g_1|g_0) = c(g_2|g_0)$, then $\mathbf{C}_0 = \{g_0\}$ and $\mathbf{C}_1 = \{g_0, g_1, g_2\}$.

65 The next section more precisely discusses how the HMT is applied.

537. The Circle Principle holds that if $c(g_j|g_0) \leq c(g_k|g_0)$, then any candidate market containing g_k must contain g_j. The word "circle" derives from visualizing candidate markets as concentric discs. Each disc is bounded by a circle of radius $c(g_i|g_0)$ centered on the focal good, g_0.

538. The Smallest Market Principle holds that the relevant market is the smallest candidate market that passes the HMT. The word "smallest" relates to the closeness metric. In practice, the Smallest Market Principle is not a strict rule. The relevant market commonly is defined by a gap in the chain of substitutes, such that the closest substitute that is not included is much further from the focal good than the most distant substitute that is included.

539. The final step in market delineation is formulating a *relevant market rule*, which describes what goods are in the relevant market by reference to objective *traits*.[66] The currently available goods in the relevant market make up a set of discrete points in a trait-space, while the relevant market is a region of the trait-space containing those points as well as infinitely many other points.[67] Entry at one of these other points would be entry into the relevant market.

540. A simple relevant market rule, i.e., a rule in a few words, is preferred to a more complicated rule because the latter smacks of gerrymandering. In the interest of a simple relevant market rule, the Smallest Market Principle often is relaxed.

541. All of the foregoing presumes that goods are sold where they are produced (e.g., that factories quote f.o.b. prices), so that the point of a good's production is one of its traits. In this case, the relevant market rule also has a part referring to the location of production.

542. If goods are sold where they are consumed and price discrimination is possible, additional price discrimination markets are delineated. The relevant market rule then refers to a location of consumption, a class of customer, or both.

V. Continuity From 1984 to 2023

543. The 1992 Horizontal Merger Guidelines,[68] released jointly by the DOJ and the FTC, clarified the HMT and its application with price discrimination.[69] The 1982–84 Guidelines were written as if the hypothetical

---

66 In the cellophane case, for example, the Supreme Court examined the substitutability for cellophane of aluminum foil, plastic products (cellulose acetate, polyethylene, polyvinyl chloride, and rubber hydrochloride), and paper products (glassine, parchment paper, and waxed paper), but defined the relevant market as "flexible wrapping materials." United States v. E.I. du Pont de Nemours & Co., 351 U.S. 377 (1956).

67 In mathematical terms, the Circle Principle is that the relevant market rule must define a "convex" and "compact" region in the trait-space. In simple terms, the region can have neither a dent nor a hole.

68 *Horizontal Merger Guidelines* (1992) ("1992 Horizontal Merger Guidelines"), https://www.justice.gov/sites/default//atr/legacy///11/.pdf.

69 The 1992–97 Horizontal Merger Guidelines' description of the HMT was quoted, paraphrased, and cited by courts. *See In re* Se. Milk Antitrust Litig., 739 F.3d 262, 278–78, 282 (6th Cir. 2014); FTC v. Tenet Health Care Corp., 186 F.3d 1045, 1053 n.11 (8th Cir. 1999); E.I. du Pont de Nemours & Co. v. Kolon Indus., 683 F. Supp. 2d 401, 412–13 (E.D. Va. 2009); Emigra Group, LLC v. Fragomen, Del Rey, Bernsen & Loewy, LLP, 612 F. Supp. 2d 330, 352 (S.D.N.Y. 2009); FTC v. Whole Foods Market, Inc., 502 F. Supp. 2d 1, 16

monopolist would set a single price, while in most instances, it would set many prices, and it would maximize profits by raising them different amounts. The 1992 Horizontal Merger Guidelines, thus, clarified when the HMT is passed.

544. First, the 1992 Horizontal Merger Guidelines stated that "the hypothetical monopolist will be assumed to pursue maximum profits in deciding whether to raise the prices of any or all of the additional products under its control." Second, the 1992 Horizontal Merger Guidelines asserted that the process of testing candidate markets "will continue until a group of products is identified such that a hypothetical monopolist over that group of products would profitably impose at least a 'small but significant and nontransitory' increase, including the price of a product of one of the merging firms."

545. The Circle Principle assures that the focal good is the good in a candidate market that is most protected from outside competition. The hypothetical monopolist, therefore, normally would increase the price of the focal good at least as much as any other price. In an exceptional case, the 1992 Horizontal Merger Guidelines assured that the HMT remained tied to the competitive effects of the merger by asking whether the price of one of the merging firms' products would increase significantly.

546. The 1992 Horizontal Merger Guidelines also elaborated the treatment of price discrimination. Separate sections on the product and geographic boundaries of the relevant market first set out the application of the HMT "[a]bsent price discrimination," then set out the application of the HMT "in the presence of price discrimination." The product market section delineated "relevant product markets consisting of a particular use or uses." The geographic market section delineated "geographic markets consisting of particular locations of buyers."

547. The 2010 Horizontal Merger Guidelines[70] dropped the pedagogic device of the iterative approach, but made no changes in the HMT or its application. The HMT was stated this way:

> The test requires that a hypothetical profit-maximizing firm, not subject to price regulation, that was the only present and future seller of those products ("hypothetical monopolist") likely would impose at least a small but significant and non-transitory increase in price ("SSNIP") on at least one product in the market, including at least one product sold by one of the merging firms.[71]

(D.D.C. 2007); Gulfstream Park Racing Assn., Inc. v. Tampa Bay Downs, Inc., 294 F. Supp. 2d 1291, 1309 (M.D. Fla. 2003); United States v. Visa USA, Inc., 163 F. Supp. 2d 322, 335 (S.D.N.Y. 2001).

70 *Horizontal Merger Guidelines* (2010) ("2010 Horizontal Merger Guidelines"), https://www.justice.gov/atr/file/810276/dl?inline.

71 The 2010 Horizontal Merger Guidelines' description of the HMT was quoted by courts. *See* FTC v. Wilhelm Wilhelmsen Holding ASA, 341 F. Supp. 3d 27, 47 (D.D.C. 2018); United States v. Anthem, Inc., 236 F. Supp. 3d 171, 198 (D.D.C. 2017); FTC v. Staples, Inc., 190 F. Supp. 3d 100, 121–22 (D.D.C. 2016); FTC v. Sysco Corp., 113 F. Supp. 3d 1, 33–34 (D.D.C. 2015); United States v. H&R Block, Inc., 833 F. Supp. 2d 36, 52 (D.D.C. 2011).

548. The Circle Principle was explicit:

> When applying the hypothetical monopolist test to define a market around a product offered by one of the merging firms, if the market includes a second product, the Agencies will normally also include a third product if that third product is a closer substitute for the first product than is the second product.

549. And the Smallest Market Principle was also articulated: "Because the relative competitive significance of more distant substitutes is apt to be overstated by their share of sales, when the Agencies rely on market shares and concentration, they usually do so in the smallest relevant market satisfying the hypothetical monopolist test."[72]

VI. Magic Market Delineation in the New Merger Guidelines

550. Section 4.3 of the 2023 Guidelines list four market delineation "tools." The first is this:

> Direct evidence of substantial competition between the merging parties can demonstrate that a relevant market exists in which the merger may substantially lessen competition and can be sufficient to identify the line of commerce and section of the country affected by a merger, even if the precise metes and bounds of the market are only broadly characterized.

551. This first tool is based on the remarkable claim that the mere fact of "substantial competition between the merging parties" is, or can be, "sufficient to identify" the relevant market in which that competition occurs. The claim suggests the conjurer's trick of misdirection. The DOJ and the FTC evidently plan to proclaim that substantial competition between the merging parties implies that they have large shares in some relevant market, so no more need be said.

552. Although market delineation does not require "precise metes and bounds,"[73] it does require boundaries. The 2023 Guidelines' first market delineation tool suggests that the DOJ and the FTC envision relevant markets without specified boundaries. Such an approach is contrary to the statutory text and controlling case law to which the 2023 Guidelines profess the agencies' slavish devotion.[74] In *Brown Shoe*, which the 2023

---

72 The 2010 Horizontal Merger Guidelines' description of the Smallest Market Principle was quoted by courts. FTC v. Rag-Stiftung, 436 F. Supp. 3d 278, 292 (D.D.C. 2020); *H&R Block*, 833 F. Supp. 2d at 59.

73 The Supreme Court made this observation in connection with geographic market boundaries. *See* United States v. Pabst Brewing Co., 384 U.S. 546, 549 (1966) (Section 7 "does not call for the delineation of a 'section of the country' by metes and bounds as a surveyor would lay off a plot of ground."); United States v. Phila. Nat'l Bank, 374 U.S. 321, 360 n.37 (1963) ("fuzziness would seem inherent in any attempt to delineate the relevant geographical market").

74 The press release accompanying the release of the draft of the 2023 Merger Guidelines asserted that they were "built around statutory text." U.S. Dep't of Justice Press Release, Justice Department and FTC Seek Comment on Draft Merger Guidelines, (July 19, 2023), https://www.justice.gov/opa/pr/justice-department-and-ftc-seek-comment-draft-merger-guidelines. And the text of Section 7 demands that any lessening of competition be located to a particular relevant market. *See supra* notes 7–8 and accompanying text.

Guidelines cite frequently, the Supreme Court declared that: "The 'area of effective competition' must be determined by reference to a product market (the 'line of commerce') and a geographic market (the 'section of the country')."[75]

553. If the merging parties compete significantly *only* with each other, the HMT leads to a relevant market in which they are the only competitors. If one or both merging parties also face competition from other sources, application of the HMT likely leads to a broader market, and it could be far broader. "Direct evidence of substantial competition between the merging parties" is never a sufficient basis for concluding that a proposed merger violates Section 7.[76]

554. The second market delineation tool listed in Section 4.3 of the 2023 Guidelines is:

> Direct evidence of the exercise of market power can demonstrate a relevant market in which that power exists. This evidence can be valuable when assessing the risk that a dominant position may be entrenched, maintained, or extended, since the same evidence identifies market power and can be sufficient to identify the line of commerce and section of the country affected by a merger, even if the metes and bounds of the market are only broadly characterized.

555. Market power generally is defined as the ability to charge more than the competitive price,[77] i.e., short-run marginal cost. Direct evidence of the exercise of market power, therefore, consists of pricing and cost evidence showing that a firm is charging more than short-run marginal cost. That evidence is available in every merger case,[78] and it is never "sufficient to identify" the relevant market.

556. The second market delineation tool asserts that "[d]irect evidence of the exercise of market power" has value in cases posing a "risk that a dominant position may be entrenched, maintained, or extended." The trick with this tool is to proclaim that some broad characterization of the relevant market follows from the fact of market dominance, since the relevant market is the part of commerce dominated. The problem is that direct proof of dominance is just an urban legend.

---

75 Brown Shoe Co. v. United States, 370 U.S. 294, 324 (1962). *See* United States v. E.I. du Pont de Nemours & Co., 353 U.S. 586, 593 (1957) ("Determination of the relevant market is a necessary predicate to a finding of a violation of the Clayton Act … .").

76 Guideline 2 in the 2023 Guidelines is that "mergers can violate the law when they eliminate substantial competition between firms," and the accompanying text hints that definition of the relevant market is not required when the merging firms are in "substantial competition." It is true that quantitative tools for assessing unilateral effects sometimes are far more useful than shares of any relevant market, but economic modeling in applying these tools requires what amounts to market delineation. *See supra* notes 15–17 and accompanying text.

77 *See* NCAA v. Bd. of Regents of the Univ. of Okla., 468 U.S. 85, 109 n.38 (1984) ("Market power is the ability to raise prices above those that would be charged in a competitive market.").

78 During 42 years in the Antitrust Division, the author observed price-cost margins in many merger cases. All were greater than 20%, and margins less than 40% were rare.

557. In cases under Section 2 of the Sherman Act, dominance is "inferred from the predominant share of the market."[79] Courts hold out the possibility of direct proof,[80] but they never find proffered proof sufficient. One reason for the unremitting failure of proof is that courts are properly skeptical of purported direct proof of dominance. Without the perspective afforded by the definition of the relevant market, any highly successful competitor could be portrayed as dominant.

VII. Zombie Market Delineation in the New Merger Guidelines

558. The practical indicia of *Brown Shoe*[81] were laid to rest by the 1982 Guidelines. Once the HMT got support from leading commentators,[82] courts were open to setting aside 1960s precedent while the Supreme Court was slowly updating antitrust law to incorporate sound economics.[83] Courts applied the HMT in contested merger cases, largely to the exclusion of the practical indicia, because the litigants agreed that it was the proper test.

559. With the third market delineation tool, the 2023 Guidelines set aside the HMT in favor of 1960s precedent:

> A relevant market can be identified from evidence on observed market characteristics ("practical indicia"), such as industry or public recognition of the submarket as a separate economic entity, the product's peculiar characteristics and uses, unique production facilities, distinct customers, distinct prices, sensitivity to price changes, and specialized vendors. Various practical indicia may identify a relevant market in different settings.

560. The 2023 Guidelines threaten to turn the practical indicia into brain-eating antitrust zombies[84] that devour the intelligence brought to market delineation by the 1982 Guidelines. The rationale for disinterring the

---

79 United States v. Grinnell Corp., 384 U.S. 563, 571 (1966). The Court cited cases in which shares of over 80 percent were sufficient for the inference.

80 In particular, courts suggest that the ability to exclude can be proved by demonstrating exclusion. *See, e.g.*, Geneva Pharms. Tech. Corp. v. Barr Labs. Inc., 386 F.3d 485, 500 (2d Cir. 2004); PepsiCo, Inc. v. Coca-Cola Co., 315 F.3d 101, 107 (2d Cir. 2002); Re/Max Int'l, Inc. v. Realty One, Inc., 173 F.3d 995, 1018 (6th Cir. 1999).

81 *See supra* note 20 and accompanying text.

82 A turning point was the first supplement to the Areeda–Turner treatise in 1986. *See* Werden, *supra* note 54, at 262–63 & n.34.

83 *See, e.g.*, Leegin Creative Leather Prods. v. PSKS, Inc., 551 U.S. 877, 889–94 (2007), *see also* Peter J. Carney & Kristen J. McAhren, *The US Supreme Court overturns its long-standing prohibition against vertical agreements between manufacturers and their dealers setting minimum resale prices (Leegin Creative)*, E-COMPETITIONS June 2007, art. No. 38050; Ill. Tool Works Inc. v. Indep. Ink, Inc. 547 U.S. 28, 43 n.4 (2006), *see also* James W. Lowe et al., *The US Supreme Court strikes down patent market power presumption in tying cases (Illinois Tool Works)*, E-COMPETITIONS Mar. 2006, art. No. 37689; State Oil Co. v. Khan, 522 U.S. 3, 15–22 (1997); Cont'l T. V., Inc. v. GTE Sylvania Inc., 433 U.S. 36, 54–59 (1977).

84 Zombies did not eat brains in the 1968 George Romero classic, *The Night of the Living Dead*, but brain eating has been a consistent meme since Dan O'Bannon's 1985 *The Return of the Living Dead*.

practical indicia must be to use them in support of market definitions that the HMT cannot adequately support.

561. As authority for use of the practical indicia, footnote 80 of the 2023 Guidelines cites the appellate decision in a recent DOJ merger case involving sugar refiners in the Southeastern United States.[85] The DOJ defined two, concentric sugar markets consisting of Southeastern states. Both were price discrimination markets, with shares assigned to refiners on the basis of sugar deliveries to the defined markets.

562. The trial court concluded that the DOJ had not met its burden, principally on the basis that price increases in the Southeast would be thwarted by supply coming from outside the alleged market.[86] The appeals court held that the trial court "did not err by considering facts on the ground rather than relying upon HMT analysis."[87] Of course, those two things should not have been alternatives.

563. The litigants disputed whether sugar distributors were competitors in the relevant markets and should be assigned market shares. The trial court mistakenly viewed this as a market delineation dispute, and the DOJ mistakenly asserted that the HMT resolved the dispute. Sound DOJ policy, as set out in both the 2010 Horizontal Merger Guidelines and in the 2023 Guidelines, separates the delineation of the relevant market from the identification of competitors and the assignment of shares.

564. In rejecting the DOJ's erroneous contention that HMT implies that distributors should not be deemed competitors, the appeals court erroneously asserted that the trial court relied instead on the practical indicia.[88] But the trial court did not allude to anything resembling a practical indicium in ruling that distributors were competitors in the relevant market. Rather, the trial court found that distributors acted as arbitrageurs to undermine price increases in the Southeast.[89]

VIII. Undermining the Application of the HMT

565. Section 4.3 of the 2023 Guidelines retains the three foundational market delineation principles articulated in the 1982–84 Guidelines, but jettisons the associated principles controlling the size and shape of the relevant market. The 2023 Guidelines use the term "candidate market" 16 times but say nothing about how a candidate market is constructed and evidently

85 United States v. U.S. Sugar Corp., 73 F.4th 197 (3d Cir. 2023).

86 United States v. U.S. Sugar Corp., 2022 WL 4544025 (D. Del. Sept. 28, 2022). Footnote 80 asserts that "unique facts of the industry" were at play, but nothing mentioned by the court seems out of the ordinary.

87 *U.S. Sugar*, 73 F.4th at 206.

88 *Id.*

89 The finding implied that the DOJ wrongly assigned market shares on the basis of current sales in Southeast. With price discrimination markets, shares must be assigned on the basis of the ability to sell in the relevant markets, and the finding implied that refineries outside the alleged markets could profitably sell far more that they currently were selling.

allow any group of products and area to be a candidate market. The 2023 Guidelines also disclaim the Smallest Market Principle.

566. The 2023 Guidelines assert that to delineate the relevant market is to "identify the 'area of effective competition,'" but they ignore the definite article: There is one area of effective competition, and yet the 2023 Guidelines assert: "Market definition ensures that antitrust markets are sufficiently broad, but it does not always lead to a single relevant market." The Circle Principle and the Smallest Market Principle eliminated agency discretion that catered to gerrymandering, and the 2023 Guidelines reclaim that discretion.

567. Footnote 77 describes the extent of the discretion the DOJ and the FTC now assert: "Multiple overlapping markets can be appropriately defined relevant markets. For example, a merger to monopoly for food worldwide would lessen competition in well-defined relevant markets for, among others, food, baked goods, cookies, low-fat cookies, and premium low-fat chocolate chip cookies."

568. To promote agency discretion even more, Section 4.3.A of the 2023 Guidelines modifies the formal statement of the HMT:

> [T]he HMT asks whether a hypothetical profit-maximizing firm, not prevented by regulation from worsening terms, that was the only present and future seller of a group of products ("hypothetical monopolist") likely would undertake at least a small but significant and non-transitory increase in price ("SSNIP") or other worsening of terms ("SSNIPT") for at least one product in the group.

569. The last eight words disconnect delineation of the relevant market from the assessment of competitive effects. That clause allows the result of the HMT to turn on how much a hypothetical monopolist would increase the price of a product that neither merging firm produces and that plays no part in the agency's theory of anticompetitive effects.

570. Posit a merger of firms selling only product *x*, which fails the HMT. Before the 2023 Guidelines, the next-best-substitute would have been added to the candidate market, and the HMT applied again. In both applications, the question would have been whether a hypothetical monopolist would significantly increase the price of *x*.

571. The Circle Principle is not observed under the 2023 Guidelines, so the agencies can expand the candidate market by adding any product, *z*. This candidate market passes the modified HMT if *z* constitutes a relevant market. The gerrymandered market of *x* plus *z* could be highly concentrated, but it is useless in assessing the posited merger.

IX. Generalizing the HMT

572. The 2023 Guidelines generalize the HMT to ask whether a hypothetical monopolist would worsen terms along any dimension of competition. Section 4.3.B of the Horizontal Merger Guidelines lists the dimensions of "quality, service, capacity investment, choice of product variety or

features, or innovative effort." This generalization introduces formidable complications without offering any advantages.

573. When price is the only dimension of competition considered, the HMT is a straightforward extrapolation of the theory of monopoly. With an approximation of the hypothetical monopolist's demand curve, the theory of monopoly permits a calculation of a monopoly price, which can be compared with the prevailing price.[90] That comparison is the HMT. Incorporating non-price dimensions of competition presents major difficulties,[91] which the 2023 Guidelines do not address.

574. The HMT rationalized market delineation by linking it to the market power concern presented by a case. Perfecting this linkage could be a rationale for generalizing the HMT, but the 2023 Guidelines do not pursue the linkage. The 2023 Guidelines do not state that the DOJ and the FTC first identify how market power would be exercised and then tailor the application of the HMT. Nor do the 2023 Guidelines state that non-price dimensions of competition are considered only if the market power created by a merger likely would be exercised in a manner that does not involve raising a price.

575. The main impetus for generalizing the HMT seems to have been a proliferation of zero-price markets. Commentators suggested implementing the HMT in such markets by focusing on consumers' non-monetary costs[92] or by positing a decrease in quality.[93] But if a merger created market power in zero-price market, it would be exercised in a related, revenue-generating activity, which should be the focus in delineating the relevant market. Section 4.3.A asserts that the agencies "assume that the hypothetical monopolist would seek to maximize profits."

576. Consider two video streaming services that require viewers to watch ads but charge no subscription fees. If the merger were anticompetitive, the merged firm almost certainly would maximize profits by raising ad rates. The non-monetary costs to viewers would fall because fewer ads would be sold at the higher rates.[94] The proper application of the HMT would focus

---

90 The hypothetical monopolist normally is assumed to operate at constant marginal cost over the relevant range, so the HMT reduces to a test of critical demand elasticity. *See* Werden, *supra* note 63, at 387–92. When constant marginal cost is a poor approximation, the analysis is different. *See* Gregory J. Werden, *Beyond Critical Loss: Tailored Application of the Hypothetical Monopolist Test*, 4 Competition L.J. 69 (2005).

91 Elements of customer choice other than price typically are discrete choices for suppliers, which renders conventional analytic tools useless. And even if all elements of customer choice are continuous variables for suppliers, competitive effects are greatly complicated by interaction between elements of customer choice. When close substitutes merge, the merged firm separates them, which reduces the incentive to raise prices. *See* Amit Gandhi et al., *Post-Merger Product Repositioning*, 56 J. Indus. Econ. 49 (2008).

92 *See* John M. Newman, *Antitrust in Zero-Priced Markets: Applications*, 94 Wash. U. L. Rev. 49, 64–69 (2016). For a quantitative implementation of the idea, see Akihiro Nakamura & Takanori Ida, *Delineating Zero-Price Markets with Network Effects: An Analysis of Free Messenger Services*, 19 J. Competition L. & Econ. 177 (2023).

93 *See* Daniel Mandrescu, *The SSNIP Test and Zero-Pricing Strategies: Considerations for Online Platforms*, 2 Eur. Competition & Reg. Rev. 244 (2018).

94 A decrease in quality is possible: The merged firm could drop some programming that had been provided due to the competition between the merging firms. But economics is unlikely to provide a basis for predicting that popular programming will be dropped. Dropping popular programming causes the loss of viewers, which reduces ad revenue.

on the demand curve for the ads, and would account for the impact of the quantity of ads on viewership, as well as the feedback from viewership to demand for ads.[95]

X. Conclusion

577. Without straying far from the trail blazed by the Supreme Court, the 1982 Guidelines led the courts, as did subsequent guidelines until 2023. And the courts welcomed the leadership, especially on market delineation[96] and the market-share-based thresholds.[97] But the 2023 Guidelines abandon the leadership role in favor of greater fidelity to case law. This posture is problematic both because the leadership of the federal enforcement agencies is needed, and because fidelity to case law is fraught.

578. The Supreme Court ruled on the merits of about two dozen Section 7 cases between 1962 and 1975, and none since.[98] These old decisions have not been abrogated, but Section 7 law today surely is not what it was in 1975. Indeed, the law began to change before the Supreme Court ceded the field to the courts of appeals. The ideological balance of the Court shifted in the early 1970s,[99] and the 1974 *General Dynamics* decision marked a turning point.[100]

579. In a 5–4 decision, the Supreme Court rejected the DOJ's appeal from an adverse judgment in a challenge to a consummated merger. The dissent was persuasive on market definition and some other issues, which made it all the more significant that the majority rejected the appeal.[101] *General Dynamics* ended the era about which Justice Potter Stewart commented: "The sole consistency that I can find is that in litigation under § 7, the Government always wins."[102]

---

95 *See* Gregory J. Werden, The Foundations of Antitrust: Events, Ideas, and Doctrines 355–59 (2020).

96 *See supra* notes 56, 59, 69, 71–72; Carl Shapiro & Howard Shelanski, *Judicial Response to the 2010 Horizontal Merger Guidelines*, 58 Rev. Indus. Org. 51, 62–63 (2021).

97 *See* Steven A. Newborn & Virginia L. Snider, *The Growing Judicial Acceptance of the Merger Guidelines*, 60 Antitrust L.J. 849 (1991); Shapiro & Shelanski, *supra* note 96, at 64–65.

98 Under the Expediting Act of 1903, ch. 544, 32 Stat. 823, district court decisions in DOJ antitrust cases were appealed directly to the Supreme Court. The Antitrust Penalties and Procedures Act, Pub. L. 93-528, 88 Stat. 1706, largely repealed the Expediting Act, but the repeal did not apply if the notice of appeal was filed on or before Jan. 15, 1975. Pub. L. 93-528, § 7, 88 Stat. 1710. The last Supreme Court decisions rendered in direct appeals of DOJ antitrust cases were announced in June 1975, and they included one merits decision under Section 7: United States v. Citizens & S. Nat'l Bank, 422 U.S. 86 (1975). The Court has never granted certiorari in a DOJ Section 7 case.

99 Chief Justice Earl Warren, who wrote the *Brown Shoe* opinion, was succeeded by Warren Burger at the end of the 1968 term. Hugo Black, who wrote the *Pabst* opinion, was succeeded by Lewis Powell in early 1972. The turnover of other seats had no clear consequence for Section 7 cases.

100 United States v. Gen. Dynamics Corp., 415 U.S. 486 (1974).

101 The critical factor to the majority was that the DOJ's market shares were faulty because they were based on current production. The Court found that the competition was for new long-term coal-supply contracts, and one of the merging firms had little uncommitted coal reserves. *Id.* at 501–04. Among the dissent's responses was that that the facts were different at the time of the merger. *Id.* at 524–25 (Douglas, J., dissenting).

102 United States v. Von's Grocery Co., 384 U.S. 270, 301 (1966) (Stewart, J., dissenting).

580. In Section 7 litigation today, the government does not always win. Defendants often assert that alleged relevant markets were gerrymandered, and courts tend to agree if they find that the alleged relevant markets make little sense. Defendants also are apt to invoke market delineation principles that the 2023 Guidelines abandoned, and courts are apt to hold that the DOJ and the FTC acted arbitrarily and capriciously in abandoning them.

Table of contents

Mergers That Increase Buyer Power and the Function of Presumptions: Two Key Issues in the Revision of the Merger Guidelines

Peter C. Carstensen

What's new in the 2023 Merger Guidelines

Joseph Farrell

Common Ownership and the Merger Guidelines

Merritt B. Fox and Menesh S. Patel

Awakening Merger Control: The New U.S. Merger Guidelines

Eleanor M. Fox

Antitrust Ideology and the 2023 U.S. Merger Guidelines

Diana L. Moss

The Missing Merger Guideline: On Efficiencies

Maureen K. Ohlhausen and Taylor M. Owings

Economics in the 2023 Merger Guidelines: Three Areas of Concern

Jeremy Sandford, Loren Smith and Nathan Wilson

The Evolution (and Devolution) of Market Structure Reasoning

Sean P. Sullivan

Market Delineation under the New Merger Guidelines: Gerrymandering Redux

Gregory J. Werden

Concurrences
Competition Laws Review

Concurrences Review

Concurrences is a print and online quarterly peer reviewed journal dedicated to EU and national competitions laws. It has been launched in 2004 as the flagship of the Institute of Competition Law in order to provide a forum for academics, practitioners and enforcers. Concurrences' influence and expertise has garnered contributions or interviews with such figures as Christine Lagarde, Bill Kovacic, Emmanuel Macron, Antonin Scalia and Magrethe Vestager.

Contents

More than 15,000 articles, print and/or online. Quarterly issues provide current coverage with contributions from the EU or national or foreign countries thanks to more than 2,500 authors in Europe and abroad.

Format

In order to balance academic contributions with opinions or legal practice notes, Concurrences provides its insight and analysis in a number of formats:

- Forewords: Opinions by leading academics or enforcers
- Interviews: Interviews of antitrust experts
- On-Topics: 4 to 6 short papers on hot issues
- Law & Economics: Short papers written by economists for a legal audience
- Articles: Long academic papers
- Case Summaries: Case commentary on EU and French case law
- Legal Practice: Short papers for in-house counsels
- International: Medium size papers on international policies
- Books Review: Summaries of recent antitrust books
- Articles Review: Summaries of leading articles published in 45 antitrust journals

Boards

The Scientific Committee is headed by Laurence Idot, Professor at Panthéon Assas University. The International Committee is headed by Frederic Jenny, OECD Competition Comitteee Chairman. Boards members include Douglas Ginsburg, Benoît Cœuré, Howard Shelanski, Richard Whish, Wouter Wils, Joshua Wright, etc.

Online version

Concurrences website provides all articles published since its inception, in addition to selected articles published online only in the electronic supplement.

Write for Concurrences

Concurrences welcome spontaneous contributions. Except in rare circumstances, the journal accepts only unpublished articles, whatever the form and nature of the contribution. The Editorial Board checks the form of the proposals, and then submits these to the Scientific Committee. Selection of the papers is conditional to a peer review by at least two members of the Committee. Within a month, the Committee assesses whether the draft article can be published and notifies the author.

www.ingramcontent.com/pod-product-compliance
Lightning Source LLC
LaVergne TN
LVHW011521200926
848484LV00001B/97
* 9 7 8 1 9 3 9 0 0 7 3 3 9 *